Instructor's Manual

to accompany

Supply Chain Logistics Management

Donald Bowersox
David Closs
M. Bixby Cooper
Michigan State University

D1418359

McGraw-Hill
Irwin

Boston   Burr Ridge, IL   Dubuque, IA   Madison, WI   New York   San Francisco   St. Louis
Bangkok   Bogotá   Caracas   Kuala Lumpur   Lisbon   London   Madrid   Mexico City
Milan   Montreal   New Delhi   Santiago   Seoul   Singapore   Sydney   Taipei   Toronto

McGraw-Hill Higher Education

A Division of The McGraw-Hill Companies

Instructor's Manual to accompany
Supply Chain Logistics Management
David Bowersox, David Closs, M. Bixby Cooper

1 2 3 4 5 6 7 8 9 0 QSR/QSR 0 9 8 7 6 5 4 3 2

ISBN 0-07-235101-2

www.mhhe.com

McGRAW-HILL/Irwin

Instructor's Manual to accompany Supply Chain Logistics Management by Bowersox, Closs, and Cooper

Please use this postage-paid form to report any errors that you find in this material. Be as complete as possible noting specifically which changes should be made. We will address them in subsequent printings and future editions. Thank you.

NOTE: An extra copy of this form appears at the end of this manual.

Attention: Scott Isenberg

Name _____   School _____

Office Phone _____

Please fold and seal so that our address is visible.

BUSINESS REPLY MAIL

FIRST-CLASS MAIL   PERMIT NO.204   OAKBROOK, IL

POSTAGE WILL BE PAID BY ADDRESSEE

ATTENTION: Scott Isenberg

THE McGRAW-HILL COMPANIES
1333 BURR RIDGE PKY.
BURR RIDGE, IL 60527-0085

(fold)

(fold)

CONTENTS

Page

Sample Syllabus 1

Challenge Questions and Answers 6

Problem Set 1 Solutions 75

Problem Set 2 Solutions 79

Case Solutions 109

Sample Exams 185

LOGA Logistics Game: Administrator's Manual I-1

LOGA Logistics Game: Participant's Manual P-1

Introduction

This Instructor's Manual provides material to support teaching with Supply Chain Logistics Management. The material includes a sample syllabus, answers to end of chapter questions, problem set solutions, case solutions, examples of subjective exams, and materials for the LOGA simulation game.

The sample syllabus includes course schedules and related assignments for a one semester graduate logistical management course.

The next three sections of the Instructor's Manual offer detailed discussions and answers for the end of chapter challenge questions, the problem sets, and the case studies. The tabular data for the case studies is provided on the website. The content includes a discussion of the conceptual issues as well as detailed quantitative analyses.

Sample subjective exams are provided. As noted in the examination instructions, we have used these to focus student study efforts and require the students to be able to answer any of the questions are part of an exam.

The final section includes the student and administrative manual for the LOGA simulation. The game is commonly used in undergraduate and graduate logistics courses to emphasize the integrated processes of logistical planning and operations. The Participant's Manual provides the game instructions for the students. Students can access the Manual on the student side of the website. The spreadsheet provides the input medium for data entry. The Administrator's Manual describes the process for using the game.

PowerPoint slides for most chapters are included on the text website for both instructors and students. The PowerPoint slides include material from the text as well as extensions that are used at Michigan State to teach the material. The PowerPoint slides are available to students on the website and can be printed out for note taking. To visit the website, go to www.mhhe.com/Bowersox

Sample Syllabus

Supply Chain Logistics Management

Instructor:

Office:

Phone:

E-mail:

Class Time:

Classroom:

Prerequisites:

Assigned Materials: Bowersox, Closs, Cooper. *Supply Chain Logistics* Management and Assigned Articles and Handouts

COURSE DESCRIPTION:

The overarching course objective is to develop an in-depth understanding of integrative managerial issues and challenges related to developing and implementing a firm's logistics strategy. Attention is directed to the logistical mission confronted by varied types of business organizations. Logistics is positioned as a value-adding process that achieves time and place synchronization of demand stimulation and operations fulfillment. Emphasis will be placed on challenges related to providing logistical support for procurement, manufacturing and market-distribution. The topics studied will span supply chain strategy, segmental positioning, service provider relationship development and maintenance, value-added services, forecasting and collaborative planning, order management, transportation, inventory, warehousing and materials handling. The course will conclude with emphasis on facility network design and integrated performance measurement.

The class will combine lecture and discussion focused on critical thinking regarding assigned topics. Advanced preparation <u>will be essential</u> for effective class participation. A limited number of problems may be assigned. Short quizzes covering key preparation assignments <u>may be</u> used at the instructor's discretion.

COURSE OBJECTIVES:

(1)   Develop an understanding of the importance of logistics in the formation of business strategy and the conduct of supply chain operations.
(2)   Develop an in-depth understanding of logistics operating areas and their interrelationship.
(3)   Strengthen integrative management analytical and problem-solving skills.

GRADING:

EVENT	PERCENT	DATE
Examination I	20	
Examination II	20	
Project Proposal		
Examination III	20	
Project	15	
Preparation/Participation	5	All Classes
Examination IV	20	Scheduled Final Exam Time:

PROJECT:

The term project centers on identification and analysis of a business situation wherein logistical performance is a significant source of competitive advantage. The assignment provides an opportunity to apply course concepts for analysis and description of how logistics impacts a firm's strategy. Particular attention should be directed to the manner by which the firm implements practices and the actual or perceived benefits. The information for this assignment can be any material in the public domain such as annual reports, trade association publications, government publications and business articles. While it acceptable to use information obtained from personal experience, THE ESTABLISHMENT OF NEW CONTACTS FOR PURPOSES OF COMPLETING THIS ASSIGNMENT IS PROHIBITED.

Each student is expected to submit a one-page work plan on October 30th. Projects are due December 6th and are limited to 8 double-spaced pages including descriptive and illustration material. EACH STUDENT IS EXPECTED TO COMPLETE THE ASSIGNMENT ON AN INDIVIDUAL BASIS AND SUBMIT ORIGINAL WORK.

PLEASE NOTE:

(1)   Makeup examinations are not given unless advanced approval is granted.

(2)   Modification to class topics and related assignments can be expected as the course progresses.

DATE	TOPIC	ASSIGNMENT

Part I - Strategic Foundations

Introduction and Class Organization

Supply Chain Strategy/Structure

SCLM Ch. 1
• *Push to Streamline Supply Chains*

Lean Logistics

SCLM Ch. 2
• *Tailored Logistics: Next Source of Competitive Advantage*
• *Rethinking Distribution*

Performance Cycle Structure and Dynamics

SCLM Ch. 2
• *Reverse Logistics Strengthens Supply Chains*
• *Reverse Logistics: A Second Chance to Profit*

Customer Accommodation

SCLM Ch. 3
• *Staple Yourself to an Order*
• *Realize Your Customers Full Profit Potential*
• *Do You Want to Keep Your Customers Forever?*

Market Distribution Strategy

SCLM Ch. 4
• *Mass Customization at Hewlett-Packard*
• *Go Downstream: The New Profit Imperative in Manufacturing*

Procurement and Manufacturing

SCLM Ch. 5
• *Economy's Power Shift*
• *Holding the Hand that Feeds*

Operational Integration

SCLM Ch. 6

DATE	TOPIC	ASSIGNMENT
	Examination - Part I	
	Part II - Information Technology	
	Information Networks	SCLM Ch. 7 • *Beyond ERP - The Storm Before the Calm* • *Are Supply Chain Systems via ERP Viable?*
	ERP, APS and Extension Systems	SCLM Ch. 8 • *A Brief History of APS* • *Packaged Application Strategies*
	Forecasting and CPFR	SCLM Ch. 9 • *State-of-the-Art Supply Chain Forecasting* • *How to Win at Educated Guessing* • *Nabisco Inc. and Wegmans Food Markets*
	Part III - Operations	
	Inventory - Level	SCLM Ch. 10
	Inventory - Deployment	SCLM Ch. 10
	Inventory Strategy	• Inventory Problem
	Review Part II and Inventory	
	Examination - Part II and Inventory	
	Transportation - Model Structure and Regulatory Framework	SCLM Ch. 11
	Transportation - Rates/Tariffs	SCLM Ch. 12 • Transportation Contract
	Warehouse Functionality	SCLM Ch. 13 • *Speeding Through the Warehouse*

DATE	TOPIC	ASSIGNMENT
	Warehouse Evaluation Case	• Hershey Chocolate Case
	Warehouse Operations	SCLM Ch. 14 • *An Inside View of the Scanning Market* • *Material Handling Guidelines*
	Review Transportation and Warehousing	

Examination - Transportation and Warehousing

Part IV - Integration

	Process Integration	SCLM Ch. 15 • *How Process Enterprises Really Work*
	Network Integration	SCLM Ch. 15
	Design Methodology	SCLM Ch. 16
	Organization and Relationship Mgt.	SCLM Ch. 17
	Performance Measurement	SCLM Ch. 18 • *Demings Message for Management Accountants*

Examination IV - Integration

Challenge Questions and Answers

Chapter 1

1. Why can the current movement toward establishing supply chains be characterized as a revolution?

Traditionally firms felt the need to cooperate with their supply chain partners. However the association was limited to an acknowledged dependency and institutional specialization. There was a lack of commitment primarily due to lack of high quality information. However during the last decade, rapid advancements have taken place in the area of information technology. This has enhanced the speed of obtaining and sharing of information between the supply chain partners and consequently increased the level of collaboration within the traditional distribution channel. This process was accelerated with the Internet and worldwide web explosion.

With this arrangement, managers were able to reduce non-value-added services, duplication, and redundancy between the consecutive stages of order fulfillment process. Moreover the managers began to believe that such sharing could be beneficial for the partners. These efforts to extend and leverage the operating range of the individual firms have propelled the manifestation of collaborative supply chains. This transformation has been so rapid and abrupt that it could be labeled as a revolution.

2. Compare the concept of a modern supply chain with more traditional distribution channels. Be specific regarding similarities and differences.

Traditional distribution channels typically had an order fulfillment time of 15-30 days. But if something went wrong, this time would increase dramatically. It was a common practice to maintain inventory at every stage of the supply chain like retailers, wholesalers, and manufacturers. The market was characterized by scarcity to the primary goal of traditional model was to ensure availability of products. However today customers want more options in product offerings. Modern supply chain is geared towards meeting the changing consumer needs. Transportation capacity and operational performance has become more reliable and economical. Logistical systems are capable of capable of delivering products at exact times. So customer orders can be fulfilled faster. With massive development in information technology, the need to maintain inventory has reduced dramatically. The occurrence of failures, characteristic of traditional supply chain, has been replaced by a commitment towards zero-defect of six sigma performance. In essence a high level of performance is achieved at a lower total cost with commitment of fewer financial resources than that in the past.

3. What specific role does logistics play in supply chain operations?

Logistics is the primary conduit of product and service flow within a supply chain arrangement. It is the work required to move and to position inventory throughout a supply chain. It is a combination of order management, inventory, transportation, warehousing, material handling and packaging as integrated throughout a facility network. Logistics is essential for effective supply chain connectivity.

4. **Describe "Integrative Management." Be specific concerning the relationship between functionality and process.**

Traditionally firms have been functionally focused. All work was performed and measured on a functional basis and the belief was that better the performance of a specific function, the greater the efficiency of the overall process. Integrative management aims to emphasis process achievement over functionality. It focuses on the total lowest process cost rather than lowest cost for each function in the process because it has become apparent that functions, individually performed best in class, do not necessarily combine to achieve the total lowest cost. Instead, lowest cost can be achieved by capturing the trade-offs that exist between the functions. Even though the underlying philosophy of Integrative Management makes logical sense, identification, measurement and implementation of the total process solutions is easier said than done.

5. **In terms of enterprise extension, describe the importance of the information-sharing and process specialization paradigms?**

Enterprise extension is based on two basic paradigms: information sharing and process specialization. Information sharing paradigm is based on the premise that in order to achieve higher cooperation, supply chain partners should be willing to share operating information and jointly plan their strategies. This information that is shared should not only be the historical or sales data but should also include strategic information about future activities in order to facilitate joint planning. The underlying philosophy of this paradigm is to have a supply chain, which can meet customers' demands faster and more efficiently.
The process specialization paradigm focuses on planning joint operations between supply chain partners with the goal of eliminating non-productive or non-value-added work. It also aims to design the overall supply chain in such a way that specific firms are responsible and accountable for each element of the value added work.
Even though enterprise extension has the capability of removing the inefficiencies of a supply chain, it introduces new challenges regarding measurement, risk sharing, trust, leadership and conflict resolution.

6. **Describe and illustrate an integrated service provider. How does the concept of integrated service provider differ from traditional service providers, such as for-hire transportation and warehousing?**

Integrated Service Providers (ISP) also known as third-party logistics providers provide a range of logistics services that includes all work necessary to service customers. With the regulatory changes in the transportation the traditional logistics services providers started offering warehousing and shared transportation services. Therefore the ISPs initiated the radical shift from single function to multifunction outsourcing. Their services include order entry to product delivery and in certain situations they also provide wide range of value-added services. For example United Parcel Services (UPS) stocks Nike shoes and warm-ups at its Louisville warehouse and processes orders hourly. All the related communication and financial administration are handled by an UPS call center in San Antonio. Therefore UPS handles the basic logistics and value-added services for Nike.

In contrast the traditional service providers, such as for-hire transportation and warehousing specialize in specific functions. For instance, the for-hire transportation industry consists of carriers who specialize in moving products between geographic locations. The companies offering warehouse services are traditionally called public warehouses and they provide storage supplemented by specialized services.

7. **Compare and contrast anticipatory and response-based business models. Why has responsiveness become popular in supply chain collaborations?**

Anticipatory and response-based business models are the two ways used by firms to fulfill customer requirements. However the fundamental difference in the two models is timing **Anticipatory model** has been the traditional business practice, which was mainly forecast driven. Since information about purchasing behavior was not readily available, and the channel partners were loosely collaborating, businesses were driven by forecasts. However the forecasts used by the manufacturers, wholesales, distributors, and retailers were often different that led to a lot of excess inventory in the system. All the work was performed in anticipation of future projections, so the likelihood of misgauging customer requirements was very high. In addition, each firm in the chain duplicated the anticipatory process. **Response-based model** aims to reduce or eliminate forecast reliance by joint planning and rapid exchange of information between supply chain partners. This model has been made possible because managers can now obtain and share accurate sales information faster. Consequently customers can be provided with their desired items faster. This model requires fewer steps and therefore less cost to complete a fulfillment process compared to the anticipatory model. Response-based model is similar to a build to order model however the former has a faster response time and allows a higher degree of customization. Responsiveness propelled by information technology development has become the cornerstone of today's supply chain collaboration. Higher responsiveness can not only increase the level of customer satisfaction but can also reduce the overall cost of doing that.

8. **Compare and contrast manufacturing and geographic postponement.**

Manufacturing and geographic postponement are strategies and practices that reduces the anticipatory risks of supply chain performance. The factors favoring one over the other form depends on the volume, value, competitive initiatives desired customer service levels. **Manufacturing or form postponement** aims at manufacturing the products one order at a time with no preparatory work or component procurement until the customer specifications are fully known and customer commitment is received. The goal of this postponement strategy is to maintain products in a neutral or non-committed status as long as possible. In an ideal situation a standard or base product is manufactured in large quantities to obtain economy of scale while deferring the finalization until the customer commitment. In this scenario, economy of scope is introduced by producing the base product to accommodate a wide range of different customers. An example of manufacturing postponement is observed in mixing paint color at retail stores to accommodate the individual customer's request. This strategy not only reduces the risks of logistics malfunction but also increases the use of light manufacturing and final assembly at logistical facilities

On the other hand, **Geographical or logistical postponement** focuses on response acceleration. This strategy aims to build and stock a full-line inventory at one or more strategic locations. Forward deployment of inventory is postponed until the customer order is received. In an ideal situation this postponement strategy eliminates the risk of anticipatory risk of inventory deployment while retaining manufacturing economy scale. An example of geographical postponement is the Sears Store Delivery System. The logistics of the appliances is not initiated till the customer order is received. An appliance purchased on Monday can be installed at customer's home as early as Wednesday. And there is a possibility that the product is not manufactured until that night or early Tuesday.

In a number of supply chains both types of postponement strategies are combined to create a highly responsive strategy.

9. **Define and illustrate cash-to-cash conversion, dwell-time minimization and cash spin. How does supply chain strategy and structure impact each?**

Cash-to-cash conversion is the time required to convert raw material or inventory purchases into sales revenue. It is directly related to inventory turn. Its benefits are realized by reducing and sharing risk and inventory investment. In traditional business the benefits were enjoyed at the expense of business partners. For example, terms of 2% net 10 meant that a prompt payment discount could be earned if the invoice is paid within ten days from the time of delivery. In a response based system these benefits can be shared by managing the inventory transfer velocity across the supply chain. To facilitate such arrangements supply chain partners often use dead net pricing, which factors discounts and allowances in the selling price. Therefore incentives of timely payment are replaced by performance commitments at a specified net price. Managing supply chain logistics as a continuous synchronized process also serves to reduce dwell time.

Dwell time is the ratio of the time that an asset sits idle to the time required to satisfy its designated supply chain mission. As an example dwell time would represent the ratio of the time inventory is in store to the time it is moving or contributing to achieve supply chain objectives. Dwell time can be reduced if the supply chain partners are willing to eliminate duplicate work. Therefore each firm could be designated to perform and be accountable for the value-added work in order to reduce the overall dwell.

Cash spin basically refers to free cash spin. This concept aims to reduce the overall assets committed to the supply chain performance. Therefore capital invested on inventory or warehouse can be made available for redeployment by revising the supply chain arrangement. Free capital can be reinvested in other projects that would have otherwise not been considered.

10. **Discuss and support the following argument: "supply chain arrangements may reduce consumer value."**

There could be potential downsides to an efficient supply chain management that may reduce the consumer value. Firstly, operating efficiency does not result into lower consumer prices. Firms collaborating within a supply chain network make higher profits and thereby increase shareholders' value. However, this mechanism does not guarantee that the benefits will be passed on to the consumers. With the increasing shift towards monopolistic supply chain structures, there is a potential of higher prices. As an example the Efficient Consumer Response (ECR) in the food industry does not show any reduction of food prices in spite of increasing collaboration.

A second argument builds on the premise that operating efficiency may not always be socially equitable. For example, if products are moved in precise quantities, there will be no overstocks or surplus to be marked down during clearance sales, etc. Therefore for the lady who buys final closeout garments at below cost price would loose out. In conclusion, firms can make reasonable profits by not being highly efficient and at the same time allow the low-end customers to realize superior values from their purchases.

Chapter 2

1. Illustrate a common trade-off that occurs between the work areas of logistics.

Any illustration that demonstrates an inherent trade-off between information, inventory, transportation, warehousing, material handling or packaging is acceptable. The following are a few examples of such tradeoffs:

Information is increasingly being used as a substitute for inventory. For instance, a warehouse manager that is in constant contact with a supplier of his/her stocks need not hold traditional, high levels of inventory. By being "connected", the supplier realizes when the warehouse is in need of product and can make accommodations of product processing and shipping accordingly. Improved, faster means of transportation also prevent manufacturers and merchandisers from holding high levels of inventory.

Poor packaging can lead to product damage in transit. Management should either improve packaging or seek a transportation mode that is more stable and less damage-inducing. Regardless, greater costs will be incurred upfront – though they are likely to be offset with reduced costs of product recollection and rework.

2. Discuss and elaborate the following statement: "The selection of a superior location network can create substantial competitive advantage."

The statement "The selection of Superior location network can create substantial competitive advantage" holds true with regard to logistical networks. The network design implies customer service and cost considerations. Added value (and perhaps a competitive advantage) may be derived from the "intimacy" of being located near customers. Networks that strive for the highest levels of effectiveness (superior service performance) often do so at significantly higher expense. Networks may also be designed for efficient product flows in order to lower transportation and inventory holding costs. Depending upon the competitive environment in which a firm operates, competitive advantage may result from either being located near the customers to provide superior service or through low cost service with the cost-efficient network design.

3. Why are market-distribution operations typically more erratic than manufacturing support and procurement operations?

Market or physical distribution operations are typically more erratic because they are initiated by the customer, whose behavior can not be controlled by the firm. Manufacturing and procurement operations, on the other hand, are initiated by the firm and considered to be within the firm's span of control. However, better communications between the logistics organization and customers can reduce the uncertainty and erratic nature of market-distribution operations.

4. How has transportation cost, as a percentage of total logistics cost, tracked since 1980?

The transportation costs as a percentage of total logistics costs in US has increased over the last 20 years. In 1980, the percentage was approximately 47% and this has gone up to 60% by 1999. Therefore transportation represents a significant portion of the overall logistics cost.

5. **Describe the *logistics value proposition*. Be specific regarding specific customer accommodation and cost.**

Logistical value proposition is a cost framework that aims to match of operating competency and commitment to meet the individual of selected groups of customers' expectations and requirements. A well-designed logistical network must have high customer response with low operational variance and minimum inventory commitment. However the combinations will be different for different groups. Well designed and operated logistical system can help firms to achieve competitive advantage.

6. **Describe the fundamental similarities and differences between procurement, manufacturing support and market-distribution performance cycles as they relate to logistical control.**

Procurement performance cycles consist of the many activities that maintain the flow of materials, parts, or finished goods into a manufacturing or distribution facility. The scope of procurement activities is limited. Although similar to the customer order processing cycle, shipments are generally larger and cycles often require much more time. Maintaining raw materials inventory is sometimes less expensive relative to finished goods, since time of delivery and material security is often less sensitive into facility than out to the customer. Another difference is that the number of suppliers of a firm is generally less than the number of customers, making the procurement cycle more direct.

Manufacturing support performance cycles serve as the logistics of production. These functions maintain orderly and economic flow of materials and work-in-process inventory to support production schedules. The goal is to support manufacturing requirements in the most efficient manner. These are internal cycles to the firm, thus they are rarely affected by behavioral uncertainty.

Physical distribution performance cycles are those associated with processing and delivering customer orders. They link the customers through timely and economical product availability. Physical distribution integrates marketing and manufacturing efforts. To improve the effectiveness of the distribution system, forecast accuracy must improve to reduce uncertainty. In addition to the value of sound forecasting methods, the firm must emphasize flexibility and responsiveness to deal with the uncertainty of customers in the physical distribution cycle.

7. **Compare and contrast a performance cycle node and a link. Give an example of each.**

Nodes are facility locations. Forms of communications and transportation represent **links** between the nodes. Most logistical work takes place at nodes whereas links represent the interface among locations. Nodes represent network facilities where materials are processed and base inventories and safety stocks are maintained. Inventory that is in between nodes is called "in transit".

8. **How does the "quest for quality" affect logistical operations? Does the concept "total quality" have relevancy when applied to logistics?**

Though logistical service quality is often in the eye of the beholder – that is, the definition of quality varies among suppliers and customers, it is possible to pursue a quest for quality. The quest requires logistics organizations to identify the service qualities that customers most highly value. Upon identifying these key dimensions of service, it is up to the firm to flawlessly execute those functions that add value. Ultimately, customers may demand "perfect order" performance, a level of service that requires suppliers to meet expectations without error.

The ideals of total quality – namely, doing things right the first time, does find relevance in logistics. It is far better in terms of customer service and low cost to provide customers with desired service on the first effort. Customers more highly value suppliers that meet their promises, delivering product on time, in proper quantities, and without damage. Costs are reduced in the process as fewer products are recollected and reworked. These costs of service or product failure can be eliminated if processes are corrected, ensuring that the problem is not a recurring one. Over time, customers tend to rely on those suppliers that provide sound service time and again.

9. **Discuss uncertainty as it relates to the overall logistical performance cycle. Discuss and illustrate how performance cycle variance can be controlled.**

One of the major objectives of logistical management is to reduce the uncertainty in performance cycles. Since the performance cycles are made up of many activities, each with its own volatility or variance, variance over the entire cycle can significantly impede the logistics organization's efficiency and effectiveness.

To control variance, the firm must conform expected cycle time to actual cycle time. If cycle time is less than expected, the delivered product becomes inventory to be stored. If the cycle time is longer than expected, then the firm must rely on safety stocks to satisfy customer demand. In either case there are costs associated with variance. The ides is to eliminate variance by equating actual cycle time to the expected cycle time. This may require adjustments in product flows into or out of the organization.

10. **What is the logic of designing echeloned logistical structures? Can echeloned and direct structures be combined?**

The echeloned logistical structure is built on the logic of stocking some level of inventory or performing specific activities at consecutive levels of supply chain. This structure utilizes warehouses to create inventory assortments and achieve consolidation economies associated with large volume transportation shipments. The inventory is position to meet the customers' requirements faster. Typical echelon systems use either break bulk or consolidation warehouses.

However the service commitment and order size economies determine the most desirable and economical structure to service the specific customer. So many supply chains use a combination of echeloned and direct structures to meet their logistical needs.

Chapter 3

1. **Explain the differences between "transactional" and "relationship" marketing. How do these differences lead to increasing emphasis on logistical performance in supply chain management?**

   Transactional marketing is generally focused towards short-term interaction with customers. Traditional marketing strategies followed this approach wherein exchanges/transactions are carried out with customers in order to increase their revenues and profits.

   Relationship marketing focuses on the long-term relations with the key supply chain partners such as the consumers, intermediate customers and suppliers. This strategy aims to develop and retain long term preference and loyalty because it has been realized in many industries that it is more important to obtain greater share of the purchases made by the existing customers than to attract new customers. This approach tries to identify the individual customers in order to satisfy their unique needs in the most cost-efficient and effective way. This requires a greater emphasis on logistical performance of the entire supply chain.

2. **Why are the four primary service outputs of spatial convenience, lot size, waiting time, and product variety important to logistics management? Provide examples of competing firms, which differ in the level of each service output provided to customers.**

   Since every customer has different requirements regarding service outputs, spatial convenience, lot size, waiting or delivery time, and product variety represent the four generic outputs to accommodate customer requirements.

   Spatial convenience measures the amount of shopping time and effort that needs to be out by the customer. Higher convenience is offered by making the product available in more number of places. As an example some household furniture manufacturers offer their products through department store, mass merchandisers and other independent department stores whereas Ethen Allen offers its products only at its own Allen retail stores.

   Lot size refers to the number of units that can be purchased in each transaction. A customer who wish to buy larger quantity of items for example 12 or 24 rolls of paper towels to get a lower unit price can get it from Sam's Club and Costco. However they can buy single rolls from grocery or convenient stores. The basic tradeoff in such purchases is between the unit price and the storage or maintenance cost of such volumes.

   Waiting time is the amount if time a customer has to wait between ordering and receiving products. The lower the waiting time, the higher is the level of service. Buying products from retail or grocery stores has no waiting time however if someone wants to order from a catalog or via the Internet, he has to wait for the product. Although higher waiting time is associated with inconvenience, customers are rewarded in the form of lower prices.

   Product variety refers to the different assortments or variety offered to the consumers and end-users. Supermarkets offer a large variety of items, whereas the warehouse stores offer a much less variety. And convenience stores offer even lesser variety.

3. **What is meant by availability in logistics customer service? Provide examples of the different ways to monitor a firm's performance in availability.**

Availability is the capacity to have inventory when desired by a customer. Typically companies stock inventory in anticipation of demand. Inventory is classified into two groups: base stock determined by forecasted and planned requirements, and safety stock to cover unexpected variations in demand. There are three performance measures of availability: stockout frequency, fill rate, and ordered shipped complete.

Stockout occurs when the firm does not have product to fulfill customer demand. However a stockout does not occur until the customer desires the product. *Stockout frequency* is the probability that a firm will not have inventory to meet an order. For example on an average retail supermarkets are out of stock eight percent of the time.

Fill rate measures the impact of stockouts over time. For example if a customer wants 100 units of an item and only 97 are available then the fill rate is 97 percent. Fill rate performance can be evaluated for a specific customer, product, or for any combination of customers, products, or business segments. This measure assumes greater importance if for critical items, where even 97 percent may not be acceptable.

Orders shipped complete is the most exacting measure of performance in product availability. For example failure to provide even one item on the customer's order leads to a zero in terms of complete shipment.

The combination of these three measures can establish the extent to which a firm's inventory strategy accommodates customers' requirements.

4. **Compare and contrast speed, consistency, and flexibility as operational performance activities. In some situation, is one activity more critical than others?**

Speed is the elapsed time from the order placement to shipment arrival. It can vary from a few hours to weeks. Not all customers need or want speed if it increases their costs. With faster performance, customers need not invest so heavily in inventory. **Flexibility** is the ability to handle extraordinary customer service requests. With logistics as a core competency, the flexible company is able to do what others consider impossible.

In certain situations speed or flexibility may be more important. For example, if the firm's product is commodity-like, easily storable, and highly standardized, flexibility may not be very important. Here, speed takes precedence, assuring availability. On the other hand, for highly customized products, customers are usually willing to wait, flexibility to satisfy special orders becomes important.

5. **Why is perfect order service so difficult to achieve?**

A perfect order refers to an order, which is delivered complete, delivered on time, at the right place, in perfect condition, with accurate and complete documentation. Alternatively, the total order cycle performance must be executed with zero defects. It is very difficult to achieve perfect order service because it requires substantial resources, so companies offer such service on a selective basis. Moreover such service cannot be based totally on inventory. It can be achieved only by a combination of customer alliances, information technology, postponement strategy, inventory strategy, transportation and selectivity programs to match the logistical resources to meet customer needs.

6. **Using the ten categories of customer expectations in Table 3-1, develop your own examples of how customers might evaluate performance of a supplier.**

Reliability refers to performance of all activities by the supplier. If Fedex promises overnight delivery and fails to do that, then it will be considered unreliable, even if it is done faster than any other provider. Customers can judge reliability in terms of all aspects of basic service platform.

Responsiveness refers to the customer's expectation of the ability and willingness to provide timely service. If Walmart experiences a stockout of certain product, its supplier's responsiveness will be measured by the time it takes for replenishment.

Access measures the ease of contact and approachability of the supplier. For example the ease of obtaining information about the status of a pending order will measure accessibility.

Communication means to proactively keeping the customer informed. If the supplier expects a shortage of raw material that can affect delivery in the future, an advance notice to the customer will not only help to explore alternative but also builds a stronger partnership.

Credibility refers to the customer's expectation that the communication from the suppliers will be believable and honest. The real essence of this measure is the completeness of the information.

Security refers to the customer's feeling of risk in doing business with a supplier. For example a customer bases its production schedule in anticipation of delivery. If the supply is delayed the customer faces the risk of changing its plans. Another aspect of security concerns the confidentiality of business dealings. For example, Solectron undertakes the manufacturing for competitors like Nortel and Cisco, so confidentiality is a major issue.

Courtesy involves politeness, friendliness and respect of contact person. Since the customer may have to deal with different individuals in the supplier's organization, failure by one person can destroy the best efforts of all the others.

Competency is judged by customers in every interaction with the suppliers. Therefore a truck drivers competency is measured when deliveries are made, customer service personnel when phone calls are made, etc. Failure by any individual can affect the customer's perception of the supplier.

Tangibles refer to the customer's expectation of the physical appearance of facilities, equipment and personnel. For example a old and dilapidated warehouse can be an indicator of the firm's overall performance to the customers.

Knowing the customer refers to the customer's expectation regarding supplier's understanding of their unique requirements and supplier willingness to adapt to those needs. For example WalMart would expect its suppliers to understand its unique need and respond to that accordingly.

7. **Which of the "gaps" in Figure 3-1 do you think represent the major problem for most firms? How can a company attempt to eliminate the knowledge gap? The Communications Gap?**

Knowledge gap, performance gap, and communication gap represent the major concerns for most organizations. The other gaps are derivatives of the above three gaps. Knowledge gap exists between the customer's real expectations and the manager's perception of those expectations. A thorough understanding of the customer's expectations, how they are prioritized and how they are formed can reduce this gap. The communication gap arises due to over-commitment, or promising higher levels of performance. Giving realistic expectations to the customers and fulfilling those expectations can reduce this gap. The customers should also be made aware of what the firm is capable of doing.

8.   **Compare and contrast the customer service, customer satisfaction, and customer success philosophies of supply chain management.**

Customer service, customer satisfaction, and customer represent three levels of customer accommodation. **Customer service** represents logistics role in fulfilling the marketing concept. It aims to provide the right amount of the right product at the right time at the right place in the right condition at the right price with right information. The fundamental attributes of customer service are availability, operational performance, and service reliability. **Customer satisfaction** measures the degree to which a customer is satisfied with the supplier's performance. However customer satisfactions depends a lot on the customer's expectations. Models have been developed to identify some of the gaps that arise due the failure of many firms to satisfy their customers. **Customer success philosophy** requires the firms to work very closely with the customers to understand their requirements, internal processes, competitive environment and try to make their customer successful. In contrast to the typical focus of basic service and satisfaction programs to meet standards and expectations of the customers, a customer success program tries to understand the entire supply chain, different levels of customers and tries to ensure that customer at each level is able to meet their customers.

9.   **What is meant by value-added services? Why are these services considered essential in a customer success program?**

Value added services refer to the unique and specific activities that firms can jointly perform to enhance their efficiency and effectiveness. Such services foster customer success. These services are typically customer specific and therefore cannot be generalized. These services enable the customers to achieve their specific objectives. These are considered essential in customer service programs because by providing unique product packages, creating customized unit loads, offering unique information services, providing VMI, etc, firms enhance their customers' success. Some of the value-added services like warehousing, transportation, proper sequencing and sorting of products involve specialists due to their flexibility and capability to concentrate on providing the required services.

10.   **How could a company use the four-stage process of cost-effectiveness, market access, market extension, and market creation to gain competitive superiority?**

Cost effectiveness is the first and most fundamental step of logistical competency to gain competitive superiority. It is essential for a firm to provide basic services at a consistently high level of performance and in a cost-effective manner. Without this basic pre-requisite there is limited possibility of building any relationship.

Market Access stage represents a higher level of commitment to the customers who are willing to cooperate. This involves sharing of basic information between the buyers and sellers to facilitate smooth operation. This stage however does not require a high degree of customer selectivity.

Market extension aims to move towards zero defects and introducing value-added services in order to build and strengthen business relationship. This stage witnesses customer selectivity since the number of customers that are willing or able to participate is limited. The companies could be involved in innovative value-added services, which are designed to increase operating efficiency and extend overall competitiveness.

Market creation is the final stage and requires full commitment for customer's success. This could involve creative arrangements like electronically linking with the customers.

Building such relationships take time and long term commitment to be successful.

Chapter 4

1.   Why is specialization so critical to distribution efficiency?

Specialization is a fundamental driver of economic efficiency. When a firm specializes in the performance of particular logistical function, it develops scale and scope to achieve operational efficiency. No matter who performs the specific work, all the functions need to be performed in order to complete the distribution process. However in order to achieve distribution efficiency, the work needs to be carried out in the most cost-effective and efficient way: and this can be achieved only by specialization.

2.   Describe how the process of assortment overcomes the problems created by specialization.

Product assortment is directly related to specialization. It is the process, which is used to eliminate any discrepancy of quantity and to create a mix of products. There are four basic steps of assortment namely concentration, allocation, customization, and dispersion. The basic purpose of *concentration* is to reduce the overall transportation cost by moving large quantities of products to concentration location. *Allocation* is also referred to as the process of break bulking because it breaks down the case quantities received from the suppliers into individual product units. *Customization* regroups the products in assortments to be sold in association with other items in order to meet the customers' unique requirement. Dispersion promises to ship the customized assortments to the customers when and where specified.

Assortment attempts to take advantage of specialization however it incorporates the economics of market distribution as well as the customers' requirements in the planning process. It overcomes some of the issues associated with specialization, like over-production to achieve economy of scale, by focusing on the lowest total cost of satisfying customer's needs.

3.   Given the principle of minimum transactions, explain why it is possible to have too many participants in a distribution channel.

Based on the economic *principle of minimum total transactions*, having more participants in the fulfillment process not only reduces the total number of transactions but also has the potential for a lower total cost. If we consider a situation in which three manufacturers supply to 10 retailers. There are a total of 30 transactions between the involved parties. Each of these transactions would involve order placement, order processing, and order fulfillment. And the cost of transportation would be typically high due to less than truckload shipments. However if a wholesaler is added in this structure, the total number of transactions reduces to thirteen. Moreover the cost of transportation also reduces because now there would be only thirteen shipments and each would be of a larger quantity than the earlier case. The intermediary (wholesaler) can also be compensated by the savings accrued by the manufacturers and retailers. Therefore it is possible to have more participants because it ultimately leads to more value creation and cost savings in the entire distribution process.

4. **What is the primary logic behind potential separation of marketing and logistics channel structure?**

Even though marketing and logistics functions represent activities that are necessary, however they need not be done simultaneously or by the same party. Therefore, in many situations it makes a lot of economic sense to separate these two channels. The marketing channel deals with the buying and selling functions related to ownership transfers, whereas logistics channel handles the function of physical distribution. Conceptually there is no need for a firm to participate in both the channels. For example, a television retailer only needs to maintain stock for point-of-sale display in its store. Upon the sale of a particular television, the item is shipped from a distributor's strategically located public warehouse directly to the consumer's home. Therefore we observe that channel separation results in low-cost delivery and effective marketing. This methodology is also very useful for direct marketing systems viz. Order placed by phone or via website.

5. **How does the risk related to inventory compare among manufacturers, wholesalers, and retailers?**

Manufacturers take the significant risk of creating the products. Even though the manufacturer's risk in the overall distribution process is considerable, it is limited to the specific product that they produce.
Wholesalers are responsible for buying merchandise from the manufacturers and selling to the retailers. They do not bear a large amount of inventory risk. Eventhough with the mergers and acquisitions happening in the manufacturing and retail sectors, it seemed that wholesaling does not have an economic justification it still flourishes in some industries.
Retailers are responsible for selling goods and services to the consumers. They perform the functions to offer the customers the right products, at the right place, at the right time, in the right quantity, and at the right price. Therefore a major component of retail strategy is merchandise assortment. Therefore the inventory risk assumed by the retailers is substantial.

6. **Why wouldn't a manufacturer desire to always have intensive distribution coverage?**

A manufacturer would not always want to have an intensive distribution coverage because if some outlets choose to sell its product at a lower price to attract customers then the other retailers may not be willing to carry this manufacturer's product. Also if some outlets are not able to provide desired level of after sale service, then the others can also be affected. Lastly, if the manufacturer wants to participate in the marketing functions then the dealers who were erstwhile doing this would be reluctant to carry this product. Therefore even though intensive distribution seems to be the logical market coverage strategy, it may not always be the right choice for the manufacturer.

7. **How could the matrix approach to design be applied to logistics activities?**

Matrix approach is a tool used in channel design. This approach uses the concept of channel separation and aims to relate activities to participants. The matrix design subdivides each function into individual activities. Each activity can be potentially performed by different channel partners for specific customer segments. .

8. **Distinguish between the four types of relational collaborative arrangements. Provide an example of each.**

The four types of Relational Collaborative Arrangements (RCA) are: 1) administered systems; 2) partnerships and alliances; 3) contractual systems; and 4) joint ventures. **Administered systems:** This is the least informal form of RCA. In this arrangement, the trading partners do not enter into any formal agreement, however the dominant firm typically assumes the leadership role. All the partners cooperate with the understanding that they will be better off by working together under the leader. A typical example would be the automobile industry wherein the auto manufacturer can assume the leadership role for the various tiers of suppliers involved in the process.
Partnerships and alliances represent arrangements that are more formalized and has greater clarity than the administered systems. In an alliance firms typically willing to give up some of their operational autonomy in order to pursue specific goals. Its primary goal is to cooperatively build on the combined resources of participating firms in order to improve the performance, quality and competitiveness of the channel. Partnerships reflect commitment far greater than an administered arrangement. They are built on the desire to work together with the intent of resolving differences and willingness to share information. Typical example of partnership can be seen in the arrangement between Ford Motor Company and Daimler-Chrysler, and their common supplier Exel Logistics resulting in efficiency improvement in distributing auto parts to the dealers.
Contractual systems are the most common form of RCA found with dealerships, franchises, and service specialists. In this arrangement the firms enter into a formal contract for conducting business mutually. This establishes a set of legal obligations for the parties. Many of the contracts are aimed towards the logistical activities necessary to complete distribution. The most common form of RCA contract involves the for-hire transportation. A typical example would be a carrier's agreement to regularly provide a predetermined amount of equipment to the shipper. The shipper in turn agrees to load and position the equipment for efficient pickup by the carrier.
Joint Venture occurs when two or more firms opt to jointly invest in an arrangement. This situation can occur when the capital investment is so high that one firm can not bear it. This occurs when a shipper decides to fully outsource all its logistical requirements and consequently establishes a joint venture with a service firm..

9. **What do you believe will be the impact of the Internet on market-distribution by the 2010?**

With the advent of internet, there have been some fundamental changes in the market distribution. We have seen the emergence of new trends like e-tailing, direct channel between consumers and manufacturers, etc. However this is only a transitional phase and a new distribution structure would emerge in the near future. *E-tailing* will be another channel for the retailers to fulfill the consumers' needs. Because of the inherent advantages of locational convenience of shopping from a computer, broader assortment of offerings, and availability of information the e-channel will be a very attractive proposition for the consumers. However companies have to find foolproof ways to overcome the challenges of physical distribution, security in credit card transactions. We are also observing a trend of *disintermediation*, whereby the need of traditional marketing channels is being eliminated and the producers and consumers directly interact for any transaction. However this may not be a ubiquitous phenomenon in the long run because historically manufacturers are not adept in completing logistical fulfillment such consumer-direct transactions. Moreover this can disrupt the long-standing relationship of these manufacturers with the retailer, who are responsible for a significant volume of the business. Also from the consumer's perspective, this arrangement does not offer the broad selection of products that is offered by the retailers. The channels are also becoming complex by *hypermediation*. Traditional retailers are taking help of such intermediaries as portals, affiliate sites etc in order to harness the potential of internet to extend their channels of distribution.

In the next 10 years, companies would primarily focus on solving the logistical issues in order to build more cost-effective and profitable business model.

10. **What is a shipper's responsibility when terms of purchase are F.O.B. origin? F.O.B. destination? Why would a shipper prefer one over the other?**

In the F.O.B. origin pricing the shipper/seller indicates the price at the point of origin. The buyer is responsible for choosing the mode of transportation, choosing a carrier, and also taking the risk of in-transit damages. Since the title of the products passes to the buyer as soon as the shipments leaves the shipper's premises, the shipper has no more liability. On the other hand, in FOB-destination pricing the title does not transfer till the delivery is complete. Therefore the shipper is responsible for transportation and associated risks.

Since transportation is outsourced, the selling companies do not have a lot of control over the physical movement of the items. Therefore for fragile/ delicate items, the sellers are better off with a F.O.B. origin pricing. However for most of the other products, the shippers can safely go for FOB destination pricing. Even though the risks are low, shipper can make some profit by build a risk-margin in its cost structure.

Chapter 5

1. **Using television receivers as an example, how could three different brands be perceived by different consumers as being the best quality brand in the market?**

   Product quality is a combination of various dimensions, how they are blended by an organization and how that blend is perceived by the customer. A television receiver brand with a remote control, picture-in-picture, on-screen programming is considered to be of a higher quality than the standard model by a customer, who perceives features to be the most important dimension of quality. For a customer for whom the performance is the most important yardstick of quality, a receiver brand even without the above features would be a high quality product. A brand, which has higher reliability and durability could be considered to be the best quality by a customer who considers these dimensions to be the most important. Therefore it is very important for brand managers of any product to understand the quality expectations of their target customers and position their brands appropriately.

2. **Why does the contemporary view of procurement as a strategic activity differ from the more traditional view of "purchasing?"**

   Purchasing has been typically viewed as a low-level managerial activity responsible for executing and processing orders for other departments of the organization. Its role was to obtain the resource at the lowest possible price from the supplier. Procurement on the other hand has a more strategic role that emphasizes on establishing relationships between buyers and sellers. The need for procurement arose due to the recognition of substantial dollar volume of purchases and the potential dollar savings from this strategic approach.

3. **How can strategic procurement contribute to the quality of products produced by a manufacturing organization?**

   The quality of the final product depends on the quality of parts or materials that goes into making it. However ensuring the quality of individual item may not be the sufficient, because it has been observed that if a standard part is procured from different suppliers, it is possible that the final product may encounter quality problems. By maintaining a quality perspective with the suppliers, strategic sourcing can make a substantial impact on the saving cost for the organization.

4. **Explain the rationale underlying volume consolidation. What are the risks associated with using a single supplier for an item?**

   Volume consolidation is one of the most common procurement strategies that is used by firms. By consolidating its purchase volume the buying company can leverage its share of the shipper's business. It also gives the buyer a greater negotiating strength. From the seller's perspective, such an arrangement can offer greater economies of scale by being able to spread the fixed costs over greater volume of output. Moreover, if the large volume of business is assured to the supplier, it will be willing to invest in improving its processes and customer service. Many companies have generated a lot of dollar savings by adopting this strategy.

There may be risks associated with having a single supplier for an item. In the event of any disruption in supply, the buying company does not have any alternative. Moreover due to lack of competition, the supplier might charge higher. Therefore companies should undertake rigorous screening to determine the strategic suppliers and rather than having only one supplier for the items, they should aim for a small pool of suppliers.

5.   How does lowest total cost of ownership differ from lowest purchase price?

Purchase price is one of the major concerns of procurement so firms typically try to negotiate for the lowest price. They also try to get quantity discounts and associated logistical benefits out of the purchase price. Apart from the standard services, there could be other value-added services that are offered by the sellers. For example a seller may deliver truckloads of material as a standard service, however delivery of smaller and more frequent shipments would represent a different level of service that would come at a cost to the buyer. It is important to understand the trade-offs between the value-added service and its price in determining the total cost of ownership. The final component of TCO is the lifecycle costs like administrative expenses, costs of rework, replacement, scrap etc that are incurred before and after the purchase of the materials.

Therefore the purchase price of a material is only a portion of the total cost of ownership for a firm. Even though the purchase price remains the most important component of cost, other cost factors like service costs and life cycle costs should also be evaluated.

6.   What is the underlying rationale that explains why firms should segment their purchase requirements?

It has been usually found that a small percentage of material purchases account for a large percentage of the total dollar spent by a firm. This shows that all procured items/services are not similar and therefore it would be more cost-effective for a firm to segment its purchase requirements and adopt different strategies. The segmentation should not only be based on the dollar expenditure but should also consider the impact that the items have on the company's competitiveness. Supply base reduction and volume consolidation can however be appropriate for all types of material classes.

7.   Explain how constraints in manufacturing are interrelated with a company's decisions regarding volume and variety.

Volume and variety provide the manufacturing competency to any firm. Volume helps a firm to take advantage of economy of scale because the cost per unit reduces with increase in the volume of the output. However if there is a capacity constraint then it may not be able to reach the demonstrated capacity of quality production to meet its volume objectives. Variety on the other hand represents the range of product variations that can be manufactured in a given manufacturing process. This represents the flexibility of the process by switching production from one product to another while retaining the efficiency, often referred to as economy-of-scope. Variety can be affected by equipment constraint caused by the range of available equipments and required sequence of work. Set-up/ changeover constraints can also affect the variety or flexibility. Therefore a firm should evaluate the various constraints before making any decision regarding volume and variety.

8. **Why would a company's costs of manufacturing and procurement tend to increase as the firm changes from a make-to-plan to a make-to-order strategy? Why would inventory costs tend to decrease?**

    Make-to-plan (MTP) is a manufacturing strategy, where production is planned on the basis of forecasted requirements. It aims to take advantage of economy of scales by having longer production runs. On the other hand, the make-to-order (MTO) strategy seeks to manufacture to customer specification. Consequently there will be smaller batch runs and greater change-overs. If a company moves from MTP to MTO, it cannot take advantage of volume and economy of scales and therefore its manufacturing and procurement costs increases. However the inventory and warehousing costs will decrease because of smaller lot sizes.

9. **How does a firm's marketing strategy impact its decisions regarding the appropriate manufacturing strategy.**

    A firm's marketing strategy can be typically classified as mass, segmental or one-to-one. This is based on the degree of product and service customization that the firm wants to offer to its customers. However for any of these strategies to be successful, the firm should choose an appropriate manufacturing strategy. The manufacturing capability has the potential to drive the feasible range of an effective marketing strategy. The marketing and manufacturing strategies in turn drive the logistical service requirements too. Therefore the goal of a company should be to have the lowest Total Cost of Manufacturing that can only be obtained by the functional integration of manufacturing, procurement, and logistics.

10. **Explain how logistics performance is crucial to a just-in-time philosophy.**

    The philosophy of JIT is to carry out activities in a time-phased manner so that the purchase materials arrive at the manufacturing point just at the time they are required for the transformation. It is not just restricted to the internal operations of the company but also involves the suppliers. Reliable logistics performance is absolutely crucial to eliminate or atleast reduce the need for buffer stocks of material. This can be achieved by close cooperation between the manufacturer's purchasing organization and the suppliers.

Chapter 6

1. **Compare and contrast economic, market, and relevancy value.**

   Economic, market, and relevancy values are created due to supply chain integration.
   Economic value represents the traditional perspective and is created by virtue of efficiency
   that is built on economy of scale. The primary focus of economic value is the efficiency of
   product/service creation. For the customer it means "high quality at a low price"
   Market value focuses on achieving economy-of-scope in product-service presentation.
   Therefore market value is about making an attractive assortment of products available at the
   right time and right place to increase effectiveness. Typical examples can be found in large-
   scale mass-merchandising retail stores, e-initiatives, etc. For the customer it means
   "convenient product-service assortment and choice".
   Relevancy value focuses on customization of value-added services and positioning itself in
   such a way that a real difference is made to the customers. It means the right product and
   services (market value) at the right price (economic value) positioned in a manner that
   creates valuable segmental distinction. For example in manufacturing and assembly, specific
   components are integrated into the products in order to increase the functionality desired by
   specific customers. For the customer it means "a unique product-service bundle".

2. **Illustrate the differences in product/service creation, presentation and positioning.**

   The focus of economic value is efficiency of **product/service creation**. It utilizes the fixed
   overhead to achieve lowest, total landed cost and seeks to do things as well as possible.
   Market value focuses on achieving economy-of-scope in **product-service presentation.**
   This is achieved by presenting attractive assortment of products at the right time and place.
   Positioning creates relevancy for the product by customizing it with value-added services. It
   aims to create a valuable segmental diversity over and above the market and economic value
   of the product/service.

3. **Explain the following statement "The methodology is systems analysis and the
   theoretical framework is the systems concept."**

   The **system concept** seeks total integration of components to achieve the desired objectives.
   The components of logistics system are called functions, which have been identified as
   order processing, inventory, transportation, warehousing, material handling and packaging,
   and facility network design. **System analysis** seeks to quantify the trade-offs between these
   functions. Its primary objective is to create an integrated system, which is greater than the
   sum of the individual components. System analysis focuses on the interaction between the
   components in achieving cross-functional integration.

4. **Why is variance reduction important to logistical integration? Illustrate in terms of
   logistical operations.**

   Variance reduction is one of the six operational objectives that need to be achieved
   simultaneously to achieve logistical integration. Variance reduction is the elimination of
   system disruptions. Variance can occur from any unexpected event in the logistical

fulfillment process. For example a delay in order processing, disruption in manufacturing, etc. are instances of variances. Typical solution to such variances is to build safety stock to buffer operations or use premium transportation for unexpected delayed delivery. However these measures are costly and can be minimized by using better information systems. The main objective of an integrated logistics management is to minimize variance, which ultimately leads to higher productivity.

5.   **What is the meaning of the phrase *cradle-to-cradle* logistics? Discuss the operational differences of original versus reverse logistics.**

A typical integrative strategy considers the original and reverse logistics of a product life cycle. **Cradle-to-cradle** logistics goes beyond the conventional focus and includes the possibility of aftermarket service, product recall and product disposal.

Original logistics refers to the movement of products from the manufacturing plants to the end customers. Reverse logistics is needed in cases of product returns due to bad quality, product expiration and responsibility for hazardous consequences. It also encompasses the return of beverage cans and packaging materials as needed by law. A sound integrative strategy cannot be formulated without a careful review of reverse logistical requirements.

6.   **How do reward systems serve as barriers to enterprise integration?**

Traditionally reward systems have been based on functional achievement, managers have strived for stand-alone performance. However enterprise integration requires cross-functional coordination. Therefore it is difficult to encourage the managers to view functions as contributing to a process rather than functional objective. To facilitate internal integration, measures like balanced scorecards are being developed because unless a suitable reward and measurement system is put in place, integration will remain more theory than practice.

7.   **In your words, describe and illustrate what the authors describe as the *Great Divide*. Do you believe the great divide phenomenon is as widely experienced as the text indicates? Support your position with an illustration.**

The *Great Divide* represents a situation wherein the supply chain integration is only partial instead of being end-to-end. This phenomenon is most commonly observed in the outbound or market-distribution side and the inbound or procurement-manufacturing side of an organization. This operational discontinuity can be generalized across different industries with similar challenges like 1) it is easier to integrate with groups external to the firm because of the relative balance of power; 2) senior managers do not have a clear vision of internal process requirements and related measures to drive enterprise-wide integration; and 3) barriers to integration within an enterprise.

A typical illustration of Great Divide is the availability of numerous forecasts within a firm. Each of the functions has to meet their target or objectives. Hence they make the projections for the future requirements in isolation, which ultimately leads to overstocking or stock-outs.

8. **What creates power in the context of supply chain collaboration? Why do many observers feel power is shifting forward or closer to end consumers in many supply chain arrangements?**

The relative power in supply chain collaboration can be due to the size of the firm, or the amount of risk a firm is willing to take or how much vital market information is available with it. The power is shifting forward towards the retailers because of four independent events. **First**, due to retail consolidation fewer retailers with extensive market coverage dominate the supply chains. **Second**, retailers have access to vital market information. By means of point-of-sale data, frequent shopper programs and credit cards information consumer trends can be identified and accommodated. The **third** factor favoring the retailers is that it is becoming difficult for high cost manufacturers to develop new brands. Finally, the logistical replenishment has become more response-based. Therefore the logistics system is driven by point of consumer purchase.

9. **Demonstrate your understanding of the relationship between logistical capabilities and competencies by tracing the evolution of logistical work to universal competencies. Does this logic have any practical application in understanding logistical sophistication? If so, what is the practical benefit?**

Capability is the knowledge and achievement level essential to developing integrated performance. Capabilities span the supply chain and are applicable to suppliers, manufacturers, wholesalers and retailers. Moreover they are observable and measurable within firms of all sizes. Fusing capabilities results in universal **competencies**. Therefore a competency is a result of the synthesis of several logistical capabilities into logistically coherent and manageable actions that achieve and maintain supply chain collaboration. Supply chains that achieve high level of integration of the competencies can gain customer loyalty and achieve competitive advantage. Identification of capabilities offers the first level of generalization. The universal competencies serve to blend logistics with the business. The positioning of logistics as a core competency expands the value generation in the supply chain integration.

10. **Compare and contrast import/export operations to local presence. What are the logistics ramifications of each state of international development?**

Export/Import and local presence represent the various stages in the continuum of global trade. **Export-import** is the initial stage wherein the organizations focus on internal operations and view internal transactions in terms of what they will do to for domestic business. Firms use service providers to conduct and manage operations in other countries. Such an orientation influences logistical decisions in three ways: *first*, sourcing and resource choices are influenced by artificial constraints like use restrictions, local content laws, and price surcharges; *second*, increases planning complexity; *third* firms attempt to extend the domestic logistics system and operating practices to global origins and destinations. This increases the complexity as there are more exceptions and the logistics management has to accommodate cultural, language, political environment, and other differences.

Local presence represents the second stage of international development where the firm establishes operations within a foreign country. The internal operations include marketing, sales, production and logistics operations. These facilities and operations increase the market presence for the firm. This stage increases the enterprise adaptability and sensitivity to unique market requirements in comparison to export-import stage.

Chapter 7

1. **Compare and contrast the role of ERP systems and planning systems in enhancing firm performance and competitiveness**

   ERP system and planning systems are kinds of information systems used by firms to operationalize their processes. **ERP systems** integrate the various operations of a firm and also maintain the integrity of data in its data warehouse. Beyond operational applications ERP systems also include financial, accounting and human resource capabilities. These systems however do not evaluate alternative strategies nor do they assist decision-making. These systems enhance the visibility across the supply chain and also make a common set data available to all the users. **Planning systems** a.k.a. advanced planning and scheduling (APS) are designed to evaluate the various alternatives and take suitable decisions based on the various constraints. There are generally two categories of planning systems: strategic and tactical. These systems enhance the competitiveness and logistical performance of the firms allowing them to better plan their activities and resource allocation for the future.

2. **Describe and contrast the role of radio frequency data communications and radio frequency identification for logistics and supply chain applications**

   Radio Frequency Data Communication (RFDC) is used to facilitate two-way information exchange. It is generally used within smaller areas like the distribution centers. This technology allows drivers to have access to real time information. Logistics RFDC applications are also used in warehouse selection cycle count verification and label printing. Advanced RFDC capabilities in the form of two-way voice communications capabilities is increasingly being used in logistics warehouse applications.
   Radio Frequency Identification (RFID) is used for identifying a container or its contents as it moves through the facilities or transportation equipments. A coded electronic chip is placed on the container or box. As the box or container moves through the supply chain, the code is canned to identify the contents. Retailers are also trying to implement such systems to scan entire loads of merchandise simultaneously.

3. **Compare and contrast the role of ERP systems and logistics execution systems.**

   ERP systems and execution systems are designed to facilitate an efficient and integrated supply chain for firms in different industries. Both these systems extensibly use technology to achieve its functionality. **ERP systems** integrate the various operations of a firm and also maintain the integrity of data in its data warehouse. Beyond operational applications ERP systems also include financial, accounting and human resource capabilities. **Execution systems** normally work in conjunction to the ERP systems to support specific logistics operations like warehouse management and transportation management. These systems are "bolted-on" or integrated to the ERP system to facilitate data exchange.

4. **Discuss the relative benefits of software purchase, use of third-party providers, and use of application software providers.**

    Even though the initial capital investment for **software purchase** could be very high, it offers higher security and low variable cost for the firm. Some firms outsource their information management to **third party providers** with the competency to implement and manage such technologies. The main advantage of this strategy is that the operational responsibility is assigned to specialist that has extensive resources to handle the hardware and software needs. Moreover these third party providers ensure security, redundancy and adequate backup support. **ASPs** are firms, which own and maintain computer hardware and software and rent clients on usage or transaction basis. They own websites that offer software, upgrades and database access to the clients. They are responsible for security, redundancy, and integrity of the website. Companies employ a combination of these three strategies depending on the criticality of the information system and the associated costs.

5. **Compare and contrast the role of EDI and the Internet for logistics and supply chain information exchange.**

    Electronic Data Interchange (EDI) enables the exchange of documents in standard formats between supply chain partners. It increases internal/external productivity, improves channel relationships, enhances the ability to compete internationally and also reduces the operating costs. The initial investment for such a system is huge, therefore it has not widely used by the small and medium-sized firms. Moreover communication and information standards are essential for any EDI transmission. The most commonly used standards are ASCX.12 and UNI/EDIFACT. However a lack of consistency in variable definition and interpretation has affected the widespread use of this medium. Internet has enhanced the possibilities of exchanging information between firms of all sizes. It offers a standard way of order entry, order status inquiry, and shipment tracking. Internet uses XML (Extensible Markup Language), which overcomes some of the sequencing problems encountered in EDI communications. The ubiquity of the internet has also led to the development of another communication medium called the exchange portals.

6. **Discuss the relative differences between contact and non-contact scanning.**

    Contact scanning using the technologies that require the scanning device to touch the bar code. This method reduces the scanning errors but also decreases flexibility. They can be either hand-held such as the wands or can be fixed type like the card readers. In contrast the non-contact scanners can scan codes without physically touching the item. This increases the flexibility of the operation. Laser guns are one of the most common non-contact type scanners used by businesses. There are some fixed-position non-contact scanners like the automatic scanners used by companies.

7. **What is a value-added network (VAN) and how does it resolve the disadvantages of different EDI transaction sets?**

Value-Added Networks (VANs) not only transfer information but also manage transactions, translate communications, and reduce the number of linkages. They commonly serve as the interface between sending and receiving systems. Functions of VANs include broadcasting of messages to subsets of suppliers, carriers or customers and the receipt of messages from the customers using different communication media. They accommodate the needs of several users simultaneously. VANs differ from EDI systems in that they difficult to duplicate since they are highly customized for particular clients.

8. **Compare and contrast the benefits and risks of firm level, industry level and cross-industry trade portals.**

   All the three levels of trade portals facilitate communication between the supply chain partners involved in business transactions. These portals have the potential to considerably reduce the transaction costs between the partners. A **firm-based portal** links a firm's customers and suppliers in order to exchange information and conduct business. A typical example could be GE's website. The **industry-based portal** aims to link the different partners within an industry. Covisint.com is an example of a industry-based portal that has been developed in the automobile industry. This portal offers a framework to exchange design information, proposal requests, commodity availability, etc between all partners of the automobile industry. A **cross-industry portal** allows the communication between firms with common interests in commodities and services. Tradematrix.com is an example of such a portal. Apart from the one-to-many kinds of transactions, these portals allow the partners to participate in auctions, reverse auctions kinds of transactions.

9. **Discuss and compare the role that EDI and the Internet will play in facilitating communication between supply chain partners**

   Same as Q5.

10. **Compare and contrast the role of supply chain ERP systems and advanced planning and scheduling systems in enhancing firm and supply chain competitiveness.**

   Same as Q1.

Chapter 8

1. **Discuss the role of the customer relationship management system in enhancing the firm's competitiveness.**

   Customer Relationship Management (CRM) helps to extend the functionality of the ERP sales and delivery applications. Beyond the traditional sales applications, these tools provide such functionalities like sales tracking, sales history analysis, pricing management, product mix management, and category management. In many cases, suppliers' sales force is made responsible for entire category of products. Such capabilities definitely help the organization to understand the needs of its customers and accordingly manage its resources to satisfy their needs in more efficient and cost-effective way.

2. **Discuss how the planning/coordination and operation flow differs for make-to-order (MTO) and make-to-stock (MTS) firms.**

   When a firm implements a **Make-To-Order strategy**, then the planning/ coordination and operations processes essentially mirror each other. It may not be necessary to schedule anticipatory raw materials and production nor to maintain buffer inventory. However in the traditional **Make-To-Stock strategy** operations are managed in anticipation of order. This requires planning for the future based on past trend and future expectation. Since there is a time difference between the production and demand fulfillment there is a build up of inventory at different stages of the fulfillment process.

3. **Discuss the rationalization for ERP implementation by firms involved in supply chain management.**

   The basic rationale for implementing ERP systems can be broken down into three factors. The first objective is to achieve **consistency** in data and processes across the regions and divisions on a global basis. The second objective is to obtain **economies of scale**. From the hardware perspective, with a centralized processor or network, there is a potential for substantial procurement and maintenance scale economies. There is some significant software scale economies since the firm could use limited number of software licenses to meet the needs of the divisions and regions. Therefore the firms needed reduced number of personnel to implement and maintain the ERP system. A centralized ERP approach also increases the potential for a multi-divisional firm to implement shared resources and services across divisions or even regions. Th final objective is enhanced **system integration** both within the firm and enterprise as well as between suppliers and customers.

4. **Compare and contrast the role of the planning/coordination and operations in improving firm competitiveness.**

   Planning/Coordination and operations represent the key processes to initiate, monitor and measure activities required to fulfill customer and replenishment orders.
   Planning and coordination include the processes necessary to schedule and coordinate procurement, production and logistics resource allocation throughout the enterprise. It includes the definition of strategic objectives, rationalization of

capacity constraints, and determination of market-distribution, manufacturing and procurement requirements. Advanced Planning and Scheduling tools are being used to enhance the planning and coordination processes and thereby improving firm competitiveness.

Operations include the processes necessary to manage customer order fulfillment including processing, inventory assignment, distribution operations, transportation operations, and procurement coordination. A coordinated, integrated operations information systems are essential for supply chain competitiveness. The ERP systems provide the integration and consistency required to support supply chain operations

5. **Compare and contrast the drivers and the role of the materials requirements planning and the distribution requirements planning system.**

    Distribution Requirements Planning (DRP) is an inventory management and process tool used to implement Logistics requirements. The future requirements are obtained from the sales and marketing forecasts, current and future committed customer orders, and the promotional activities. The current inventory is the product available to ship. Periodically logistics requirements are determined as the demand less the inventory-on-hand plus planned receipts. An ideal situation would be zero inventory available, but this may not be possible to achieve.

    Manufacturing Requirements Planning (MRP) time phases the purchase and arrival of materials and components to support the desired manufacturing plan.

    Both the planning processes operate in parallel and they need to be synchronized with the capacity constraints and manufacturing capabilities in order to achieve optimal system performance. In a demand flow or market paced strategy, a total integration of MRP and DRP is necessary

6. **Discuss the driver and role of the inventory deployment and management system.**
    Inventory management and management system is the primary interface between planning/coordination and operations. One of its major roles is the forecast process in order to predict the product requirement by customer and DC to support enterprise-wide planning. The second process are the inventory allocation decision aids. These aids help the inventory planners to decide when and how much to order.

    The primary drivers of inventory deployment and management systems are the customer service objectives established by management. Service objectives typically define the target fill rates for customers and products.

    In addition to initiating basic inventory decisions, inventory deployment and management also has to measure inventory performance by monitoring the inventory levels, turns and productivity. It estimates the future demand in the form of implicit or explicit forecasts. With the underlying premise that more integrated information facilitates inventory deployment and management resulting in lower inventory.

7. **Discuss why it is important to coordinate the arrival of procurement shipments with the dispatching of customer shipments.**

For integrated supply chain management, procurement needs to track and coordinate the receiving and shipping activities in order to optimize facility, transport, and personnel scheduling. Typically loading and unloading docks are critical resources, therefore by coordinating the arrival of procurement shipments with the dispatching of customer shipments firms can better utilize the facility. Moreover they can use the same carrier for both deliveries and shipments, which would allow them to use a smaller and more manageable pool of carriers. However effective coordination can be achieved through receipt and shipment visibility and electronic integration with the suppliers

8. **Discuss how advanced WMS functionality will change the role of the distribution center in the supply chain.**

Historically warehouse systems have been involved in receiving shipments, stock putaway, and order picking. However the modern warehouses are expected to perform some light manufacturing. They are also required to manage inventory on a just-in-time basis. The DCs would also be required to offer value-added services like packaging, labeling, kitting, and setting up displays for some types of products. With increasing emphasis on reducing inventory, there would be greater instances of planned cross-docking and merge –in-transit of different parts of customer's order. Therefore DCs will have to undertake a lot more activities over and above the core WMS functionality with the sole objective of creating more value.

9. **Discuss the major challenges a firm should expect when implementing an integrated ERP system including financial, supply chain, service, and human resource applications.**

The various applications of an integrated ERP system are the financial, service, human resource, and reporting. Traditional each of these functions had their own way of maintaining information. So the biggest challenge in integrating all these modules would be finding a common format. Moreover information sharing could be an issue in situations where, the priorities of the different functions are based on their unique objectives, which may not be common. Firms trying to implement and maintain an integrated system has to address the control issues across different regions.

10. **Discuss the rationale and risks associated with using a common forecast to drive the firm's planning/coordination flow.**

Historically an enterprise had a number of independent forecasts for its different functional areas. Since most of these forecasts, this led to inconsistencies that created excess manufacturing and logistics inventory and other operational inefficiencies. A common forecast can eliminate this problem. However there are some risks involved with such a common forecast. A traditional sales forecast tends to be ambitious in order to motivate the sales force while the logistics forecasts are more conservative to avoid building unnecessary stock. A common forecast would simply average out these forecasts and therefore cannot fulfil the intended objectives of each organizational function.

Chapter 9

1. **Discuss the primary differences between top-down and bottom-up forecasting process.**

   The **top down approach** develops a national level, SKU forecast and distributes demand across locations according to historic patterns. This approach is centralized and appropriate for stable demand situations or when the demand changes are uniform. The **bottom-up approach** is decentralized. Each distribution center develops independent forecasts. The demand fluctuations within specific markets are tracked more accurately, though data manipulation is more difficult with this approach.

2. **Describe the major rationale and anticipated benefits for implementing advanced planning and scheduling.**

   Historically, planning systems have been functionally centric with limited data and process integration between the functions. Independent performances of a single function typically results in reduced performance in other functions and the overall system as well. APS systems seek to integrate information and coordinate overall logistics and supply chain decisions while recognizing the dynamics between functions and processes. The four factors driving APS development and implementation are: planning horizon recognition, supply chain visibility, simultaneous resource consideration, and resource utilization.

3. **Discuss overall information flow and the major role of each APS system component.**

   APS incorporates spatial and temporal considerations in planning and executing strategies. The spatial considerations include the movement of between raw materials providers, manufacturing plants, distribution centers, distributors, retailers, and end-customer. The temporal considerations focus on the timing and scheduling of these movements.

   The four major components of APS are:
   Demand management develops the requirement projections for the planning horizon. It generates the sales forecast based on sales history, scheduled activities, and customer information.
   Resource management coordinates and records supply chain system resources and constraints. This module includes the databases to store the product and customer definitions, resource definitions, system constraints, and planning objectives as well as the processes to validate and maintain the information.
   Requirements optimization uses mathematical programming and heuristics to analyze the output of the two modules in order to determine the best way to meet the customers requirements while utilizing resources effectively.
   Resource allocation refines the resource assignments and communicates them to he ERP systems to initiate appropriate transactions. It also provides product information regarding ATP (Available to promise) and CTP (Capable to promise).

4. **Discuss the major supply chain APS applications with particular focus on the role and anticipated benefits for each application.**

The following applications are typically used for many supply-chain planning environments. **Demand planning** integrates the history-based forecasts and future plans to prepare an integrated statement of requirements. It also focuses on creating forecast consistency across products and distribution centers.

Production planning aims to satisfy the necessary requirements at the minimum total production cost without violating any constraints. It results in a time-sequenced plan that leads to the manufacturing the correct items in a timely manner while operating within facility, equipment, and labor constraints.

Inventory requirements planning uses evaluative techniques to trade-off the costs of production, storage, and transportation. Its primary aim is to satisfy customer demand, minimize overall cost, and remain within the supply chain's physical constraints.

Transportation planning integrates transportation requirements, transportation resources, and relevant costs into a common tactical decision support system that seeks to minimize the overall freight expenses. It identifies the various ways of shifting freights amongst the carriers and also facilities information sharing between the partners.

5. **Discuss the major considerations that a firm must address when implementing APS.**

The major considerations that need to be addressed prior to implementing an APS system include: 1)integrated versus bolt-on application; 2) data integrity; 3) application.

1) The company can use its own resources to maintain such a system or it can integrate third party softwares with its ERP system. The other alternative could be to use bolt-on or best-of-breed approach that identifies the best APS system for the firm based on the feature and functionality and then bolt it on the firm's ERP system.

2) Data integrity is more critical for APS as missing and inaccurate data can dramatically impact decision-making process. One most-often cited integrity problem deals with the cube and weight issue. Having accurate data also adds more credibility to this new concept.

3) The application education should be broader than existing training approaches. The users can be given experience with the tool by job-shadowing approach or by simulation methods. Such educational experience provides a solid foundation for a successful APS.

6. **Compare and contrast the basic logic differentiator of time series and causal forecast techniques. Under what conditions would each be appropriate?**

The **time-series approach** uses the information consistent with a variable's historical behavior to predict its future behavior. Time series are appropriate when historical data are available. It can identify trends, seasonality, and cyclical patterns in the data set. **Causal forecast techniques** estimate variables based on the value of other independent factors. They are not appropriate if demand has a random pattern or fluctuates wildly. They are appropriate for long-term or aggregate forecasting.

7. **Compare and contrast the role of the forecast support system, forecast technique, and forecast process.**

Forecast technique is the mathematical or statistical computation used to translate numerical parameters, including history, into forecast quantity. Even though these techniques do a good job of connecting the historical trends into future forecasts, they do not do as well at incorporating the input of anticipated future events.

Forecast Support System includes the data manipulation capability to gather and analyze data, develop the forecast and communicate the forecast to relevant personnel and planning systems. It supports the maintenance and manipulation of data and allows consideration of external factors like promotion, price changes, etc.

Forecast administration includes the organizational, procedural, motivational, and personnel aspects of forecast management functions and its integration into the other functions of the firm.

In order to obtain an accurate and optimal forecast/demand management all the three components need to be integrated.

8. **Identify and discuss the major forecast components. Why is it important to decompose demand into these components when developing new forecasts?**

The major forecasting components are 1) **base demand** that represents an appropriate forecast of items without the impact of seasonality, trend, cycle or promotional components; 2) **seasonal** component is the generally recurring upward and downward movement in the demand pattern, usually on an annual basis; 3) **trend** component is the long range movement in periodic sales over an extended period of time; 4) **cyclic** component is characterized by swings in demand pattern that lasts more that a year; 5)**promotional** component characterizes the demand swings initiated by the company's marketing efforts, such as advertising, deals or promotions; 6) **irregular** component represents the random quantities that do not fit any categories.

Each one of them has different impact on the overall demand and it operates over different time horizons. Therefore by decomposing the total demand into these components, it is easier to track and control each of the components.

9. **Discuss how a minor change in demand at the retail level can significantly impact supply chain variation at distributors, manufacturers, and suppliers.**

There is a tendency for any anticipation or speculation to amplify as it proceeds down a supply chain. Each change/ error in the demand creates a disturbance for the total logistics demand. In a study done by Forrester Research, it was found that an increase in retail demand by 10 percent without clear communication to the other members of the supply chain leads to an inventory swing of 16 percent for the distributor, 28 percent for the factory warehouse, and 40 percent for factory production. Such a phenomenon obviously increases the supply chain variance, increases costs and reduces asset utilization.

10. **Discuss how error accountability can be a major factor in improving forecast performance.**

Error accountability or feedback is helps to motivate the demand management process. The improvements can occur by motivating the individuals to identify the problems and improvement opportunities. With suitable incentives managers can identify major sources of error and develop techniques and information sources that can reduce error.

Chapter 10

1. **How does the cost of carrying inventory impact the traditional earnings statement of the enterprise?**

   Inventory carrying cost is not apparent in the traditional profit-loss statement. However, it has obvious effects of lost opportunity (money that could be invested in areas guaranteeing higher returns) and interest expense that directly detracts from revenue.

2. **Discuss the relationship between service level, uncertainty, safety stock, and order quantity. How can trade-offs between these elements be made?**

   Two of the most important factors regarding the level of service delivered are availability and speed. Availability and speed of service are affected by the uncertainties of demand and replenishment cycles. To maximize certainty in service levels, safety stocks are often maintained at logistical facilities across the network. Hefty quantities of safety stock significantly increase inventory carrying costs and the total cost. Should orders be submitted in larger quantities by customers, uncertainties may be reduced, alleviating the need for safety stock. Close communications between suppliers and customers perhaps most substantially reduces uncertainty.

3. **Discuss the disproportionate risk of holding inventory by retailers, wholesalers, and manufacturers. Why has there been a trend to push inventory back up the channel of distribution?**

   Holding inventory is risky because of the tied-up capital investment and the potential for obsolescence. The nature and the extent of the risk varies depending on the position of the company in the supply chain. Manufacturers' inventories have a long-term dimension. Their inventory commitment is relatively deeper and of longer duration. Wholesalers have a more broad exposure, but a shorter duration compared to the manufacturers. For retailers, inventory management is no more than a buying-selling process. Retailers have an extensive breadth of inventory and their inventory holding costs are typically higher than those of the manufacturers and wholesalers. Thus, they try to push the inventory responsibility back up the channel to avoid those high costs.

4. **What is the difference between the probability of a stock-out and the magnitude of a stock-out?**

   The **probability of a stockout** is the frequency of stockout occurrences. This figure gives no indication of how severe the particular stockout is – that is, it does not tell us how many units the on-time shipment is below order quantity. The **magnitude of the stockout,** usually measured by fill rate, tells us how many more units were needed when the stockout occurred. Generally, for a given safety stock level, the greater the order quantity, the lesser the magnitude of the stockouts and the lesser the stockout probability.

5. **Data suggest that while overall average inventory levels are declining, the relative percentage being held by manufacturers is increasing. Explain why you think this observation is either true or false. Describe how such a shift could benefit the operations of the entire channel and how manufacturers could take advantage of the shift.**

Although a logistical system that depends upon the continuous flow of goods is possible, it is not very probable that all the uncertainties in the systems will be eliminated. There will always be unexpected events and since customer service is becoming more and more competitive, even the probability of 0.001 for service failure may result in a competitive loss. To avoid this, companies will still hold inventory.

6. **Discuss the differences between reactive and planning inventory logics. What are the advantages of each? What are the major implications of each?**

The **reactive inventory system** responds to the channel members' inventory needs by drawing the product through the distribution channel. The replenishments are initiated when the stock level falls under a specified limit. It assumes that all customers, markets and products are equal contributors to profit. It also assumes infinite availability at the source and infinite capacity at the holding site, as well as predictable and independent performance cycle times. Reactive systems operate best when customer demand patterns are predictable. On the other hand, **inventory planning** methods use a common information base to coordinate inventory requirements across multiple locations. They improve effectiveness and efficiency of the inventory in terms of quantity and placement. They require accurate, time-placed forecasts across distribution centers. Though consistent and reliable performance cycles are often prerequisite, plans are always subject to frequency rescheduling.

7. **Illustrate how fine-line inventory classification can be used with product and market segments. What are the benefits and considerations when classifying inventory by product, market, and product/market?**

The objective of **product/ market inventory classification** is to focus and refine inventory management efforts. It groups products with similar qualifications, in terms of sales, profit contribution, inventory value, usage rate, and nature of the item to facilitate inventory management. Once the items are classified, they are labeled as A,B and C. Each designation has its own inventory control policy.

8. **What advantage does DRP have over a fair share method of inventory deployment?**

DRP reduces freight costs, making use of coordinated shipments. Since it can accurately determine when and where product is needed, it reduces inventory levels and warehouse space requirements. In addition, it improves inventory visibility and makes budgeting easier. Customers potentially benefit from improved service and lower costs.

9.   **Discuss the importance of collaboration in the developing of supply chain inventory strategies. Provide an example.**

The basic intent of collaboration in developing supply chain inventory strategies is to reduce the reliance on forecasting demand, and instead, allow suppliers to respond to demand on a just-in-time basis. It requires extensive cooperation and information sharing among distribution channel participants. Some techniques commonly used include quick response, continuous replenishment, vendor managed inventory and profile replenishment.

Quick Response (QR) is a cooperative effort between retailers and suppliers to improve inventory velocity by providing merchandise supply that closely matched the consumer buying patterns. The point of sale information about specific products is exchanged between the retailers and manufacturers. For example, instead of operating on fifteen-to thirty day order cycles, QR arrangement can replenish inventory in six or fewer days. With a faster and dependable order response, inventory can be committed as required, resulting in increased turnover and improved availability.

10.   **Customer-based inventory management strategies allow the use of different availability levels for specific customers. Discuss the rationale for such a strategy. Are such strategies discriminatory? Justify your position.**

Though allocation may sometimes be discriminatory, companies should take into consideration the needs of heir core customers. If the company will have an obvious loss in marketing its products in one demand segment, it may reconsider further pursuing that segment. Some products of societal importance such as food stocks and healthcare are particularly sensitive to needs. Inventory is sometimes required in sites that are relatively inefficient.

Chapter 11

1. **Compare and contrast the transport principles of economy-of-scale and economy-of-distance. Illustrate how they combine to create efficient transportation.**

   Economy of scale and economy of distance are two fundamental principles that impact transportation efficiency. These scaling principles are very important when various transportation alternatives are evaluated.

   Economy of scale means that the cost per unit of weight decreases as the size of the shipment increases. Therefore, truckload (TL) shipments that utilize the total vehicle capacity have a lower cost per pound than less than truckload (LTL) shipments. The economies-of-scale exists because the fixed costs associated with moving the load is distributed over the increase weight.

   Economy of distance refers to a decrease in the transportation cost per unit of weight as the distance increases. Therefore, a shipment for 800 miles will cost less to move than two shipments of the same weight each moving 400 miles. This principle is also called as the tapering principle. Longer distances allow fixed costs to be spread over more miles resulting in lower per mile charges.

2. **Describe the five modes of transportation, identifying the most significant characteristic of each.**

   Five modes of transportation and their main characteristics are the following:

   Rail: Railroads dominated intercity tonnage until after World War II. Their low variable cost gave them the ability to transfer large shipments at a low per unit price. Recently, rail shipment shifted from transporting a broad range of commodities to a focus on agricultural commodities. Although it has a low variable cost, rail transportation has a high fixed cost. Facilities and equipment are readily available between most destinations within the U.S. and rail has the ability to handle many kinds of shipments.

   Motor: Highways have low fixed costs, which are covered by public support, and medium variable costs. They are readily available between any two destinations in the U.S. and developed nations abroad. They are dependable and offer more frequent delivery than rail transport. They may not be able to handle very large shipments. Short distances and high value products are usually carried by motor carriers.

   Pipelines: Pipelines have very high fixed costs. However, once they are constructed, they incur the lowest variable costs. Their ability to handle a variety of products is very limited. The products should be either liquid, gas or slurry. To switch from one product to another is too costly and is not usually done. Their speed and infrastructure availability are low, but they are dependable.

Air: This is the newest mode of transportation. Though very fast, air transport has very high variable costs and low fixed costs. Weather conditions may decrease its dependability to a great extent and it is not capable of carrying various types of shipments.

Between origin and destination of a product, there are paths that one of these modes may be more appropriate than the other. **International operations** use multiple modes to take advantage of the inherent economics of each mode to provide integrated service at the lowest cost.

3. **Why is motor carrier freight transportation the most preferred method of product shipment?**

Motor transportation is usually readily available for any origin and destination in the U.S. It serves as a link for all other modes of transportation. Motor carriers have low fixed costs and medium variable costs which makes their services fairly cheap. They are useful in handling small shipments, which makes up a large proportion of wholesaler-retailer shipments. It is fairly fast, frequent, flexible, and dependable. These characteristics make it the most common method of shipment.

4. **What is the economic justification for the recent rapid growth of premium package services?**

In today's business world, competition is shifting towards time-based competition. Given this fact, though service is expensive, premium package services can justify their costs wit the incredible speed they offer. That value of speed may exceed the business or personal shipper's costs, especially in emergency situations. Most times, business shippers parlay those costs to customers that value time and are willing to pay the premium package cost.

5. **Why is it important for a logistics manager to have a degree of understanding of transportation regulatory history?**

Logistics managers should be aware of the transportation regulatory history to get some insight and appreciation about the background of transportation. In today's market regulation is limited to safety and social issues. Thus, eventhough executives are free from the historical burden of explicit transportation regulation, executive actions are accountable to FTC and Justice Department.

6. **Why have railroad miles declined during a period of national growth?**

Although railroads once ranked first in terms of the number of miles in service, this status changed basically due to the extensive development of roads and highways that support the growth of automobiles and trucks after World War II. Liberalization abandonment provisions in Staggers Rail Act were also a factor

7. **Railroads have the largest percentage of intercity freight ton-miles, but motor carriers have the largest revenue. How do you explain this relationship?**

The characteristic of railroad transport is that very large shipments can be carried at low costs. Thus, the rates they charge are relatively low. On the other hand, motor carriage can handle small, but valuable shipments. Motor carriers can charge higher rates because of higher speed and flexibility, The fact that they are more readily available also lets them charge more, thus increasing their revenue per ton relative to railroads.

8. **Discuss the fundamental difference between TOFC and COFC. Why was double stacking considered a major innovation in multi-modal transportation?**

Trailer (TOFC) or container (COFC) on a flatcar is the most widely used form of intermodal system. Containers are boxes used for storage and movement between motor freight, railroads and water transportation. They are typically 8 feet wide, 8 feet high, 20 or 40 feet long and do not have highway wheels. Trailers on the other hand are of similar width and height but can be as long as 53 feet and have highway wheels. **Double stacking** is a major innovation as the containers can be stacked thereby reducing the space requirement for moving shipments.

9. **Explain the value proposition offered by freight forwarding. Provide an example that illustrates why shippers would be attracted to using the services of a freight forwarder as contrasted to arranging their own transportation.**

Freight forwarders can offer a lower rate per hundredweight for large shipments, and in most cases, faster transport of small shipments than what individual customer can obtain by directly dealing with the common carrier. They consolidate shipments from various customers and then utilize a common surface or air carrier for transport. At destination, they split the bulk shipment into original smaller shipments. Freight forwarders accept full responsibility for shipment performance. Therefore it is beneficial for shippers to use such intermediaries.

10. **The five basic modes of transportation have been available for well over fifty years. Is this the way it will always be or can you identify a *sixth* mode that may become economically feasible at some time in the foreseeable future?**

Intermodal transportation could be another mode of transportation in the future. It takes advantage of the inherent economies of each mode and provides an integrated service at lower total cost. The most widely used intermodal system is the trailer (TOFC) or container (COFC) on a flatcar.

Chapter 12

1. **Seven economic drivers that influence transportation cost were presented. Select a specific product and discuss how each factor will impact determination of a freight rate.**

The following are the factors that affect the cost of a product:

Distance: Generally, transportation costs increase the distance, though at a decreasing rate. Since there are fixed costs involved regardless of distance, real costs are never zero – even if product is not moved. Generally speaking, if the product is moving in the city, transportation cost/distance would be much higher than that of intercity transportation.

Volume: Generally, transportation costs per pound tend to decrease as the total weight is distributed across a number of transportation facilities and equipment, each having its own fixed costs to cover. The more a unit of equipment is utilized (filled), the lower the variable cost per product unit. The relationship is repetitive for each truck load.

Density: In terms of weight and space, the individual vehicle is more constrained by space, unless the product is extremely dense –- creating limitations based on weight. The transportation rates are quoted per weight, while the actual fuel and labor expenses are not dramatically influenced by weight. Therefore, higher density products usually have lower transportation costs per unit of weight. The cost/density relationship is similar to the cost/volume relationship.

Stowability: Items with standard rectangular shapes that do not have odd lengths, sizes and weights are easy to stow. This factor is directly related to the shipment shape.

Handling: The way products are packaged, the need for special handling equipment, and the physical grouping of products serve as handling cost elements.

Liability: Carriers should either have insurance to protect against damage claims or accept responsibility for damage. Improved packaging and reduced susceptibility to loss and damage can be a solution to reduce risks.

Market Conditions: The imbalance of movement between the destination and the origin causes vehicles to sometimes return empty. This is also increased by the seasonality effect of demand. The logistical system should be designed so that backhaul movement is integrated in systematic movements when possible.

Students should give a specific example illustrating how a product's freight rate is influenced by the above factors.

2. **Compare and contrast cost-of-service with value-of-service as alternative rate making strategies.**

These are two pricing strategies that are most commonly followed by carriers to set rates for charging the shippers.

Cost-of-service strategy is a build-up approach where the carrier establishes a rate based on the cost of providing the service plus a profit margin. This approach is most commonly used as a pricing approach for low-value goods or in highly competitive situations.

Value-of-service is a strategy that charges a price based on value as perceived by shipper rather than the carrier's cost of actually providing service. For example transporting 1000 pounds of electronics equipments is perceived as more critical than 1000 pounds of coal hence is charged higher. Carriers use this strategy for high-value items or when limited competition exists.

Normally a combination of these two strategies is used in order to consider the trade-offs between cost of service incurred by the carrier and value of service to the shipper.

3.   **What is the purpose of freight classification: Does the concept of classification have relevancy given deregulation of transportation?**

Not all types of freight should be considered the same and charged according to weight only. Some types of freight are more delicate than others. Like glass, many products require special handling. Like frozen foods, many products require special packaging. Shipping size is another factor that may influence the transportation costs. Thus, for all factors that influence transportation costs, rate should be established to determine the market price for the shipment of specific product types. The freight classification system establishes standards that simplify the negotiation of freight charges.

4.   **Describe the difference between a rate and a rating.   How do they relate to classification?**

Rate is the price in dollars and cents per hundredweight to move a specific product between two locations. It is also known as tariffs. All products transported by common carriers are classified into class rates for pricing purposes. Determination of class rates involves two steps : classification or grouping of the products and determination of the rate or price based on the classification and the origin-destination points of shipment

Rating, on the other hand, is the particular class that a product or commodity receives based on their characteristics. This is the product classification, which is used to determine the freight rate. However, this classification does not identify the price charged for movement of a product; it only refers to a product's transportation characteristics in comparison to other commodities.

5.   **What is the role of the freight bill and the bill of lading in a transportation transaction?**

The **Bill of lading** is the basic document in purchasing transport services. It serves as a a receipt and documents the type and amount of products shipped. In case of damage or fire, the bill of lading is the basis for damage claims. It determines the specifications of the service and to whom the delivery will be made. The **Freight Bill** represents the transportation provider's way of charging for the services it provided. The two documents can be combined to reduce the paperwork involved in transactions. Since every detail of the transportation service is actually on the bill of lading, the freight bill can be redundant.

6. **Discuss the concept of net pricing. What advantage does net pricing provide to carriers and shippers?**

With **net rate pricing,** carriers are able to simplify pricing schedules by customizing them to an individual customer's needs. Carriers can replace individual discount sheets and class tariffs with a single price sheet, applicable for that customer. This approach replaces the complex and burdensome discount pricing structure that has been common practice since deregulation. Carriers hope to win over customers by taking much of the calculation out of finding the rice and by providing billing accuracy and clarity. Shippers are attracted to he simplification because it provides billing accuracy and provides a clear understanding of how to generate savings in transportation. However, this method is not a way of determining what price to charge the transportation service. It should be combined with other price determining methods, such as cost of service and value of service, to calculate the charged rate.

7. **Compare and contrast variable, fixed and joint costs.**

Variable costs are those that are directly related to the required level of activity during a time period. They can be avoided by not executing the activity. Transport rates should at least cover variable costs. Variable transaction costs basically consist of labor, fuel and maintenance costs.

Fixed costs are those that do not change in the short run. Even if activities are not carried out, these costs still exist. They consist of terminals, vehicles, information systems, and rights-of-way-costs not directly associated with activity levels. In the short term, expenses related to fixed costs must be covered with contributions exceeding variable costs.

Joint costs are the expenses that are created unavoidably to provide a particular service. These basically consist of backhaul costs. They can either be covered by the original shipper or by another backhaul shipper. They have a significant impact on transportation charges, and should not be neglected when developing total cost measures.

8. **What is the basic concept of multi-vendor consolidation? How do integrated service providers help achieve such consolidation?**

Multi-vendor consolidation refers to the concept of grouping different shipper's freight. This requires joint planning of warehousing and order processing across different companies to facilitate the consolidation. These kinds of services are provided by a umber of integrated service providers. Similarly, firms are also endorsing arrangements to pool with their competitors to achieve logistical efficiency.

9.   **Compare and contrast reactive and proactive consolidation. Provide of example of each.**

Each of these consolidation types is important for achieving transportation efficiency. **Reactive Consolidation** seeks to take shipments as the come and then combines freight into larger shipments for line-haul movement. An example of such a consolidation can be seen in UPS's nightly sorting and consolidation of package freight for inter-city movement. There are three ways of achieving effective freight consolidation : a) market area; b) scheduled delivery; c) pooled delivery.

Proactive consolidation requires the pre-order planing of order quantities and timing to facilitate consolidated freight movement. In essence, the order creation should not be restricted to standard buying times and inventory replenishment rules. Buyer participation helps in such type of freight consolidation. The driving forces behind such consolidation has the creation of larger number of smaller shipments and the desire for shippers, carriers, carriers and consignees to participate in the consolidation savings.

10.   **Four aspects of transportation operations management were identified as: (1) equipment scheduling; (2) load planning; (3) routing; and (4) carrier administration. Identify a commercial transportation movement you are aware of and discuss how each managerial aspect was involved.**

A typical grocery store like Meijers has to handle such an issue on a daily basis. In order to prevent the waiting time for loading and unloading the trailers/trucks, it uses cross-docking arrangements as one of its methods of **equipment scheduling**. It is more important for the fresh produce and the perishables because they cannot be stored for a long time.

Since the system has to handle products of different physical characteristics, it has to sequence the shipments in order to load the trailers optimally. **Load planning** also drives the timing of product selection and the work sequence at warehouses.

Routing of the shipments is done with due consideration of the customer's requirements and the need for efficient use of transportation equipment. Meijers has strategically built its DCs in order to meet its routing objectives.

Carrier administration involves carrier selection, integration, and evaluation. This has to be done regularly in order to maintain high levels of performance and availability of products.

Chapter 13

1. **Provide a definition and an example of strategic storage from a logistical system you are familiar with.**

   Strategic storage is the network's warehousing component that supports the logistical strategy of the company. With changes in customer expectations, the primary purpose of strategic storage has shifted from merely matching products with customers to grouping products into assortments that enhance customers' operational benefits.

   For example, in today's market environment, a warehouse should be ale to combine the products of different manufacturers into a single consolidated shipment to a retailer, reducing the customer's transportation and handling costs. Any example that demonstrates how warehouses are used to maintain an organization's strategic position is acceptable.

2. **Under what conditions could it make sense to combine private and public warehouses in a logistical system?**

   A **private warehouse** facility is owned and managed by the same enterprise that owns the merchandise stored at the facility. A **public warehouse** is facility that provides services to the clients as an independent business. Private warehouses operate wholly under the guise of the firm. Though not always as efficient or proficient as public warehouse operators, they have no markup. Utilizing private warehouses offers financial flexibility since they require no fixed investment. With public warehouses, it is easier to change location, size and the number of warehouses. A combination of both is used to satisfy the product demand change patterns during the year and among geographic locations, taking the financial resources of the company into consideration.

3. **Discuss and illustrate the economic justification for establishing a warehouse.**

   Warehouses offer many economic benefits for companies. One economic benefit of a warehouse is derived from the ability to consolidate products from a number of production plants into large, consolidated shipments delivered to customers. Also, big shipments from production plants are often broken into smaller shipments and arranged for local delivery. This is called **break bulk.** Break bulk shipments significantly reduce freight costs. In addition, warehouses allow production to be postponed or delayed until actual demand is certain. Once demand is determined in terms of product type and quantity, minor processing can quickly make final products available, reducing inventory requirements. Warehouses also provide buffers for seasonality, improve production efficiency, and support marketing efforts that often send logistics managers scrambling to meet surges in demand.

4. **Why would a warehouse be described as a "necessary evil"?**

   Though keeping inventory at any stage of the supply chain has well-known costs, inventory and the warehouses that maintain stocks serve many necessary purposes. Finished goods inventory ensures that customer demand is met, regardless of market uncertainty and volatility in today's competitive environment. The same can be said for raw materials warehouses that ensure that inputs are readily available for manufacturing. Whether warehouses are truly necessary is becoming an issue of debate. Information technologies and just-in-time delivery systems are reducing the necessity of maintaining vast amounts of inventory. Fewer warehouses must be utilized under these considerations, lessening the "evil", costly nature of their existence.

5.   How do warehouses perform assortment?

Assortment is done to reconfigure freight as it flows from origin to destination. There are three types of assortments performed in the warehouses namely – cross docking, mixing, and assembly. The objective of *cross-docking* is to combine inventory from multiple origins into an assortment for a specific customer. This operation is used by retailers for the fast moving store inventories. *Mixing* is performed at an intermediate location between shipment origin and destination. In this process the inbound products are combined with those regularly stored at the warehouse. The net effect is to reduce the overall product storage in a logistical system while achieving customer specific assortment and minimizing transportation cost. *Assembly* supports manufacturing operations. The components from a variety of second tier suppliers are assembled in a warehouse located close to the manufacturing plant. Like cross-docking and mixing, assembly serves to achieve a process grouping of inventory at a precise time and location.

6.   What is the concept of market presence, and how does it relate to the functionality of warehousing?

The customer often perceives that warehouses located close to their operations, having **market presence,** will be more responsive to their needs. As a result, it is expected that nearby warehouses will increase sales and gain market share as customers in the vicinity choose the close, responsive warehouse operator. There is also the promotional value of having a presence within a market.

7.   Discuss and illustrate the role warehouses play in reverse logistics.

Warehouses play an important role in performing reverse logistics. Most of the physical work related to product recall, reclamation and disposal of overstock and damaged inventory is performed at warehouses. Reverse logistics involves the handling of controlled and regular inventory. *Controlled* inventory consists of hazardous materials and product recalls that might have potential health or environmental implications. The controlled inventory needs to be reclaimed under strict scrutiny to prevent possible redistribution or improper disposal. *Regular* inventory represents products that are damaged or aged beyond the recommended sale-by-date. Reverse logistics offer typical challenges because the packages are often broken or not packaged properly, it also requires significant manual sorting and inspection. However, the opportunity to recover cost by reimbursement and recycling is significant.

8.   What role can a warehouse play in postponement strategies?

A warehouse with light processing, packaging and/or labeling capacity allows for the postponement of final product placement until actual demand is known. These capabilities enable the producer to finalize production only after the firm knows which products and quantities to produce. This provides two economic benefits: 1) risk is minimized as product's final form is only committed after an order has been received, which leads to 2) a reduction in total inventory, since only basic product configurations need to be maintained order receipt.

9. **Illustrate the relationship between the size and shape of a distribution warehouse and the material-handling system. Why do some warehouses have square design while others are rectangular?**

The size and the shape of a warehouse, together with the consideration of material handling equipment appropriate for the products and facilities, determine the most efficient/effective layout can be applied to the warehouse. According to these factors, the most suitable shape, whether it be square or rectangle, would be the one that assures the best fit and flow with regard to space and movement restrictions. The layout must be spacious enough for storage and selection as well as for receiving and shipping activities.

10. **Explain the following statement: "A warehouse should merely consist of walls enclosing an efficient handling system."**

Warehouses need not be considered facilities in which goods are merely stored. As the text discusses, warehouses can serve as centers for value-added activities to be performed, such as sorting, labeling, and processing. However, warehouses should be kept simple. The primary reason for warehouses is still storing materials and products. Though expanding the functional scope of warehouses often improves delivery effectiveness, minimizing total costs may mean utilizing the warehouse for simply handling and sorting goods. A set of walls can accomplish this though material-handling equipment is vital too.

Chapter 14

1. In terms of basic material handling, what is the role of a unit load?

A **unit load** is the smallest quantity of product readily available for shipment. Unit loads are usually combined together to make larger, more economical shipments. Since it is the smallest shipment quantity, its shape and size serves as the standard determining appropriate suitable packaging material, and the appropriate selection and usage of handling equipment for the warehouse. It can thereby be implied that the unit load has far-reaching effects in capital investments for facility accommodations and variable costs for packaging.

2. Until recently, why have automated handling systems failed to meet their expected potential? What changed to encourage automation in the 1980's?

The motive for automated handling systems is typically to replace manual operations in the warehouse with the advantages of lower variable coats and accurate, faster product storage and retrieval. However, the capital investment required of an automated warehouse is very high., serving as the most significant barrier to consideration and installation. With the enhancements in communication technology and information-directed systems of the 1980s, automation became even more reliable and efficient, further reducing variable costs. In addition, the manufacturing market of automated systems grew, slowing the rate of price increases. In sum, it became easier for warehouse operators to achieve payback on their investments in automation.

3. Compare and contrast order selection and unit-load automation.

Order selection systems integrate mechanized and automated handling components to reduce labor requirements in the order selection process. Automation is spread throughout the handling system and merchandise stacked in the form of master cartons. In **unit load automation**, however, stock keeping is based on unit loads rather on unit loads rather than master cartons. Storage areas are high (sometimes rising up to 120 feet) with system-wide automation and handling equipment that is relatively fast. Greater control system sophistication is required of unit load automaton to achieve full utilization of equipment.

4. What is the logic of a "live rack"?

The logic of **"logic rack"** is to reduce manual labor while ensuring the flow of products to desired positions. The natural force of gravity is used in place of human or machine power with inclined storage racks. Live racks are commonly used for energy savings, reduced demand of manual and mechanical requirements, and first-in-first-out replenishment.

5. What type of products and logistics applications are most suitable to ASRS handling?

AS/RS (Automated Storage/ Retrieval Systems) handling systems are becoming better able to handle diverse products and achieve different objectives. However, today's systems are able to maximize storage density only when products are packaged in standardize, rectangular units. Dissimilar and odd-shaped packages pose a problem for most systems. When AS/RS capabilities match storage and retrieval needs, they can perform tasks more efficiently with less damage.

6. **Provide an illustration that highlights the differences between consumer and industrial packaging.**

    Consumer packaging focuses on customer convenience, market appeal, retail shelf utilization, product protection, and on-the-shelf advertising. **Industrial packaging,** on the other hand, focuses on the economic balance between packaging costs and costs of potential product damage considering product's size, weight, fragility, packaging material. Storage and handling conditions. Any illustration that demonstrates the distinct differences in purpose and function between consumer and industrial packaging is acceptable.

7. **What is the primary purpose of bar coding in packaging? Is the role of bar coding different in material handling?**

    Bar coding is used in packaging for product identification, tracking, and price determination. In material handling, bar coding is used to determine the route the product should follow in the warehouse to fulfill a specific customer order. Tracking may also be achieved in the warehouse with bar coded goods.

8. **Discuss the differences between rigid and nonrigid containers. Discuss the role of load securing in unitization.**

    Rigid containers serve as a device for master cartons or loose products to be transferred during warehousing and transportation. The distinct purpose of rigid containers is to better protect merchandise and enhance material handling. They reduce packaging requirements and transportation costs since the potential for damage is lessened. **Non-rigid containers** do not protect the product during storage and transfer by complete closure. It is a cheaper method of unitization though more careful packaging of the product is often required since it is more prone to handling disturbances.

    To decrease damage potential, the unit load must be restrained during handling and transportation. Simply stacking containers is usually insufficient to secure a unit load. To improve stability, techniques such as rope ties, corner posts, steel strapping, taping, anti-skid treatment, adhesion, and wrapping are widely used.

9. **What benefits do flexible unit-load materials have in contrast to rigid containers? How do return or reverse logistics considerations impact the two approaches?**

    Flexible unit load materials have many benefits over rigid containers. First, necessary unloading time and congestion at the dock are minimized. Second, material handling is facilitated by unit load quantities. Third, inbound shipment and inventory positioning is easier. Also, in-transit damage is lowered by using unit load shipping and specialized transportation. **Rigid containers,** however, provide a shipment unit that can be reused, reducing waste and the need to dispose of the container. Since rigid containers are reusable, logistics managers must determine how to best utilize them to keep them in motion without cluttering the warehouse.

10. **What trade-offs are involved in the use of returnable racks?**

Returnable racks require greater investment relative to those that are disposable, though they do not have to be purchased continuously and have little to no disposal costs with each use. In addition, they improve housekeeping and reduce the probability of damage. On the other hand, they do have incumbent costs of sorting, tracing, and cleaning. Thus, a cost-benefit analysis of gains and losses should be calculated before deciding whether to use returnable or disposable racks.

CHAPTER 15

1. **Describe in your words the meaning of spatial-temporal integration in logistical system integration.**

    Logistics is the process that provides customers with time and place utilities, ensuring that the right product is available at the right place. The term "right time" and "right place" provide indications of the **temporal/spatial** structure of logistics. It is the challenge of logistical management to provide customers with these desired utilities at the lowest possible cost to the firm.

    Inventory shapes logistics' temporal structure through product availability. Availability implies that goods and services are ready for consumption <u>when</u> demanded, providing time utility. Transportation provides logistics with spatial structure by fulfilling place utility. It allows manufacturing to occur in one place and ultimate consumption to occur in a distant location, for instance. It is this ability to cover distance that permits specialization of skills and resources. In other words, geography does not prevent us from consuming only what we can produce.

    Students are encouraged to express these general concepts in their own words. Responses may vary somewhat, but the basic unity of time and space achieved trough logistics must be demonstrated.

2. **What justification of logic can be presented to support the placement of a warehouse in a logistical system?**

    There are two main reasons for placing a warehouse within a logistical system: 1) to enhance customer service, and/or2) to establish cost advantages. Warehouses facilitate the firm's objective of providing place and time utilities. They should only be established when the value of these utilities exceeds the cost they add to the system. As long as the combined cost of warehousing and local delivery is less than the cost of shipping directly to customers, new warehouses should be added to the system.

3. **Why do transportation costs decrease as the number of warehouses in a system increase? Why do inventory costs increase as the number of warehouses in a system increase?**

    Warehouses serve as centers for consolidation. Thus, transportation costs decrease as the number of consolidation points increases. As discussed in earlier chapters, transportation economies through consolidated shipments result in lower rates per hundred-weight mile. However, beyond the maximum consolidation point, this advantage begins to diminish, creating an optimal breakpoint number of warehouses.

    Additional warehouse locations generally imply higher system-wide average inventories. More facilities and higher levels of inventory lead to higher costs. Higher average inventory levels result from the growth in the number of performance cycles. Each performance cycle creates a need for safety stock. These subsequent demands for safety stocks lead to an increase in the average inventory level.

4. **In your words, what is the locational impact of inventory? How does it differ for transit inventories and safety stocks?**

The locational impact of inventory is the value derived by customers for having goods and materials readily available when demanded. The availability of inventory helps the firm to provide high levels of customer service. As for customers, the locational impact of inventory means fast replenishment and a reduction in inventory requirements – both of which result in higher levels of service for their customers and lower costs.

The locational impact of inventory differs for **transit inventories** in that it cannot be physically utilized by customers, not deriving place utility. However, if transportation times are consistent, customers can plan purchases accordingly and satisfy needs when demand is not volatile. **Safety stock,** on the other hand, provides the firm with a locational impact by accommodating uncertainties in performance cycles and demand patterns, tough it increases the average inventory and costs considerably.

5. **What is meant by the level of threshold service of a least-cost system?**

Threshold service of a least-cost system is the standard of service performance in terms of inventory availability and capability. Threshold service serves as the starting point in the process of defining customer service policy, establishing the basic service platform and determining which value-added services might be valued by specific customers. Threshold service seeks to maximize service given constraints of the network design and the pursuit of least total cost.

6. **Why does customer service not increase proportionately to increases in total cost when a logistical system is being designed?**

The relationship between service value and the costs required to achieve subsequently higher levels of service is non-linear. That is, the value derived from higher levels of service is not constant relative to costs that also lack constancy. Marginal improvements in service derive diminishing improvements in value but continually rising costs. This principle is based upon the law of diminishing returns found in economies. The further you pursue an activity the more difficult it is to achieve each additional increment of change. To continually improve customer service logistics, the firm must shorten performance cycles and meet needs more proficiently, generating higher levels of quality for the customer. This requires investment in more facilities (fixed costs) while also generating higher variable costs. At some point, it becomes unreasonable to seek greater output regardless of the level of inputs (materials, facilities, links, and labor) within the network design.

7. **In Table 15-5, why does customer service speed of performance increase faster for customers located greater distances from a warehouse facility? What is the implication of this relationship for system design?**

Quite naturally, customers located near warehouse locations already receive high levels of service, providing little room for improvement. Additional locations should dramatically enhance the level of service (shorten the performance cycle) received by the one-time distant customers. Meanwhile, those customers already located near warehouses benefit from the reduced demand placed on the particular location catering to their needs as some of its original burden is displaced to other warehouses.

This relationship implies that there is a delicate equilibrium to achieve between the number of inventory locations, transportation costs and speed, and the ultimate level of service delivered. More facilities typically result in shorter performance cycles for all customers (higher customer service), more points for shipment consolidation, but significantly higher levels of average inventory. The challenge of network design is to determine the number and placement of warehouse locations that meet customer expectations and minimize cost in an ever-changing environment (customer needs change as do cost drivers)

8. **Discuss the differences between improving customer service through faster and more consistent transportation, higher inventory levels and/or expanded numbers of warehouses.**

Customer service improved with faster, more consistent transportation still requires adequate inventory during replenishment periods. However, less safety stock is needed to be maintained in the field as performance cycle uncertainty lessens. Also, premium transportation modes are typically required to provide quick, consistent delivery.

Customer service improved with higher inventory levels is typically very expensive. Therefore, it is important to establish consolidation is transportation. Movement of large quantities creates transportation economies. These economies can be readily achieved when plentiful levels of inventory are maintained.

Improving customer service with more warehouses increases the average inventory level and system-wide inventory carrying costs. However, transportation costs will decrease with more consolidation points. Closer proximity to the customer results in less uncertainty as the order replenishment time decreases.

9. **What is the difference between minimum-total cost and short-range profit maximization policies in system design?**

The **minimum-total cost approach** does consider the potential marginal revenues of adding more warehouses to the system. Rather, this perspective emphasizes minimizing transportation and inventory holding costs given the logistical network design. On the other hand, **profit maximization approach** considers the cost-profit relationship of adding more warehouses to the network. When the marginal revenues exceed marginal costs with each additional facility, warehouse locations are added (though they need not be privately owned). Networks developed under profit maximization typically utilize more warehouse locations than those using the minimum-total cost method. More warehouses imply higher levels of service to customers in peripheral market areas outside those of high demand density.

10. **In what ways can customer service performance be improved by incorporating flexible distribution operations into a logistical system design?**

Flexible distribution operations give the firm the capacity to choose which facility of multiple possibilities will supply a specific customer order. The primary benefit of a flexible system is that any of several warehouses are capable of satisfying that customer demand, providing alternatives. Flexibility helps the firm to reduce stockouts and service breakdowns while accommodating special customer requirements.

Chapter 16

1. **What is the basic objective in a logistics design and analysis study? Is it normally a one-time activity?**

The basic objective of a logistics design and analysis study is to determine the best utilization of logistical resources so that customer service goals are achieved at minimum total costs. The current status and future demands of the logistical system and customer service levels must be taken into consideration. Since the logistical environment changes continuously, system design and analysis cannot be a one-time activity despite efforts to build a flexible system capable of meeting customer needs for the longest possible period of time.

2. **What is sensitivity analysis, and what is its role in systems design and analysis?**

Sensitivity analysis involves the testing of effects beyond those conventionally under the firm's control. They often examine changes in demand, supply, competitive action, and regulation under different assumptions of organizational capabilities. Sensitivity analysis is often used to test how alternative actions react to manipulations within a setting as a result of uncertainty. It is a helpful tool in systems design and analysis allowing the designer to see how much certainty needs to be "built into" the system (assuming it can be achieved) and which types of data require higher levels of accuracy.

3. **Why is it important to develop supporting logic to guide the logistical planning process?**

Upon concluding situational analysis, management has a better understanding of the firm's current capabilities and the future demands of the environment. These conclusions are based upon internal and external reviews as well as technology assessments. The purpose of **supporting logic development** is to integrate the findings of the situational analysis to determine whether further investigation and execution toward logistics improvement opportunities is worthwhile. It comprehensively and factually evaluates current procedures and practices to ultimately list system adjustment priorities into primary and secondary categories and short and long range planning horizons. Finally, a formal supporting logic development clarifies potential redesign alternatives.

4. **Both internal and external review assessments must consider a number of measures. What are they and why are they important?**

Internal review assessments must consider the following broad measure: customer service, material management performance, transportation performance, warehouse performance and inventory performance. **External review assessments** consider measures such as supplier performance, response to customer purchasing patterns, conformance to customers' performance requirements, and benchmarking best-in-class practices. These measures are important since they provide the firm with a basis of comparison. They help the firm to answer the questions: Are we doing what we should be doing? Are we doing these things as well as we can? Are we doing these things as well as our competitors or as well as our customers expect? Are we doing these things at the lowest possible cost? Answers to these questions justify necessary changes and measure the potential value of improvements.

5.   Why is a cost-benefit evaluation important to logistical systems design efforts?

Cost-benefit evaluation is important when making any form of business investment. However, the strategic implications of investments in the firm's logistical network are widespread. The cost-benefit evaluation serves as the final form of assessment prior to the conclusive determination and implementation of recommendations. It typically examines potential service improvements, cost reductions, and cost prevention. A substantial challenge in this analysis is accurately determining opportunity costs and benefits as well as those that are actual or realized. Despite efforts to make these estimates as accurate as possible, figures and ultimate decisions are largely subject to judgment.

6.   What is the key objective in freight lane analysis?

The key objective of **freight lane analysis** is to identify imbalances in the logistical system that may offer opportunities for enhanced productivity upon solution. Upon identifying these imbalances, the analysis' focus becomes the shifting of over-utilized resources toward those that are under-utilized.

7.   In a general sense, what are the essential differences between analytic and simulation techniques?

Analytic techniques are employed to determine the solution of a single warehouse location problem. The methods of determination may be either mathematical or non-mathematical. As discussed previously, analytic models are known as center of gravity models. It is possible to optimally locate a warehouse according to criteria based on centers of tons, miles, ton-miles, or time-ton-miles.

Simulation techniques are used to replicate the real world environment for the purpose of better understanding the logistical system and testing alternative strategies under certain conditions. Simulations can be either dynamic or static depending on whether the model considers the interaction among time intervals. Simulations are useful in predicting the outcomes of strategies under real world conditions. These models tend to incorporate more variables than analytic models and represent the logistical system and its environment more realistically.

8.   What is the main advantage of the typical optimization technique in comparison to simulation?

The main advantage of optimization models over simulation is that they provide the analyst with the best mathematically-determined alternative. Assuming the logistical system is modeled carefully, there is no better solution than those determined by the linear program. However sometimes the solutions may not be practical. But in addition to finding the absolute best alternative, optimization models are generally less complicated to develop than comprehensive simulation models.

9.   **At what point in the typical analysis does the technique give way to the managerial review and evaluation process?**

In a typical analysis, the technique gives way to managerial review and evaluation only at the conclusion. By the analysis's end, it is often too late to determine whether the technique is reliable and practical solutions are derived. To avoid this dilemma, managerial participation is important in earlier stages of analysis, including model selection and development.

10.   **Compare and contrast strategic and tactical transportation decisions.**

Strategic transportation decisions are concerned with long-term resource allocations. They identify routs that may be used for a number of months or even years. Meanwhile, **tactical transportation decisions** are concerned with short-term resource allocations such as daily or weekly routs. Typically, the firm will formally develop strategic decisions on a regular basis and implement tactical decisions based on contingent situations, where the strategic determinations fail to address minor or unforeseen circumstances.

Chapter 17

1.   **Describe why teams are being formed more frequently in business today. What are some of the special considerations required for a team to be successful?**

A main reason for the common formation of teams in business today is the realization that multiple view points are better than one. Though not a new idea, only in recent years have corporate cultures emphasized the importance of employee empowerment and broken down the structures preventing cross-functionality. " Downsizing" and reengineering efforts have paved the way for increased use of teams as well. Roles and responsibilities of employees have expanded out of necessity.

For a team to be successful, there must be clearly defined roles for team members, specific performance goals for the team, commitment to teamwork, the freedom to work independently as a group within the organization, and the empowerment to implement whatever is deemed best for the firm.

2.   **Compare and contrast the five stages of functional aggregation.**

The first stage of **functional aggregation** consists of merging two or more functions, without any significant change in the overall organization hierarchy. The text demonstrates that in logistics example, line and staff operations begin to shift toward integration though structural separations remain among most relevant functions.

In the second stage, functions are grouped together to be managed independently of previous departmental assignments. In the example, physical distribution is segmented from other functional areas and elevated in the organizational hierarchy based on the nature of the enterprise's primary business.

In keeping with our logistics example, the third stage involves the formalization of the integration with its management under the guise of a logistical executive.

In the fourth stage, the newly formed logistical organization is radically restructured and redirected to shift from management by functions to a process perspective. Through this integration, the operational potential and impact of logistics is expanded. Logistics becomes a central contributor to initiatives involving new product development, customer order generation, fulfillment and delivery.

In the fifth stage, a virtual organization is formed where the traditional, hierarchical command structure is replaced by a network of relations that focus on work rather than structure. The virtual organization achieves integrated performance though it belongs as no identifiable unit of the formal organizational structure. These "transparent" organizations remain largely a topic of theoretical discussion, though the idea holds promise for the future.

3.   **What is the functional aggregation paradigm and why is it important?**

When managers recognized the need for total cost control, they combined logistics function into a single managerial group to accomplish integration. The **functional aggregation paradigm** is the idea that functional proximity facilitates an understanding of how decisions and procedures in one area affect performance in others. This paradigm led to logistics being viewed as process rather than a set of individually-managed functions, and helped derive substantial service and efficiency improvements as a result of integration.

4.   **Discuss the three challenges logistics faces as it manages on a process, rather than a functional basis. Describe each challenge and give an example of how it may be overcome.**

Logistics faces three challenges as it manages on a process, rather than functional, basis:

The first challenge is that all effort must be focussed on the **value added** for the customer. Managers can meet the demands of this new mind set by focussing on the needs of customers.

The second challenge is to match skills necessary to complete a particular job regardless of functional assignments. This difficulty can be overcome by establishing a horizontal structure.

The third challenge is that the work performed should simulate **synergism**. Systems integration considers functional trade-offs and coordinates activities to achieve maximum output from minimal required inputs.

5.   **Defend a position on the following question: Does radical organizational change require disintegration of existing structures?**

Students may assume a position on either side of this issue though, as long as it is adequately supported. A central issue in the text is the uncompromising, constant need for change. Rarely is radical change through structural disintegration necessary, but in those instances where shifts and adjustments in functional work prove fruitless due to structural limitations, disintegration is not only warranted but necessary.

6.   **What is a horizontal company and how would this type of company be organized? What are the strengths to this type of organizational structure?**

A **horizontal company** is characterized by its organization around processes, not tasks. The horizontal company's hierarchy is flattened, with unnecessary tasks eliminated. Emphasis is placed on management by teams, with team performance rewarded appropriately. In addition, customer satisfaction serves as the entire firm's primary performance objective. To ensure optimal performance, feedback loops are maintained with suppliers and customers. Finally, extensive employee training and information accessibility are important.

The dominant strength associated with this type of organization structure is the empowerment of front-line managers who are closer to the realities of operations, enabling them to do whatever is necessary to secure customer satisfaction on the spot. This flexible structure and its customer service implications can create an important differential advantage for the firm.

7. **Describe a situation where empowerment has been used. What are the benefits and drawbacks to empowerment in the situation?**

    Empowerment refers to the delegation of authority to lower-level management and employees. Students are asked to describe a situation where empowerment is utilized and determine potential benefits and drawbacks to empowerment in the situation. The scenario should first demonstrate how authority is passes from a higher – to lower-level employee, giving that employee or group of employees the ability to execute work as they deem appropriate.

    Benefits typically include improved customer responsiveness, less duplication of effort, and less reliance on managerial attention when it is not necessary. As well as offering quicker solutions to problems, empowerment allows the employee with more customer contact to implement better decisions than might otherwise be handled down from upper management.

    Drawbacks to empowerment typically point toward derivation of suboptimal decisions or poor execution. However, much of the blame in such situations can be place back on upper management that fails to : 1) properly train employees, and 2) provide empowered employees with necessary information and tools for performing on-the-spot decision making and implementation of solutions.

8. **What is meant by the term "Structure Compression?" How does this term affect logistics?**

    "Structure compression" refers to redesigning the organization so that required work can be performed as well or better with the utilization of fewer human resources.

    Logistics has traditionally been one of the more labor-intensive functional groups found within organizations. The emergence of new information technologies and innovative logistics equipment has made structural compression a considerable option in logistical operations. Readily available information creates less uncertainty in demand cycles and performance cycles, allowing for better planning and less redundant, unnecessary work. Similar to manufacturing environments, automation in logistics is increasingly being used in applications previously left to human labor. In addition, decline in strength of labor unions has permitted firms to establish more autonomous labor policies, allowing for greater flexibility in labor deployment.

9. **Describe four reasons why alliances fail. How can these failures be avoided?**

One reason that alliances fail is **"fuzzy goals"**, or a lack of common, clear goals between the two organizations. The very idea of creating an alliance is to create synergy in operations. When each firm strives for objectives in different directions, it is impossible to derive the chemistry that leads to success.

A second reason alliances fail is the **inadequate trust** among parties. Only when an organization feels free to treat alliance partners as extensions of the firm itself can alliances achieve success meeting their potential. This is a great deal to ask of the traditional organization that is protective of information and resources.

A third reason is what is referred to as **"lip-service commitment"**. Often firms enter into close relationship without making the mutual commitment needed for successful alliances. It is often done merely to secure a long-term relationship with customers or suppliers. In order to build successful alliances with customers and suppliers, they must be viewed as more than merely receivers or providers of products/services, but rather participants in product development, creation, and delivery.

A fourth reason is **human resource incompatibility.** Occasionally, two or more firms simply cannot work together due to differences in cultures, beliefs, or practices. The effort required to overcome such barriers may exceed the potential benefits derived from the relationship.

The fifth reason alliances fail is the placement of an **inadequate operating framework.** Successful alliances require clear knowledge of the individual firm's responsibilities and contribution to the relationship. This is, each firm must know exactly what is expected of it and all activities must be appropriately coordinated between partners.

A sixth reason is **inadequate measurement**. Each participating firm should know how each individual firm and its partners are performing relative to the alliance's common goals. Without adequate measurements, there is uncertainty of achievement on behalf of both parties and a lack of direction for the future.

These failures can often be dissolved by building an alliance between firms with complementary strengths and compatible strategies. These commonalities should be reinforced through a clarification of goals and the use of adequate performance measurements and feedback mechanisms.

10. **What is the distinction between centralization and decentralization? How do these concepts relate to logistics with the advent of information technology?**

The distinction between centralization and decentralization is the degree of authority and profit responsibility delegated to specific operating units. **Decentralization** is represented by units functioning in a highly autonomous manner. Meanwhile, in **centralized operations,** functional units rely significantly upon the organization's core planners as a source of direction and information. Centralization allows for better coordination among the organization's parts. Decentralization is more conducive to market responsiveness, giving each unit the ability to meet demand as it sees fit.

Information technology is managing to blur the once clear-cut classification of an organizations centralized or decentralized. Information is allowing for better central planning and ready placement of decision-relevant information in the hands of field managers simultaneously.

Chapter – 18

1. Briefly discuss the three objectives for developing and implementing performance measurement systems.

The first objective for developing and implementing performance measurement systems is **monitoring.** Monitoring involves the historical taking of logistics system performance for management and customers. Monitoring measures are typically focused on service levels achieved and logistics cost components. The second objective of performance measurement is **controlling.** Controlling tracks ongoing performance and helps to refine a logistics process in order t bring it into compliance with he standards. The third objective is **directing.** Directing measures are designed to motivate personnel to achieve higher levels of productivity.

2. Compare and contrast the various metrics for product availability. Why is orders shipped complete considered the most stringent metric?

Availability is typically reflected by an organization's fill rate. It is critical to note, however, that fill rate may be measured in a variety of ways:

$$Item\ Fill\ Rate\ =\ \frac{number\ of\ items\ ordered\ by\ customer}{number\ of\ items\ delivered\ to\ customers}$$

$$Line\ Fill\ Rate\ =\ \frac{number\ of\ purchase\ order\ lines\ ordered\ by\ customer}{number\ of\ purchase\ order\ lines\ delivered\ complete\ to\ customers}$$

$$Value\ Fill\ Rate\ =\ \frac{total\ dollar\ value\ of\ customer\ orders}{total\ dollar\ value\ delivered\ to\ customers}$$

Availability may also be measured by orders delivered complete which is:

$$\frac{number\ of\ customer\ orders}{number\ of\ orders\ delivered\ complete}$$

Orders delivered complete is the most stringent measure of a firm's performance relative to product availability. In this metric, an order that is missing only one item on one line is considered to be incomplete. It is the ultimate objective of any logistician however it calls for a perfect order approach.

3. Why is it important that a firm measure customer perception as a regular part of performance measurement?

Understanding buying behavior is very important for the firm when it considers that the customer ultimately determines the firm's success and failure. Developing this understanding can best be achieved with concise **customer perception measurement.** By keeping track of how customers perceive performance, operational strengths can be promoted and weaknesses can be dealt with as the firm sees fit.

4. **Is the ideal of a perfect order a realistic operational goal?**

The **perfect order** is the ultimate, integrative measure of quality in logistics. It measures whether an order proceeds smoothly through every step of the logistical system, without fault. However, as mentioned previously, service quality is in the "eye of the beholder." Even operationally " perfect" execution can result in "faulty" delivery if the customer <u>perceives</u> an inadequacy. Therefore, though the perfect order represents an ideal, it can rarely be achieved in reality.

5. **Why are comprehensive measures of supply chain performance such as total supply chain cost so difficult to develop?**

Traditionally companies have focussed inwardly in order to reduce the costs. The comprehensive measures like total supply chain costs primarily focus on reducing the aggregate of costs across all firms in the supply chain, not an individual organization. It requires that those companies whose cost is reduced to share benefits to fair compensate those, whose cost is increased. It is challenging to equitably distribute the gains/ benefits amongst the partners.

6. **Why is Flexible budgeting a more valuable tool for logistics managers than Fixed-dollar budgeting?**

Flexible budgets are based on standardized costs, or expected norms for particular activities. They require sophisticated information systems to track activity levels and costs. Flexible budgeting provides a means of accommodating for unexpected changes in production volume during an operating period. It manages to compare activity costs with standard, expected costs despite these fluctuations. The value of flexible budgets is their ability to maintain focus and detect problem areas during periods of great demand variance.

7. **Compare and contrast the contribution approach with the net profit approach in cost-revenue analysis.**

The Contribution approach and net profit approach are two widely used frameworks for effective costing.
Contribution approach requires all costs to be identified as fixed and variable according to the cost behavior. It also specifies which are direct costs and which are variable costs. In this approach, income statements are prepared to identify profitability of each segment by determination of fixed, variable, direct, and indirect costs.
Net Profit approach requires all operating costs be charged or allocated to an operating segment. This approach is based on the fact that all of a company's activities exist to support the production and delivery of goods and services to

customers. Moreover, in many firms most costs are joint or shared costs. Therefore in order to determine profitability of a channel, territory, or product, each segment is allocated its fair share of these costs.

8. **Do you believe that activity-based costing represents an equitable basis for allocating indirect expenses?**

The primary purpose of **activity based costing** is to track all relevant costs associated with the performance of value-added activities. The basic premise is that all the costs should be assigned to activities that consume resources. It is a metric used within the framework of **total cost analysis.** Traditional accounting methods fail to properly identify cost drivers in logistics, ABC seeks to identify the cost drivers of logistical work across specific customers and products, lending to explorations of cost trade-offs. Therefore ABC attempts to allocate indirect expenses on an equitable basis.

9. **Suppose you have been asked by a firm to assess the impact on return on assets of outsourcing transportation. Currently the firm uses a private truck fleet and is considering a switch to a third-party transportation company. Which aspects of the Strategic Profit Model would be affected?**

The Strategic Profit Model demonstrates that a firm can increase its return on assets by managing net profit margin and/or managing asset turnover. By outsourcing transportation to a third party provider, the company is reducing its investment in assets (truck fleet). Since Asset turnover is measured as the ratio of total sales to the total assets, this initiative will reduce the denominator thereby increasing the asset turnover.

10. **How can the Strategic Profit Model be integrated with cost-revenue analysis for the purpose of analyzing the return on assets from servicing a specific customer account?**

The Strategic Pricing Model can be integrated with the cost-revenue analysis for analyzing the return on assets from servicing a specific customer account. Contribution for each product is calculated using only those expenses directly traced to each product. Similarly asset investments directly attributable to specific products are identified. In some situations, accounts receivable and other direct asset investments attributable to specific customer need to be included. Other segment profitability and return o investment analysis can be conducted using the SPM framework. This gives a very powerful tool to the mangers to identify how logistics process, activities and decisions impact the financial objectives of the organization.

Problem Set 1 Solutions

Information and Forecasting

1a. To determine if EDI will pay for itself within the first five years, we must begin by determining the annual costs associated with the current, manual system over this period:

Yr.	(Order volume x cost/order)	+ (errors x cost/error)	= Annual Cost
1	(20,000 x $2.50)	+ ((20,000 x 0.012) x $5.00)	= $ 51,200
2	(20,000 x $2.50)	+ ((22,000 x 0.012) x $5.00)	= $ 56,320
3	(25,000 x $3.00)	+ ((25,000 x 0.012) x $5.00)	= $ 76,500
4	(30,000 x $3.00)	+ ((30,000 x 0.012) x $5.00)	= $ 91,800
5	(36,000 x $3.00)	+ ((36,000 x 0.012) x $5.00)	= $110,160

The cumulative total cost of the manual system is $385,980

Now calculate the cost of EDI over the same period

EDI System Costs

Yr.   (Order volume x cost/order) + (errors x cost/error) + salary= Annual Cost

0	Upfront implementation cost = $100,000
1	(20,000 x $.50)+((20,000 x 0.003) x $8)+($38,000 x 1.03^0) = $ 48,480
2	(22,000 x $.50)+((22,000 x 0.003) x $8)+($38,000 x 1.03^1) = $ 50,668
3	(25,000 x $.50)+((25,000 x 0.003) x $8)+($38,000 x 1.03^2) = $ 53,414
4	(30,000 x $.50)+((30,000 x 0.003) x $8)+($38,000 x 1.03^3) = $ 57,224
5	(36,000 x $.50)+((36,000 x 0.003) x $8)+($38,000 x 1.03^4) = $ 61,633

The cumulative cost of the EDI system is: $371,439

By comparing the two total five-year costs, we can see that EDI would pay for itself within the specified period. It is, in fact, in the fifth year that EDI pays itself off.

Note: This problem, like most other cost comparison problems in the textbook, does not consider the time value of money.

1b. This is a creative thinking question. Responses might include but are not limited to: improved customer service through increased productivity, higher order accuracy, and better order tracking. Mr. McNealy might also expect improved relations with all channel members through better coordination and cooperation in the order process and delivery.

2.   Order placement as orders wait to be bundled for processing. However, the decision should consider customer service requirements. Batch processing better allows a supplier to allocate current inventory, yet real-time processing is more responsive.

3.   This is a creative thinking question. Responses may include but are not limited to: Point-of-Sale applications can help Quikee Stop track sales, reducing inventory uncertainty and the need for buffer stock, and readily provide strategic marketing information. Material handling and tracking applications provide valuable information regarding the movement, storage, shipment and receipt of product. All of these benefits may have cost and customer service implications.

4a.   June's anticipated demand at each DC is show below:

DC location	Historical % x		Aggregate Demand	=	DC Demand
Los Angeles	(25%	x	12,000)	=	3,000 pairs
Memphis	(30%	x	12,000)	=	3,600
Dayton	(35%	x	12,000)	=	4,200
Topeka	(10%	x	12,000)	=	1,200
TOTAL					**12,000 pairs**

4b.   The aggregate forecast for July is 12,720 pairs of socks (12,000 x 1.06). July's anticipated demand at each DC is shown below:

DC location	Historical % x		Aggregate Demand	=	DC Demand
Los Angeles	(25%	x	12,720)	=	3,180 pairs
Memphis	(30%	x	12,720)	=	3,816
Dayton	(35%	x	12,720)	=	4,452
Topeka	(10%	x	12,720)	=	1,272
TOTAL					**12,720 pairs**

5a.   To find the forecasted sales for the third quarter of 1999 under the moving averages technique, sum the actual sales from quarter 4 or 1999 and quarters 1 and 2 of 2000 and divide by 3:

$$F_{Qtr3,00} = \frac{1000 + 1300 + 800}{3} = 1{,}033 \text{ Units}$$

5b.   The forecasts of 1999 quarterly sales by exponential smoothing ($\alpha = 0.10$) are:

F_t:
2000, Qtr. 1 = 0.10 (1000) + 0.90 (900)   = 910
2000, Qtr. 2 = 0.10 (1300) + 0.90 (910)   = 949
2000, Qtr. 3 = 0.10 (800) + 0.90 (949)   = 934
2000, Qtr. 4 = 0.10 (250) + 0.90 (934)   = 866

5c.   The revised forecasts for the 1999 sales by exponential smoothing ($\alpha = 0.20$) are:

F_t: 2000, Qtr. 1 = 0.20 (1000) + 0.80 (900)   = 920
        2000, Qtr. 2 = 0.20 (1300) + 0.80 (920)   = 996
        2000, Qtr. 3 = 0.20 (800) + 0.80 (996)   = 957
        2000, Qtr. 4 = 0.20 (250) + 0.80 (957)   = 816

Students should note that higher alpha values place more emphasis on the previous period's actual results and less on the previous period's forecast. In our case it appears to have made the forecasts more sensitive to actual fluctuation though not necessarily more accurate.

5d.   The moving averages and simple exponential smoothing techniques do not work well in Ms. Boyd's situation. Ms. Boyd's product experiences a seasonal fluctuation that is ineffectively represented in both simple techniques. Adding a seasonality factor would help. Regression analysis with seasonal dummy variables and ratio-to-moving averages techniques more adequately perform forecasts with seasonal variations.

6a.   Compare costs associated with the two alternative plans:

	Old system	New System
Monthly Inventory Carrying Cost:	$3,000	$1,800*
Additional systems costs (monthly):	0	1,000
Total associated monthly costs:	$3,000	$2,800

*found by reducing the old system's monthly cost by 40% ($3,000 x (1.0-.0.4)) = 1,800

By Mr. Gregory's estimations, he should implement the system improvements for a monthly savings of $200 ($3,000 - $2,800).

6b.   This is a creative thinking question. Reponses may include but are not limited to: potential cost savings to Muscle Man customers should inventory cost savings be passed along to them as less is invested in material and storage, or perhaps better service through higher order fulfillment and quality.

Problem Set 2 Solutions

Operations

1. a. Use the reorder point to find the order quantity:

$$R = D \times T + SS$$

$$= 400 \times 14 + 500$$

$$= \textbf{6,100 spatulas}$$

    b. The average inventor is one-half the order quantity:

$$\text{Average inventory} = \frac{6,100}{2} = \textbf{3,050 spatulas}$$

2. a. The economic order quantity (EOQ) is the square root of the product of the numerator (two times order cost and demand) divided by the product of the denominator (inventory carrying cost times unit cost):

$$\textbf{EOQ} = \sqrt{\frac{2 C_o D}{C_i U}} = \sqrt{\frac{2(8)(44,000)}{(.12)(.75)}} = \sqrt{\frac{704,000}{.09}} = \textbf{2,797 cups}$$

    b. Annual total cost with order quantities of 2,797 cups (calculated in part (a)):

Inventory Carrying Costs $= \dfrac{2,797}{2} \times .75 \times .12 = \$\ 125.87$

Order Costs: determine the number of whole orders/yr.

$$\frac{44,000}{2,797} = 15.73 \text{ or } \textbf{16 whole orders/yr.}$$

16 orders x $8 per order   =   128.00

Transportation Costs = 44,000 units x $ .05 / unit =   <u>2,200.00</u>

Total Cost (q_e = 2,797 units)   **$ 2,453.87**

Annual total cost with order quantities of 4,000 cups:

Inventory Carrying Costs $= \dfrac{4,200}{2} \times (.75) \times (.12) = \$\ 180.00$

Order Costs : determine the number of whole orders/ yr.

$$\frac{44,000}{4,000} = 11 \text{ whole orders/ yr}$$

11 orders x \$8/order   =   88.00

Transportation Costs = 44,000 units x (\$ .04/unit) = 1,760.00

Total Cost (q_e = 4,000 units)   **\$ 2,028.00**

The order quantity of 4,000 units costs (\$2,453.87 – 2,028.00) **\$425.87** less annually than 2,797 order quantity found in part (a) when transportation costs are considered.

c.   We found that the low cost alternative in part (b) was the order quantity of 4,000 units. Therefore, the number of orders per year required to meet demand can be calculated as follows:

Orders per year   = $\frac{44,000}{4,000}$ =   **11 orders**

From the number of orders we can find the order interval:

Order interval = $\frac{12 \text{ months}}{11}$ =   **1.1 months**

-or-

Order interval = $\frac{365 \text{ days}}{11}$ =   33.18 =   **33 days**

3.   a.   Reorder point under perpetual review:

R   =   D x T +   SS

=   100 x 8 + 0 =   **800 watches**

b.   Average inventory = Q/2 + SS = 1,200 + 0   =   **600 watches**

c.   Reorder point under weekly review:

R = D (T + P/2) + SS

= 100 (8 + 7/2) + 0 = 100 (11.5) = **1,150 watches**

d.   Average inventory   = Q/2 + (P x D)/2 + SS

= (1,200/2) + (7 x 100) /2 + 0

$$= 600 + 350$$

$$= \textbf{950 units}$$

4. a. Common days' supply of chocolate chewies:

$$DS = \frac{A + \sum I_j}{\sum D_j} = \frac{(42{,}000 - 7{,}000) + 18{,}500}{4{,}500}$$

$$= \textbf{11.89 days}$$

b. Fair Share Allocation Logic:

Allocation = (Days' Supply x Daily Requirements) - Inventory

$$A_{Cincinnati} = (11.89 \times 2{,}500) - 12{,}500 = \textbf{17{,}225 units}$$

$$A_{Phoenix} = (11.89 \times 2{,}500) - 6{,}000 = \textbf{17{,}780 units}$$

Note: Together, the allocations equal 35,005 units (17,225 + 17,780) which is 5 more than the plant warehouse's allocation supply. The difference rests with the rounding of the days' supply figure.

5. a.

Dallas Distribution Center

On Hand Balance: 220   Performance Cycle: 1 week
Safety Stock: 80   Order Quantity: 200

	Past Due	Week 1	2	3	4	5	6	
Gross Requirements		60	70	80	85	90	80	
Scheduled Receipts				200		200		
Projected On hand	220	160	90	210	125	235	155	DC1
Planned Orders			200		200			

Lexington Distribution Center

On Hand Balance: 420   Performance Cycle: 2 weeks
Safety Stock: 100   Order Quantity: 400

	Past Due	Week 1	2	3	4	5	6	
Gross Requirements		100	115	120	125	140	125	
Scheduled Receipts				400			400	DC2
Projected On hand	420	320	205	485	360	220	495	
Planned Orders		400			400			

Evansville Warehouse

On Hand Balance: 900   Performance Cycle: 2 weeks
Safety Stock: 250   Order Quantity: 650

	Past Due	Week 1	2	3	4	5	6
Gross Requirements	0	400	200	0	600	0	0
Scheduled Receipts							
Projected On hand	900	500	300	300	350	350	350
Master Sched.- Rcpt.					650		
Master Sched.- Start			650				

b.   This question is for the purpose of discussion. Should student's DRP schedules in part (a) be completed correctly, the question draws relevance by noting that in week 4 the Evansville warehouse has an expected demand of 600 units (with an order of 200 from Dallas and an order of 400 from Lexington).

From purely a potential revenue standpoint it would make sense to ensure that Lexington's needs are satisfied though special customer considerations may be made. Stay safe would be wise to see that its preferred customers' needs are met.

We must assume that the manufacturing breakdown cannot be predicted and, hence, no anticipatory action will be made on behalf of the DC managers. This is, in part, why safety stocks maintained. With the expectation of a possible breakdown, one DC manager (or both) might increase safety stock levels in the preceding week(s).

There is not enough information provided to quantify the potential dollar loss should deliveries be delayed until all requirements can be satisfied. This missing piece of data is Lexington's week 7 requirements. The Lexington DC should still have 95 units left(in safety stock) after week 6 to serve 7 demand, but this figure is not provided for us.

We can provide as estimate of potential lost sales from the Dallas DC though we cannot compare it to that of Lexington for reasons detailed above. Dallas would loose 45 sales units in week 6 (having only 35 units of inventory after week 5 to meet week 6's demand of 80 units). The dollar loss would be $540 (45 units x $12/unit).

6.   a.   Yes, the distribution is normal. The sample's mean, median and mode are all equal:

$$\text{mean} = \frac{\sum d_j}{n} = \frac{150}{25} = 6$$

$$\text{median} = \frac{2+10}{2} = 6$$

mode = **6** (seven of the 25 observations are 6 units).

b.   The calculation of standard deviation for daily demand is:

$$\sigma_{dd} = \sqrt{\frac{\sum F_i D_i^2}{n}}$$

$$= \sqrt{\frac{1(4)^2 + 1(3)^2 + 3(2)^2 + 4(1)^2 + 7(0)^2 + 4(1)^2 + 3(2)^2 + 1(3)^2 + 1(4)^2}{25}}$$

$$= \sqrt{\frac{16 + 9 + 12 + 4 + 0 + 4 + 12 + 9 + 16}{25}} = \sqrt{3.28}$$

$$= 1.81$$

c. Yes, the distribution is normal as well. Look a the mean, median and mode:

$$\text{Mean} = \frac{4(10) + 8(11) + 6(12) + 8(13) + 4(14)}{40} = \frac{480}{40} = 12$$

$$\text{Median} = \frac{10 + 14}{2} = 12$$

Mode = **12** (since it has the greatest frequency).

d. The calculation of the standard deviation of the performance cycle is:

$$\sigma_{pc} = \sqrt{\frac{\sum F_i D_i^2}{n}}$$

$$= \sqrt{\frac{4(2)^2 + 8(1)^2 + 16(0)^2 + 8(1)^2 + 4(2)^2}{40}}$$

$$= \sqrt{\frac{16 + 8 + 0 + 8 + 16}{40}} = \sqrt{1.20} = 1.10$$

e. The safety stock at one combined standard deviation is :

$$\sigma_c = \sqrt{T S_s^2 + D^2 S_t^2}$$

$$= \sqrt{12(1.81)^2 + 6^2(1.10)^2} \qquad = \sqrt{(39.31) + (43.56)}$$

$$= \sqrt{82.87}$$

$$= 9.10$$

As instructed, round to nearest whole units, **9 units.**

Therefore, a safety stock of 9 scoreboards is required to protect approximately 68% of all performance cycles.

f. Average Inventory with no safety stock : $Q/2 = 36/2 = 18$ units

Average Inventory with <u>one</u> standard deviation :   18 + 1 (9) = 27 units

Average Inventory with <u>two</u> standard deviation :   18 + 2 (9) = 36 units

Average Inventory with <u>three</u> standard deviation : 18 + 3 (9) = **45 units**

To protect at three standard deviations (99.73% level), average inventory would be 45 scoreboards.

g.   Combine the given elements and the answer to part (e) to find f(k);

     $f(k)$ = (1 - Service Level) x (Order Quantity / σ_c)

     = (1 - .99) x (36/9) = .01 x 4 = **.04**

h.   From Table of Normal Loss, we determine that K is approximately 1.3.

     Now plug in this value for K and multiply by the combined standard deviation found in part e) to determine the safety stock:

     $SS = K \times \sigma_c$

     = 1.3 x 9 = **11.7 scoreboards**

     As noted in the text, there may be confusion between the probability of stockout and the magnitude of stockout. Here, we are estimating the safety stock to protect against the probability of stockout .

i.   First, find a new value for f(k):

     $f(k)$ = (1 - service Level) x (order quantity / σ_c)

     = (1 - .99) x (30/9)   = .01 x 3.33 =   **.033**

     From table 8-15, we determine that K is approximately 1.4.

     Again, plug in this value for K and multiply by the combined standard deviation found in part e) to determine the safety stock:

     $SS = K \times \sigma_c$

     = 1.4 x 9   = **12.6 (or round to 13 scoreboards)**

The smaller order quantity requires that an additional scoreboard be kept in safety stock at 99% service level, comparing answers to part h) and i).

7.   a.   The cost of each alternative is illustrated below:

Motor (truck): 2 tank trucks required @ $600 per tank truck

$$2 \times \$600 = \mathbf{\$1200}$$

Rail: 1 rail tankcar can cover shipment @ 41000 tankcar

$$1 \times \$1000 = \mathbf{\$1000}$$

Rail offers the least cost transportation for the shipment, $1000.

b.   A shortlist of qualitative factors includes: time, route flexibility, railcar fleet utilization, safety and security of product, regulations, backhaul opportunities, and contractual agreements which may require a specific volume of traffic. A number of other factors may also be considered.

8.   a.   The correct LTL and TL product classifications are:

	LTL	TL
i.	70	45
ii.	70	40
iii.	100	40

b.   The freight charges are calculated as follows:

i.   Applicable rate is 416.61 /cwt. Calculate: $52 \times 416.61 = \mathbf{\$863.72}$

ii.   Applicable rate is $6/41 / cwt. Calculate: $320 \times \$6.41 = \mathbf{\$2051.20}$

iii.   Applicable rate is $36.84/cwt. Calculate: $2 \times \$36.84 = \$73.68$, **BUT** the table shows that there is a minimum charge of $81.00. Therefore, the answer is **$81.00.**

iv.   Look at the rates for 10,000 lbs. and 20,000 lbs. On this problem since it may be cheaper to pay for 20,000 lbs. At 20,000 lb. Rate than 19,000 lbs. At 10,000 lb. rate:

10,000 lb. Rate is 421.30/cwt and 20,000 lb. Rate is $13.20/cwt.

19,000 lbs @ 10,000 lb. rate: 190 x $21.30 = **$4047**

19,000 lbs @ 20,000 lb. rate: (190 x $13.20) + (10 x $13.20) = **$2642**

It is less expensive for the shipper to accept the 20,000 lb. rate with a 1000 lb. deficit charge tacked on. Therefore, the correct change is **$2642.** The shipper should be charged this lower amount.

v.   The applicable linehaul rate found in Table 12-2 is $50.16/cwt. The total charge is :

$50.16/cwt x 25 = $1254 x 1.05 (surcharge) = **$1316.70**

9.   Three individual shipments cost:

$ 18.94/cwt x 50 = $ 947.00
$ 14.73/cwt x 100 = 1473.00
$ 18.94/cwt x 70 = <u>1325.00</u>
$3745.80

vs

One bundled shipment of 22,000 lbs. With stopoffs in Lansing:

$9.22/cwt x 220 = $2028.40
<u>+ 100.00</u>   (2 stopoffs @ $50.00 each)
$2128.40

A single bundled shipment is ($3745.80 - $2128.40), **$1617.40** cheaper than the three individual LTL shipments.

10. a.   The calculation of the current freight bill can be;

<u>Per shipment:</u>

Class Rate x Discount = After-discount Rate x Weight factor = Rate/Shipment

5,000 lbs., cl 65: $13.84/cwt x (1 - .45) = $7.62 x 50 = $381.00

1,200 lbs., cl 400: $118.58/cwt x (1 - .45) = $65.22 x 12 = $782.64

10,000 lbs., cl 100: $14.73/cwt x (1 - .45) = $8.11 x 100 = $811.00

<u>For all shipments:</u>

$$200(4381.00) + 40(\$782.64) + 30(\$811.00) = \mathbf{\$131{,}835.60}$$

The total freight bill for the given shipments is **$131,835.60.**

b.   The simplest way to determine the freight bill with an FAK rate is to first find the sum of the shipment weights:

Total weight = 200 (5,000 lbs.) + 40 (1,200 lbs.) + 30 (10,000 lbs.) = 1,348,000 lbs

Apply the FAK rate of $10/cwt:

$10/cwt x 13,480 cwt = **$134,800**

Hence, with price as the sole determinant, Mr. Harris should not accept the $10 FAK rate, but negotiate a lower rate given the nature of his traffic (number of shipments and class of those shipments). The break-even FAK rate would be ($131,835.60 / 13,480 cwt), **$9.78/cwt.**

c.   The FAK rate simplifies rate audits for the bill recipient and simplifies billing for the transportation provider. Future business expectations will shape the rate Mr. Harris should negotiate. For instance, if a heavier volume of high-class traffic is anticipated in the future, it might be wise for Mr. Harris to accept the $10/cwt FAK or, perhaps, a slightly higher rate. On the other hand, a lower rate should be sought if lower class products are expected to assume a larger proportion of the traffic.

11.   a.   the cost associated with motor carriage is comprised of two components: 1) the line-haul charge, and 2) the opportunity cost associated with tardy delivery. The cost is calculated as follows:

Line haul:	1940 miles @ $1.65 /mile	=	$3,201
+ late fee: (1/2 day, 150 units) = .5($6 x 150)		=	600

The associated cost of motor carriage is **$3,801**

b.   The costs associated with the rail option are consistent with the components found with motor carriage; both a line-haul charge and late fee exist. The calculation follows:

Line haul:	Flat line-haul charge	=	$1,500
+ late fee: (2.5 day, 150 units) = .5($6 x 150)		=	2,250

The associated cost of rail transport is **$3,750**

c.   The intermodal problem differs from parts a. and b. in that the shipment is made within the standardized transit time allocated (2.5 days), yet has a loss/damage component. In addition, 1/3 of the loss is said to be readily reimbursed. Hence, (2/3 of 3%), 2% of the dollar value of goods results in a loss.

Line haul:	Flat line-haul charge	=	$2,500.00
+ loss/ damage: (3% of $29,250)		=	877.00
	Cost before reimbursement is		$3,377.50
- amount reimbursed: (1/3 x 3% x $29,250)		=	292.21
	The associated cost of intermodal transport is		**$3,085.29**

12.   a.   Class 100, 1000 lbs = $33.15/cwt (10) = $331.50

            Class 85,   1000 lbs = $29.07/cwt (10) = $290.70

                     Per shipment cost difference of   **$ 40.80**

     b.   Compare the savings associated with lower transportation costs over one year to the $10,000 packaging investment:

            Savings = 300 shipments x 440.80 = **$ 12,240.00**

The first year savings exceed the 410,000 investment, therefore Moving hands <u>should</u> expect full payback in the first year. The break-even number of shipments is:

$$\frac{\$\ 10,000}{\$\ 40.80} = 246\ shipments.$$

13.   a.   Each El Coquistador shipment requires speedy to cover the route diagrammed below:

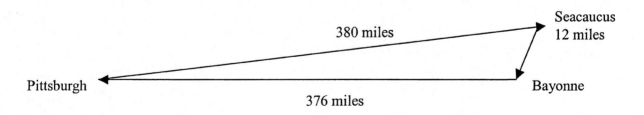

            Revenue per trip: $850.00

- Cost per trip: $1.20/mile x (12 + 376 + 380 miles) = $\underline{921.60}$

$ 71.60 loss/trip

Mr. Berry should negotiate a new, higher rate or defer the business. This trip is not profitable. For Speedy, a loss of $71.60 results from each trip. Over the course of a month, speedy would loose (12 x $71.60), $ 859.20.

b.   The Conquistador/ super tread combined move will follow the route shown below:

Revenue per trip; $850.00 + ($1.30/mile x 430 miles) = 41,409.00

- Cost per trip: $1.20 x (12 + 376 + 65 + 430 + 12 miles) = $\underline{1,074.00}$

$335.00 loss/trip

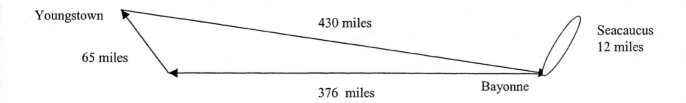

c.   As calculated in part b) above, Speedy will receive a profit of $335 per trip with the backhaul arrangement coupled with the original Conquistador agreement. Over the course of a month (12 trips/month), speedy can expect profits of (12 x $335), **$4,020.**

d.   A comparison of respective profits calculated in parts a. and b. illustrates the importance of creating backhaul opportunities for the carrier. Mr. Berry faced a per trip loss of $71.60 with the Conquistador fronthaul, but a profit of $335 was possible when the trip was coupled with a backhaul arrangement. Neither shipment alone represents a profitable utilization of resources. Yet, coupling the fronthaul move with a revenue-generating return trip is a worthwhile arrangement for Mr. Berry.

14.   a.   <u>Direct Shipping Plan</u> (annual costs)

Storage costs: $6,000/month x 12 months = $ 72,000

Shipping costs:	=	300,000
		$372,000

Storage costs: fixed $200,000/ 10 years	=	$ 20,000
Operations cost	=	48,000
Shipping costs: ($300,000)(1 - .25)	=	225,000
		$293,000

The consolidated warehouse can be operated for $79,000 less per year over the agreement's ten year life.

b. This is a creative thinking question for the purpose of discussion. Responses may include but are not limited to: better customer service (in various forms) to Ace, synergy through coordination with partners, SPP may be able to utilize/share assets not financially feasible on their own.

c. This too is a creative thinking question. Some responses might be: added risk through ownership (part-ownership), potential difficulties with coordination across partners, incongruent objectives may lead to tribulations, and possible cash flow difficulties due to fixed investment disbursement(s).

15. a. Look at the annual costs associated with each plan to determine the least cost alternative:

<u>Single consolidated warehouse</u>

Determine the best transportation mix (van types) for this plan:

How many refrigerated trucks are needed for weekly barrel demand?

$$\frac{300 \text{ barrels / week}}{72 - \text{barrel capacity}} \quad = \quad 4.16 \text{ refrigerated trucks}$$

How many non-refrigerated trucks are needed for weekly case demand?

$$\frac{5,000 \text{ barrels / week}}{400 - \text{case capacity}} \quad = \quad 12.5 \text{ non-refrigerated trucks}$$

The least cost transportation mix for this alternative would be to use 4 refrigerated, 12 non-refrigerated, and 1 half-refrigerated truck.

Weekly transportation costs = 4($550) + 12($400) + 1($500) = **$7,500**

Now find the annual costs of the single warehouse:

Capital: $3,500/week x 52 weeks   = $182,000

Labor: $3,200/week x 52 weeks   =   166,400

Transportation: $7,500/week x 52 weeks =   <u>390,000</u>

Total Costs: =   **$738,400**

Now look at the annual cost of the two-warehouse alternative (one for cases and one for barrels):

Transportation: Low cost option is:

$$\frac{5{,}000 \text{ cases / week}}{400 - \text{case capacity}} = 12.5 \text{ or } \textbf{13 non-refrigerated trucks}$$

Weekly transportation cost: 13 x $400   = $5,200

Annual costs for case warehouse:

Capital: $1,250/week x 52 weeks   = $ 65,000

Labor: $2,500/week x 52 weeks   =   130,000

Transportation: $5,200/week x 52 weeks =   <u>270,400</u>

Total annual cost of **case warehouse:**   =   **$465,400**

<u>The barrel warehouse:</u>

Transportation: Low cost option is:

$$\frac{300 \text{ barrels / week}}{72\text{-barrel capacity}} = 4.16 \text{ or } \textbf{4 refrigerated and 1 half -refrigerated truck}$$

Weekly transportation cost: 4($550) + 1($500) = $2,700

Annual costs for barrel warehouse:

Capital: $2,500/week x 52 weeks   = $ 130,000

Labor:	$1,600/week x 52 weeks	=	83,200
Transportation:	$2,700/week x 52 weeks	=	140,400
Total annual cost of **barrel warehouse**:		=	**$353,600**

Now add the total cost of each warehouse for the alternative's total annual cost:

Case warehouse	$465,400
Barrel warehouse	353,600
Total cost	**$819,000**

<u>Conclusion:</u> The consolidated warehouse costs (819,000 – 738,400), **$80,600** less per year to operate.

b. Compare the revised consolidated option with the $819,000 found above for the two-warehouse option in part a.:

How many multi-compartmented (half-refrigerated) trucks are needed to meet weekly shipping demand?

Cases:	5,000 cases / week	=	25 trucks
	200- case capacity		
barrels:	300 barrels / week	=	8.33 trucks
	36- barrel capacity		

Under the assumption that cases cannot be stored in the refrigerated compartment, we will need 25 multi-compartmented trucks each week.

Weekly transportation costs: 25 ($500) = $12,500

Now find the revised annual costs of the single warehouse:

Capital:	$3,500/week x 52 weeks	=	$ 182,000
Labor:	$3,200/week x 52 weeks	=	166,400
Transportation:	$12,500/week x 52 weeks	=	650,000
Total Costs :		=	**$998,400**

Conclusion: In the revised scenario, maintaining two individual warehouses is the least cost alternative, costing ($998,400 - $819,000), **$179,400** less than a consolidated warehouse served solely by multi-compartmented trucks.

16.   a   <u>Annual costs of the private warehouse:</u>

Fixed:	$\dfrac{\$300,000}{10 \text{ years}}$	=	$ 30,000

Variable:

Warehouse: 24,000 units x $5.00/unit		=	120,000
Transportation; 24,000 units x $12.50/unit		=	<u>300,000</u>
Total cost private warehouse		=	**$450,000**

b.   <u>Annual costs of the public warehouse:</u>

Variable:

Warehouse: 24,000 units x $8.00/unit		=	192,000
Transportation; 24,000 units x $17.50/unit		=	<u>420,000</u>
Total cost public warehouse		=	**$612,000**

*The $17.50/unit transportation charge is a combination of the $5.00 transshipment of the mattresses from the plant to the warehouse and the $12.50 outbound charge from the warehouse.

c.   <u>Annual costs of the outsourced logistics system:</u>

Fixed:	$\dfrac{\$150,000}{10 \text{ years}}$	=	$ 15,000

Variable:

Warehouse and transportation	= 24,000 units x $20.00/unit =		<u>480,000</u>
Total cost, outsourced logistics		=	**$495,000**

c.   This is a creative thinking question. Assuming (a) was chosen as the least cost alternative, responses may include the firm's ability to specifically design the warehouse to meet its needs and those of its customers such that the optimal flow of goods is maintained. The firm also has full control of the facility's utilization, providing the means for internal logistics process integration. Plus, operating one's own warehouse can sere as a form of market presence, a perceptual comfort often deemed valuable by customers. Instructors should be open to other responses, should (a) have not been chosen as the least cost alternative.

17. a.   Look at each system's accompanying cash flow (next ten years):

Mechanized Handling System

Year	labor expenses		system maintenance		Payment on equipment		Total Annual Cost
0	(20 x $13/hr x 2,000 hrs)	+	($18,000)	+	($25,000)	=	$563,000
1	(20 x $13/hr x 2,000 hrs)	+	($18,000)	+	($25,000)	=	$563,000
2	(20 x $13/hr x 2,000 hrs)	+	($18,000)	+	($25,000)	=	$563,000
3	(20 x $13/hr x 2,000 hrs)	+	($18,000)	+	($25,000)	=	$563,000
4	(20 x $13/hr x 2,000 hrs)	+	($18,000)	+	($25,000)	=	$563,000
5	(20 x $13/hr x 2,000 hrs)	+	($18,000)	+	($25,000)	=	$563,000
6	(20 x $13/hr x 2,000 hrs)	+	($18,000)	+	($25,000)	=	$563,000
7	(20 x $13/hr x 2,000 hrs)	+	($18,000)	+	($25,000)	=	$563,000
8	(20 x $13/hr x 2,000 hrs)	+	($18,000)	+	($25,000)	=	$563,000
9	(20 x $13/hr x 2,000 hrs)	+	($12,000)	+	($35,000)	=	$567,000
10	(20 x $13/hr x 2,000 hrs)	+	($12,000)	+	($35,000)	=	$567,000

Automated Handling System

Year	labor expenses	specialist's salary	system maintenance	Total Annual Cost
0	Upfront investment of $1.2 million + $125,000 sale of old		=	$1,075,000
1	(8 x $16/hr. x 2,000 hrs.) + ($56,000)1.02^0 + ($60,000)$1.03^0$		=	372,000
2	(8 x $16/hr. x 2,000 hrs.) + ($56,000)1.02^1 + ($60,000)$1.03^1$		=	374,920
3	(8 x $16/hr. x 2,000 hrs.) + ($56,000)1.02^2 + ($60,000)$1.03^2$		=	377,916
4	(8 x $16/hr. x 2,000 hrs.) + ($56,000)1.02^3 + ($60,000)$1.03^3$		=	380,991
5	(8 x $16/hr. x 2,000 hrs.) + ($56,000)1.02^4 + ($60,000)$1.03^4$		=	384,147
6	(8 x $16/hr. x 2,000 hrs.) + ($56,000)1.02^5 + ($60,000)$1.03^5$		=	387,385
7	(8 x $16/hr. x 2,000 hrs.) + ($56,000)1.02^6 + ($60,000)$1.03^6$		=	390,708
8	(8 x $16/hr. x 2,000 hrs.) + ($56,000)1.02^7 + ($60,000)$1.03^7$		=	394,119
9	(8 x $16/hr. x 2,000 hrs.) + ($56,000)1.02^8 + ($60,000)$1.03^8$		=	397,619
10	(8 x $16/hr. x 2,000 hrs.) + ($56,000)1.02^9 + ($60,000)$1.03^9$		=	401,212

Now look at the cumulative ten-year costs of each system:

Year	Mechanized	Automated
0	$ 0	$1,075,000
1	563,000	1,447,000
2	1,126,000	1,821,920
3	1,689,000	2,199,836
4	2,252,000	2,580,827
5	2,815,000	2,964,974
6	3,378,000	3,352,359*
7	3,941,000	3,743,067
8	4,504,000	4,137,186
9	5,071,000	4,534,804
10	5,638,000	4,936,017

*By comparing cumulative costs for each system, we can see the mechanized system surpasses the automated system's operating expenses in the sixth year ($3,378,999 vs. $3,352,359).

The specific payback period would be : $5 + \left(\dfrac{\$2,964,974 - \$2,815,000 + \$387,385}{\$563,000} \right)$

$$= \textbf{5.954 years}$$

b.   Automated systems have the potential to operate faster and more accurately than mechanized systems. In addition, the automated system requires less building space and can perform warehouse operations with greater certainty and less product damage.

18.   a.   the number of workers needed under each plan:

Hourly Compensation Plan

$$\dfrac{17,280 \text{ units}}{20 \text{ units/hr x 40 hrs}} = 21.6 = \textbf{22 workers*}$$

Incentive Plan

$$\dfrac{17,280 \text{ units}}{28 \text{ units/hr x 40 hrs.}} = 15.4 = \textbf{16 workers*}$$

* recall that union restrictions prevent the hiring of part-time workers.

The base wage expense under the incentive plan would not be affected by the number of workers hired to fill the weekly orders since pickers' earnings are based on individual contribution. It does mean that hiring sequentially more workers would cause average earnings to decrease. In a more realistic environment, benefits and training expenses would encourage the firm to hire enough labor to cover demand.

b.   Compare the weekly cost of each compensation package:

Hourly Compensation Plan

Labor Expense:

22 workers x $13/hr. x 40hrs.	=	$11,440

Lost Revenue:

Error rate = 17,280 units x .005 = 86.4 errors*

87 errors x $60/error	=	5,220
		$16,660

Incentive Plan

Labor expense:

17,280 units x $ .40/unit	=	$ 6,912

Lost Revenue:

Error rate = 17,280 units x .01 = 172.8 errors*

173 errors x $60/error	=	10,380
		$17,292

Though labor expenses far exceed those of the incentive plan, it is ($17,292 - $16,660), **$632** cheaper in the typical week for Dandy to utilize an hourly compensation plan with the consideration of lost sales due to errors.
*NOTE: The number of errors is rounded up in each case under the premise that Dandy does not distribute partially filled orders.

19.   First, find the cost associated with the going rate of pilferage (with no added security):

Cost = volume x pilferage rate x lost revenue/bottle

9,600,000 volume x .004 x $4.50/bottle =   **$172,800**

a.   Total cost with four security guards (Plan A);

Added cost:

Wages and benefits:

$14.50/hr. x 24 hrs/day x 365 days + 4 ($2,000) = $135,020

Product still pilfered:

9,600,000 volume x .002 x $4.50/bottle   =   86,400

Total Annual Cost of Plan A: **$221,420**

b.   Total cost with bar code technology (Plan B);

Added cost:

Wages and benefits:

Specialist's salary and benefits: = $ 49,000

Equipment: $120,000 + $8,000 + (4800/mo. X 12 mos) =   25,600
                   8 years

Product still pilfered:

9,600,000 volume x .001 x $4.50/bottle   =   43,200

Total Annual Cost of Plan B: **$117,800**

c.   Total cost with video surveillance and four security guards (Plan C):

Added cost:

Wages and benefits:

$12/hr. x 24 hrs/day x 365 days + 4 ($1,000)   = $109,120

Equipment: $\dfrac{(6 \times \$1,200) + \$36,000}{12 \text{ years}}$ = 3,600

Product still pilfered:

9,600,000 volume x .0005 x $4.50/bottle = 21,600

Total Annual Cost of Plan C: **$134,320**

From the total cost analysis above, bar code technology (Plan B) offers the lowest combination of added investment and remaining product pilferage ($117,800). Video surveillance (Plan C) offers the next best option ($134,320), still better than $172,800 expected loss associated with no remedial action. Hiring four security guards (Plan A) represents the least preferable option with associated costs of $221,420.

20. a. Compare the additional cost of providing double-wall corrugation for the X-100 with its potential loss and damage savings:

Additional cost:

Additional cost = cost/unit x forecasted sales

= [($.80)(1.20) - ($.80)] x 12,000 = **$1,920**

Savings:

First find the number of whole units lost:

Units lost = .5(.005) x 12,000 = 30 units

Now find potential savings:

Savings = 30 units x $40 = **$1,200**

From a low-cost (and product-segmented) perspective at the given forecasted sales volume, Chronotronics would not utilize double-wall corrugation with the X-100 next year. The additional cost of providing the extra protection exceeds the savings from loss and damage by ($1,920 – 41,200), **$720.**

b. Compare the additional cost of providing double-wall corrugation for the X-250 with its potential loss and damage savings:

Additional cost:

Additional cost   =   cost/unit x   forecasted sales

                    =   [($.80)(1.20) - ($.80)] x 7,000 (1.05) = **$1,176**

Savings:

First find the number of whole units lost:

Units lost = .5(.005) x 7,000 (1.05) = 18.375 units

Note that we must round up to 19 units lost.

Now find potential savings:

Savings = 19 units x $70   = **$1,330**

Yes, the higher market value of the X-250 makes it a good idea to use double-wall corrugation from a low-cost perspective as its expected savings exceed the costs by ($1,330 - $1,176), **$154.** Of course, Chronotronics should consider the system and channel-wide impact of making potential package improvements. Utilizing double-wall protection with one product might create efficiencies, making it less expensive for the firm to apply similar packaging to other product lines. Customers would likely approve of greater product protection measures so long as their costs are not affected significantly.

    c.   The transportation text discussed how measures to improve product protection lower the product's NMFC classification, the relative measure of a product's sensitivity of damage and hazard. These classifications affect the transportation rates charged to shippers. By improving packaging, the shipper can lower the likelihood of damage and appeal for lower transportation rates Note, however, that packaging alternatives can also affect the weight of a package, another dimension of transportation cost.

21.   a.   With the given information, we will first calculate the combined uncertainty (σ_c)

$$\sigma_c = \sqrt{T\,S_s^2 + D^2\,S_t^2}$$

$$= \sqrt{7 \times (3)^2 + (20)^2 \times 2^2}$$

$$= 40.8$$

Service Level (SL) $= 1 - \dfrac{f(k) \times \sigma_c}{OQ}$

With a case fill rate of 95% and order quantity of 200 units, we can calculate the loss factor, $f(k)$.

$f(k) = 0.245$

From the table for Normal loss, we observe that this value lies between 0.2667 and 0.2304, so we can choose $k = 0.4$.

Safety Stock (SS) $= k \times \sigma_c$

$= 0.4 \times 40.8$

$= 16.32$

Average Inventory $= \dfrac{OQ}{2} + SS + \text{In transit}$

$= 200/2 + 16.32 + 0$

$= 116.32$ units

b. Service level (SL) $= 99\%$

Using equation for SL as in part a), we calculate $f(k)$

$f(k) = 0.049$

from the table, we would choose $k = 1.3$

$SS = \sigma_c \times 1.3$

$= 53.04$ units

Average Inventory $= 100 + 53.04 = 153.04$ units

c. If replenishment is done daily then $T = 1$.

Therefore $\sigma_c = \sqrt{1 \times (3)^2 + (20)^2 \times (2)^2}$
$= 40.1$

With the given information, we can calculate $f(k) = 0.0498$. Correspondingly the value of $k = 1.3$.

$$SS \quad = \quad k \times \sigma_c$$

$$= \quad 52.14 \text{ units}$$

Average Inventory $\quad = \quad 100 + 52.14 \quad = \quad 152.14$ units.

As long as the uncertainties remain the same, the replenishment cycle does not impact the inventory position.

22. a.   With the given information, we will first calculate the combined uncertainty (σ_c)

$$\sigma_c \quad = \quad \sqrt{T \, S_s^{\,2} + D^2 \, S_t^{\,2}}$$

$$= \quad \sqrt{10 \times (250)^2 + (1000)^2 \times 4^2}$$

$$= \quad 4077.37$$

Since the customer orders weekly, the base stock should be 7000 (based on weekly ordering of 1000 units/day).

$$\text{Service Level (SL)} \quad = \quad 1 - \frac{f(k) \times \sigma_c}{OQ}$$

With a case fill rate of 99% and order quantity of 7000 units, we can calculate the loss factor, f(k).

$$f(k) \quad = \quad 0.01716$$

From the table for Normal loss, we observe that this value lies between 0.0232 and 0.0142, so we can choose k = 1.7

Safety Stock (SS) $\quad = \quad k \times \sigma_c$

$$= \quad 1.7 \times 4077.37$$

$$= \quad 6931.53$$

Average Inventory $\quad = \quad$ Cycle stock $+$ SS $+$ In transit

$$= \quad 7000 / 2 + 6931.53 + 0$$

$$= \quad \textbf{10431.53 units}$$

Inventory carrying cost $\quad = \quad \$ 25 \times 0.2 \times 10431.53$

$$= \$ 52{,}157$$

b. If the performance cycle variation is reduced by 2 days, then $S_T = 2$ days. So σ_c can be calculated using the above formula.

$$\sigma_c = 2150.58$$

$$f(k) = \frac{0.01 \times 7000}{2150.58} = 0.0325$$

⇨ $k = 1.4$

Safety Stock (SS) $= k \times \sigma_c$

$$= 1.4 \times 2150.58 = 3010.8 \text{ units}$$

Average Inventory $= 7000/2 + 3010.8$

$$= 6510.8 \text{ units}$$

Inventory Carrying Cost $= \$25 \times 0.2 \times 6510.8 = \mathbf{\$32{,}554}$

c. If the performance cycle is reduced by 2 days, then $T = 8$ days. So σ_c can be calculated using the above formula.

$$\sigma_c = 4062.02$$

$$f(k) = \frac{0.01 \times 7000}{4062.02} = 0.017$$

⇨ $k = 1.7$

Safety Stock (SS) $= k \times \sigma_c$

$$= 1.7 \times 4062.02 = 6905.43 \text{ units}$$

Average Inventory $= 7000/2 + 6905.43$

$$= 10{,}405.43 \text{ units}$$

Inventory Carrying Cost $= \$25 \times 0.2 \times 10405.43 = \mathbf{\$52{,}027}$

Therefore a reduction in performance cycle uncertainty has a greater impact on the average inventory and the Inventory carrying cost compared to a reduction in the cycle time.

23.   The following table shows the distances between the cities

Origin	Destination	Distance
St. Louis, MO	Lansing, MI	487 miles
St. Louis, MO	Detroit, MI	552 miles
St. Louis, MO	Toledo, OH	499 miles
Lansing, MI	Detroit, MI	88 miles
Detroit, MI	Toledo, OH	65 miles
St. Louis, MO	Ypsilanti, MI	521 miles

Daily shipment to each plant is 3000 pounds

Presently Spartan Plastics ships directly from its plant in St. Louis, MO to the 10 assembly plants. LTL rate from the plants to the assembly plants is $0.0013 per pound per mile.

Total cost of transportation   = Cost for St. Louis- Lansing + St. Louis – Detroit (8 plants)
                                                      + St. Louis-Toledo

= 3000 x 0.0013 x 487 miles + 3000 x 0.0013 x (8 x 552) miles
+ 3000 x 0.0013 x 499miles

= $21,067

Option 1 : Milk- run approach

Unit cost = $1.30 per truck mile plus $100 / stop.

Total cost of transportation = Cost for St. Louis-Lansing + Lansing–Detroit + Detroit-Toledo
                                                    + Stoppage costs (excluding Toledo)

= $1.3 x 487miles + $1.3 x 88miles + $1.3 x 65miles + $100x 9

= **$1,732**

Option 2 : Consolidate truck to Ypsilanti,MI and cross dock to the assembly plants.

Unit cost = $1.30 per truck mile and cost of delivery to each plant is $200.

Total cost of transportation = Cost for St. Louis-Ypsilanti + Cost of delivery

= $1.3 x 521miles + $200 x 10

= **$2,677**

b.   The first option is cheaper but since the delivery to the assembly plants is made sequentially, there is greater uncertainty involved. Disruption at any leg could affect the delivery to all the subsequent assembly plants.

The second option reduces the delivery uncertainty for the individual assembly plants and also takes advantage of the benefits of cross-docking.

24.   a.   Option 1: Using corrugated boxes.

Presswick needs 5000 corrugated boxes for shipping its containers and tubes.

$$\text{Total cost} = \text{Cost of boxes} + \text{Cost of disposal}$$

$$= \$\,0.05 \times 5000 + \$\,0.02 \times 5000$$

$$= \$\,350$$

Option 2: Using recyclable containers.

Due to uncertainty of the return of the boxes from the customers, Presswick needs to maintain a 3-month(25% more than the annual requirement) supply. The Inventory carrying costs is determined to be 20% of the cost of the containers.

Let us assume that the number of recyclable containers be X

$$\text{Total cost} = \text{Cost of the container (one time)} + \text{Cost of transportation} + \text{Inventory carrying cost}$$

$$= 0.25\,X + 0.01 \times 5000 + \$.25 \times 0.2 \times (25\% \text{ of } X)$$

$$= 50 + 0.2625\,X$$

Equating the costs from the two options , we get $X = 1143$

So Presswick would need atleast 1143 recyclable containers in order to meet its annual shipment needs.

b.   Other qualitative factors that should be considered include cleanliness, tracing, and theft. Since corrugated is only used once, it would likely be cleaner. Although there would probably not be a big demand for such containers, there should be some consideration for the tracking and pilferage that would result from usage of returnable containers. A plus for the use of returnable containers is that it would allow for return trips for some carriers which may allow for a reduced round-trip freight rate.

25.   a.   The following is the total volume shipped to the three DCs.

Columbus, OH   = 1.75 million cases
St. Louis , MO   = 2.00 million cases
Minneapolis, MN   = 1.25 million cases

Annual costs for each DC = Acquisition cost + Annual fixed cost + Variable cost

Columbus, OH

Annual cost for mechanized handling system
= $1,000,000 x 1.75 + $50,000 x 1.75 + $0.30 x 1,750,000 = **$2,362,500**

Annual cost for semi-automated handling system
= $3,000,000 x   1.75 + $200,000 x 1.75 + $0.08 x 1,750,000 = $5,740,000

Annual cost for information directed handling system
= $1,500,000 x 1.75 + $150,000 x 1.75 + $0.15 x 1,750,000 = $3,150,000

St. Louis, MO

Annual cost for mechanized handling system
= $1,000,000 x 2.0 + $50,000 x 2.0 + $0.30 x 2,000,000 = **$2,700,000**

Annual cost for semi-automated handling system
= $3,000,000 x 2.0 + $200,000 x 2.0 + $0.08 x 2,000,000 = $6,560,000

Annual cost for information directed handling system
= $1,500,000 x 2.0 + $150,000 x 2.0 + $0.15 x 2,000,000 = $3,600,000

Minneapolis, MN

Annual cost for mechanized handling system
= $1,000,000 x 1.25 + $50,000 x 1.25 + $0.30 x 1,250,000 = **$1,910,000**

Annual cost for semi-automated handling system
= $3,000,000 x 1.25 + $200,000 x 1.25 + $0.08 x 1,250,000 = $4,100,000

Annual cost for information directed handling system
= $1,500,000 x 1.25 + $150,000 x 1.25 + $0.15 x 1,250,000 = $2,250,000

Based on the above cost estimates, Forest Green Products should choose the **mechanized handling system**

–   If we use the NPV analysis to determine the cost, based on the usage life span of the systems, we the following results:

Columbus, OH

Annual cost for mechanized handling system (usage life of 10 years)
= $1,000,000 x 1.75 + [$50,000 x 1.75 + $0.30 x 1,750,000] x [Annuity,10%,10yrs]
= 1,000,000 x 1.75 + [$50,000 x 1.75 + $0.30 x 1,750,000] x 6.145
= $5,510,000

Annual cost for semi-automatic handling system (usage life of 5 years)
= $3,000,000 x 1.75 + [$200,000 x 1.75 + $0.08 x 1,750,000] x [Annuity,10%,5 yrs]
= $3,000,000 x 1.75 + [$200,000 x 1.75 + $0.08 x 1,750,000] x 3.791
= $7,100,000

Annual cost for information directed handling system (usage life of 7 years)
= $1,500,000 x 1.75 + [$150,000 x 1.75 + $0.15 x 1,750,000] x [Annuity,10%, 7 yrs]
= $1,500,000 x 1.75 + [$150,000 x 1.75 + $0.15 x 1,750,000] x 4.868
= **$5,180,700**

St. Louis, MO

Annual cost for mechanized handling system (usage life of 10 years)
= $1,000,000 x 2.0 + [$50,000 x 2.0 + $0.30 x 2,000,000] x [Annuity,10%,10yrs]
= 1,000,000 x 2.0 + [$50,000 x 2.0 + $0.30 x 2,000,000] x 6.145
= $6,300,000

Annual cost for semi-automatic handling system (usage life of 5 years)
= $3,000,000 x 2.0 + [$200,000 x 2.0 + $0.08 x 2,000,000] x [Annuity,10%,5 yrs]
= $3,000,000 x 2.0 + [$200,000 x 2.0 + $0.08 x 2,000,000] x 3.791
= $8,120,000

Annual cost for information directed handling system (usage life of 7 years)
= $1,500,000 x 2.0 + [$150,000 x 2.0 + $0.15 x 2,000,000] x [Annuity,10%, 7 yrs]
= $1,500,000 x 2.0 + [$150,000 x 2.0 + $0.15 x 2,000,000] x 4.868
= **$5,920,000**

Minneapolis, MN

Annual cost for mechanized handling system (usage life of 10 years)
= $1,000,000 x 1.25 + [$50,000 x 1.25 + $0.30 x 1,250,000] x [Annuity,10%,10yrs]
= $1,000,000 x 1.25 + [$50,000 x 1.25 + $0.30 x 1,250,000] x 6.145
= $3,940,000

Annual cost for semi-automatic handling system (usage life of 5 years)
= $3,000,000 x 1.25 + [$200,000 x 1.25 + $0.08 x 1,250,000] x [Annuity,10%,5 yrs]
= $3,000,000 x 1.25 + [$200,000 x 1.25 + $0.08 x 1,250,000] x 3.791
= $5,070,000

Annual cost for information directed handling system (usage life of 7 years)
= $1,500,000 x 1.25 + [$150,000 x 1.25 + $0.15 x 1,250,000] x [Annuity,10%, 7 yrs]
= $1,500,000 x 1.25 + [$150,000 x 1.25 + $0.15 x 1,250,000] x 4.868
= **$3,700,500**

Based on the above calculations, the least-cost alternative for each of the DCs is as follows:

Columbus, OH = Information-directed handling system
St. Louis, MO = Information-directed handling system
Minneapolis, MN = Information-directed handling system

b. If Forest Green Products wants to use only one system for all its DCs, the best alternative would be Information-directed handling system. The overall cost would be $10,139,300.

c. Other qualitative factors that should be considered include standardization/consistency, purchasing and operating economics, and training. A single system would result in standardized operations and training which would make it easier to implement consistent policies and procedures and allow for exchange of management between facilities. A single system would also allow for purchasing and operating synergies which should provide leverage with the vendor.

Case 1

Integrated Logistics

Overview

This case finds Tom Lippert, sales representative for DuPont Engineering Polymers (DEP), in a situation common to today's competitive sales environment. His company, as a supplier to a major manufacturer (GARD), is faced with changing times. GARD is in the midst of a "changing of the guard" as Mr. Lippert's long-time contact, Mike O'Leary, retires. O'Leary's successor, Richard Binish, brings a new set of supplier expectations to the fore of GARD's purchasing strategy. Over the years, the quality of competitors' products began to match DEP's. Firms now compete based on logistics quality. To keep the GARD business, DEP must improve its logistical performance to meet the customer's rising expectations.

The textbook illustrates a concept called the "shrinking service window." The idea behind the shrinking service window is that customers have begun to expect higher levels of service (higher fill rates) in less time (shorter order cycles). In GARD's case, a change in leadership is responsible for the new, higher expectations. The change, however, is indicative of the realization that logistics has become a strategic weapon. The case illustrates that DEP must either match competitors' service or face losing a major customer.

Solutions to Questions

1.   A diagram of the DEP-GARD supply chain is provided on the next page.

Stages that are adding value:

- Inbound transportation from the suppliers
- DEP packaging
- manufacturing
- product delivery

Stages that are not adding value:

- "dwell time" at the remote warehouse
- matching orders to paperwork
- materials receiving
- materials inventory

DEP-GARD supply chain

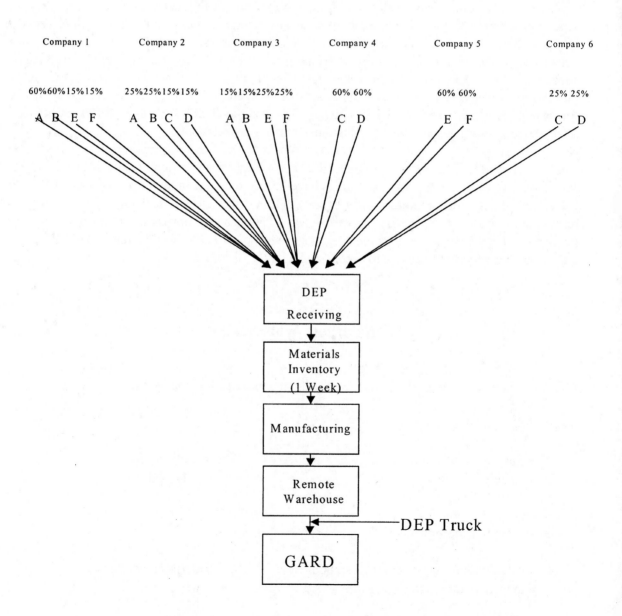

2.   Minimum order cycle time: 8 days

        Maximum order cycle time: 25 days

3.   Yes, it appears that the performance cycle can be improved through the use of 25% and 15% suppliers. For example, Company 2 offers better service levels and less variability than Company 1. Using more reliable suppliers may result in higher prices on materials but this can be mitigated by reducing DEP's material inventories. Greater certainty on the part of suppliers reduces the need to maintain high stocks of inventory.

4.   This is a question of opinion. People's resistance to change should be considered. In particular, manufacturing personnel will be tough to convince due to past experience.

5.   The means of "selling" the idea to Mr. Binish is matter of opinion -- more of an art than science. Regardless of the specific effort, it should demonstrate why Binish should keep DEP as a core GARD supplier. This will involve conveying clear guidelines for making the desired service improvements while maintaining a competitive price -- providing Binish with the value he demands.

Below are samples of "Qualifying" and "Order winning" criteria.

"Qualifying criteria"

1) Good product quality

2) Competitive price

3) Service capability that exceeds the minimum standards

"Order winning criteria"

1)   Consider changes that demonstrate that DEP is practicing the very service expectations that Binish is trying to implement. This would illustrate DEP's conceptual understanding of Binish's ideas.

2) Position GARD for electronic data interchange (EDI) or other asset- and information-sharing processes. EDI would allow Binish with "real time" information from DEP. These investments also help to solidify relationships.

These criteria will likely change over time. The shrinking service window illustrates how customers continue to expect more until eventually service approaches 100% fill rates and very short performance cycles.

This case suggests that supply chain management increases in sophistication with higher levels of performance. Unless these areas of improvement are addressed, supplying firms will be left behind as competitors strive to meet customers' ever-changing needs.

```
┌────────────────────────────────────────────────────────────┐
│                                                              │
│                          Case 2                              │
│                                                              │
│        Whitmore Products:  Time Based Logistics at Work      │
│                                                              │
└────────────────────────────────────────────────────────────┘
```

Overview

From Whitmore's perspective, the HomeHelp partnership offers substantial rewards, but at a price. This case demonstrates the all-encompassing change that is sometimes required for a firm to maintain long-term competitive success. Change is very difficult to achieve in organizations large and small. Laborers, managers and executives alike establish "comfort zones" that are difficult to break. The case follows John Smith as he first studies the potential benefits of refocusing production and logistics strategies before promoting the idea to top management.

Solutions to Questions

1.   As the supplier, Whitmore is faced with the ultimatum of effecting the change (implementing the time based service strategy) or losing the HomeHelp business. To implement the time based strategy will require new approaches to production and logistical operations as well as significant, constant investments in technology. The changes are likely to affect the way Whitmore conducts business with other customers and channel participants (suppliers, transportation providers, etc.).

As the customer, HomeHelp has issued the ultimatum to Whitmore Products. However, should Whitmore elect to turn down the opportunity, HomeHelp will have to look elsewhere for products and service.

Though the issue is open to debate, it seems that both firms stand to benefit from the time based strategy. Both firms stand to gain potential competitive advantages by being the first in their respective industries to adopt time-based logistics practices. Ideally, alliances should create synergy, where the dynamics of the whole is greater than the sum of the parts -- both firms succeed at levels unachievable when alone. As noted above, significant investment is required of each firm to see the strategy reach fruition.

2.   Whitmore Products

<u>Benefits</u>

- An exclusive relationship with HomeHelp that ensures generous revenues well into the future.

- The time based strategy may create competitive advantage that carries over into other business.

- Replacing inventory with information improves customer service and can lower costs.

<u>Barriers</u>

- The generous revenues derived from the HomeHelp relationship will require significant change and investment. The very nature of the potential competitive advantage offered by the time based strategy is that it is unique -- no one in the industry is doing it. Therefore, the challenge of figuring out how to implement the strategy effectively rests with the first mover, requiring trial-and-error efforts and investment. Change is almost always difficult to implement.

- The failure experienced with Happy Home & Living plagues future close relationships.

- Management's belief that the "additional cost" of providing service to HomeHelp will be pushed on to other customers.

HomeHelp

<u>Benefits</u>

- Reduced inventories in regional warehouses.

- Improved service from Whitmore that translates into better service delivered to HomeHelp customers in terms of availability, and quality.

<u>Barriers</u>

- The time based strategy will require commitment and investment. The time and resources required to implement such momentous change between two channel partners is substantial.

- Investment in technologies is required upfront and throughout the relationship.

3.   Suggestions may include but are not limited to:

• Reduce the role of the distribution centers. Direct shipment from the manufacturing facility would be most effective, reducing the time spent intransit and eliminating the sorting process at the distribution center. This would also reduce Whitmore's inventory holding investment significantly.

• Deliver incomplete orders when necessary rather than holding up the order at the distribution center until complete.

• Include HomeHelp's in-stock figures in data that is transmitted daily. In addition, more frequent data transmission may be worthwhile.

• The purpose of the central information service may be in question though little is said about it. It would be worthwhile to determine the role to transportation as well.

• To achieve competitive advantage is difficult. Once it is achieved, however, it should be fully exploited to benefit the firm. Perhaps Whitmore should develop the time based strategy to serve all customers.

4.   There is no clear-cut determination of right and wrong in this question. Students should assume a position on one side of the issue and justify their decisions with well-supported arguments. Discussion should encompass advantages/disadvantages of the proposal with any suggestions for change.

Case 3

Zwick Electrical: Developing a Global Logistics Strategy

Overview

This case illustrates a difficulty common to firms throughout the world that find themselves unprepared to compete in the global marketplace. The Zwick brothers and their father before them enjoyed success in the electric and power industry when the U.S. was the largest single market for the goods, and the premiere manufacturer. Suddenly, firms that have not foreseen the economic and technological development of nations around the world, realize that they no longer hold sole industry leadership.

The Zwick brothers find that reestablishing a strong market presence is far more difficult than achieving success in the domestic market. Though opportunities exist overseas they realize that establishing success in the different market environment will involve entirely new ways of doing business. They have called in a group of professionals to help institute the new mind set.

Solutions to Questions

1.   Descriptions of each company's level of sophistication in international activities:

ZEI: ZEI is in the infantile stages of global operations. Typical with firms that initially venture into new markets, the company has hired a manufacturer's representative (OVM) to peddle products abroad. The plan is being met with little success in its first three years of the agreement. Currently, ZEI has no overseas manufacturing operations. Consultants indicate that manufacturing, marketing and logistics must change for Zwick to make inroads in foreign markets and salvage competitiveness in the domestic market as well.

ABB: The merger of Swedish Asea AB and Swiss BBC Brown Boveri Ltd. demonstrates the international sophistication of this industry giant. The merged corporation has continued to expand operations throughout the world with plans apparently in place for even further expansion. ABB has an organization structure that caters to the individual needs of product managers in each country, what Barnevik refers to as a "multidomestic" approach. In addition, information systems are in place to coordinate and review the vast scope of products and nations within which ABB operates.

Siemens AG: Like ABB, Siemens has managed to acquire international manufacturing and marketing operations though it largely remains a "Euro-centered" organization. As sales data illustrate, 75% of the company's sales are derived from European markets. As the world's second largest manufacturer of electrical goods, it is anticipated that Siemens has the savvy to maintain its position in the global market.

2.   Sales are certainly at the heart of any plan for greater international activity, but perhaps even more fundamental is the ability to survive in the long-term within the competitive global environment. Industries that were once national strongholds must now compete for every sale with rivals from abroad. Zwick finds itself in this situation. It could once count on a share of the domestic market but larger domestic and foreign manufacturers are pushing them out. It should also be noted that engaging competitors in their domestic markets drains them of potential revenues that might be used to support entry into foreign markets. Assuming an active role in the international arena is no longer viewed as merely a supplement to sales at home but rather a necessity for survival.

As investment portfolio management would dictate, it is wise to spread the risk of business dealings across a number of options. Hence, the common expression: "Don't put all your eggs in one basket" finds application in international dealings. Building a portfolio of markets prevents the manufacturer from becoming dependent upon any single market.

"Cross-pollination" -- This involves gathering concepts and practices from foreign markets and cultures that might be implemented elsewhere. Zwick could harvest ideas from these foreign markets and apply them at home to possibly gain a competitive advantage.

There is also a degree of prestige associated with overseas success. Brand recognition is often enhanced at home with news of international achievements.

3.   Entering into relations with either of the large international corporations is likely to have its advantages and disadvantages for Zwick. Zwick's long-term survival would certainly be enhanced with a partnership with either organization though the firm would lose the independent identity (autonomy) that it now enjoys. It is also probable that downsizing of the Zwick organization would result from a merger, raising the issue of employee-employer loyalty. Zwick products would benefit from advanced research and development resources though products might not carry the Zwick label. Zwick would benefit from well-developed channels of marketing and distribution with either partner. Many of the advantages and disadvantages would only become known after the negotiation process and over time.

4.   Aside from a potential alliance with ABB or Siemens, Zwick might consider any number of alternatives. Responses are not limited to, but might include:

Establish alliances with firms other than ABB or Siemens: Though the two targeted firms are dominant forces in their chosen markets and have the global presence that Zwick aspires to have, ABB and Siemens are not the only firms that might offer benefits to Zwick. Perhaps they should look to other parties for potential partnerships.

Make acquisitions of its own: Though the Zwick brothers have no desire to relocate outside the United States, they may consider acquiring small Western or Central European manufacturers and distributors. Just as Zwick is being "squeezed out" of the market in the U.S. and abroad, manufacturers of the same size in Europe are likely experiencing the same problem in their domestic and international efforts as well. Much of this decision would rely on Zwick's financial position which is said to be particularly strong at the present time. An acquisition might achieve any or all of the three primary objectives: 1) maintenance of Zwick's market access in regional trading blocs, 2) increased international sales as a percentage of total sales, 3) complementary products from overseas suppliers.

Look to new products: Zwick might seek to "cut its losses" in the electric and power industry altogether and look to emerging products and markets to make an impression. As the case notes, however, Zwick's investments in research and development have been limited which would make it difficult for the firm to make a presence in anything but complementary product lines.

Address the changing economic-political environment in North America. The North American Free Trade Agreement (NAFTA) may create sizable markets for Zwick products in Canada and Mexico.

5.   The suggested course of action is entirely a matter of opinion. Each option will have its distinct advantages and disadvantages (which should be identified). There is no conclusive right or wrong answer to the question though the student's ultimate course of action should have ample support.

Case 4

Alternative Distribution Strategies

Overview

Sugar Sweets, Inc. finds that it must adjust its distribution strategy to increase market coverage and sales volume without threatening the service levels that customers have come to expect. The traditional channels of distribution for SSI products is undergoing significant change, forcing the candy company to reevaluate its current system. Candy and tobacco jobbers were becoming fewer in number. Those distributors that remained dominated wholesale operations that were not serviced by warehouse club stores. In all, the retail customer was in for a loss in product variety and high service levels, both of which were traditionally offered by the now diminishing jobbers.

To respond to the changing business environment, SSI has determined that a new approach to marketing its products is necessary. In large part, the new approach consists of an expansion of retail targets to include outlets that enjoy high traffic volumes but rarely offer snack products. The new sales sites include dry cleaners, barber/beauty shops, hardware stores, and drinking establishments. The case questions require the student to analyze the costs and benefits associated with the new distribution strategy.

Solutions to Questions

1. From the data in Table 2:

    Total number of target retailers (320,000 + 290,000 + 210,000)   =   820,000

    Number of retailers initially contacted (820,000 x .20)   =   164,000

    Anticipated number of participating retailers:

pre-trial period	(164,000 x .30)	=	**49,200**
post-trial period	(49,200 x .55)	=	**27,060**

2.   Based on Table 2 data for the average retailer:

Daily calculations

Expected number of paying customers (100/day x .10)   =   10 customers

Projected unit sales per day (10 customers x 1.12 units)   =   **11.2 units**

Projected sales dollars per day (10 customers x $1.40)   =   **$14.00**

Annual calculations

Expected number of paying customers (10/day x 260 days)   =   2,600 customers

Projected units sales per year (11.2 units/day x 260 days)   =   **2,912 units/year**

Projected sales dollars per year ($14.00/day x 260 days)   =   **$3,640/ year**

3.   Based on answers to question 2 and data from Table 3:

Number of <u>large packs</u> necessary for average retailer annually:

   2,912 units/year ÷ 180 units/large pack   =   16.18 (**16 orders/year**)

Number of <u>small packs</u> necessary for average retailer annually:

   2,912 units/year ÷ 92 units/small pack   =   31.65 (**32 orders/year**)

4.   The following calculations apply for the six-month <u>trial period</u>:

Total initial participants (from question 1)   =   49,200

The number of large pack retailers (49,200 x .45)   =   22,140

The performance breakdown of the 22,140 large pack retailers:

         High performers (22,140 x .40)   =   8,856 retailers
         Medium performers (22,140 x .20) =   4,428 retailers
         Low performers (22,140 x .40)   =   <u>8,856 retailers</u>
         Total large pack retailers   22,140 retailers

On the basis of expected orders per year from question 3, average large pack retailers should place 16 orders per year, or 8 over each six-month period. The first order of the trial period is considered the "initial order" and the remaining 7 are called "reorders."

The number of initial orders from large pack retailers:

High performers (8,856 retailers x 1 order)	=	8,856 orders
Medium performers (4,428 retailers x 1 order)	=	4,428 orders
Low performers (8,856 retailers x 1 order)	=	8,856 orders
Total number of initial large pack orders		**22,140 orders**

The number of reorders from large pack retailers:

High performers (8,856 retailers x 7 reorders)	=	61,992 reorders
Medium performers (4,428 retailers x 5 reorders)	=	22,140 reorders
Low performers (8,856 retailers x 3 reorders)	=	26,568 reorders
Total number of large pack reorders		**110,700 reorders**

The number of small pack retailers (49,200 x .55) = 27,060

The performance breakdown of the 27,060 small pack retailers:

High performers (27,060 x .40)	=	10,824 retailers
Medium performers (27,060 x .20)	=	5,412 retailers
Low performers (27,060 x .40)	=	10,824 retailers
Total small pack retailers		27,060 retailers

On the basis of expected orders per year from question 3, average small pack retailers should place 32 orders per year, or 16 over each six-month period. The first order of the trial period is considered the "initial order" and the remaining 15 are called "reorders."

The number of initial orders from small pack retailers:

High performers (10,824 retailers x 1 order)	=	10,824 orders
Medium performers (5,412 retailers x 1 order)	=	5,412 orders
Low performers (10,824 retailers x 1 order) =		10,824 orders
Total number of initial small pack orders		**27,060 orders**

The number of reorders from small pack retailers:

High performers (10,824 retailers x 15 reorders)	=	162,360 reorders
Medium performers (5,412 retailers x 10 reorders)	=	54,120 reorders
Low performers (10,824 retailers x 7 reorders)	=	75,768 reorders
Total number of small pack reorders		**292,248 reorders**

The following calculations apply for the six-month <u>post-trial period</u>:

Remaining participants (49,200 original retailers x .55)   =   27,060 retailers

The remaining large pack retailers (27,060 x .45)   =   12,177 retailers

The performance breakdown of the 12,177 small pack retailers:

High performers (12,177 x .40)   =   4,871 retailers
Medium performers (12,177 x .20) =   2,435 retailers
Low performers (12,177 x .40)   =   <u>4,871 retailers</u>
Total large pack retailers   12,177 retailers

All orders taken in the second six-week period are reorders.

The number of reorders from large pack retailers:

High performers (4,871 retailers x 8 reorders)   =   38,968 reorders
Medium performers (2,435 retailers x 6 reorders) =   14,610 reorders
Low performers (4,871 retailers x 4 reorders)   =   <u>19,484 reorders</u>
Total number of large pack reorders   **73,484 reorders**

The remaining small pack retailers (27,060 x .55)   =   14,883 retailers

The performance breakdown of the 14,883 small pack retailers:

High performers (14,883 x .40)   =   5,953 retailers
Medium performers (14,883 x .20) =   2,977 retailers
Low performers (14,883 x .40)   =   <u>5,953 retailers</u>
Total small pack retailers   14,883 retailers

All orders taken in the second six-week period are reorders.

The number of reorders from small pack retailers:

High performers (5,953 retailers x 16 reorders)   =   95,248 reorders
Medium performers (2,977 retailers x 11 reorders) =   32,747 reorders
Low performers (5,953 retailers x 8 reorders)   =   <u>47,624 reorders</u>
Total number of small pack reorders   **175,619 reorders**

Total first-year orders:

Pack type	Initial orders	Reorders	Total
Large	22,140	183,762	205,902
Small	27,060	467,867	494,927

5.   Based on answers from question 4 and data from Tables 3 and 4:

The following calculations apply to a network of <u>three</u> distribution centers:

Annual revenues:

Revenue from large packs ($205/pack x 205,902 packs)	=	$42,209,910
Revenue from small packs ($115/pack x 494,297 packs)	=	$56,916,605
Total annual revenue		**$99,126,515**

Logistics costs:

Large packs: $10.11/order x 205,902 orders	=	$2,081,669
Small packs: $10.11/order x 494,927 orders	=	$5,003,712
Total logistics costs		**$7,085,381**

Production costs:

Large packs: $190/order x 205,902 orders=		$39,121,380
Small packs: $98/order x 494,927 orders	=	$48,502,846
Total production costs		**$87,624,226**

Display costs:

Large packs: $35/display x 22,140 initial orders	=	$774,900
Small packs: $18/display x 27,060 initial orders	=	$487,080
Total display costs		**$1,261,980**

Total costs   **$95,971,587**

Profits   **$3,154,928**

The following calculations apply to a network of <u>four</u> distribution centers:

Annual revenues:

The total annual revenue will be the same regardless of the network, **$99,126,515**

Logistics costs:

Large packs:	$9.86/order x 205,902 orders	=	$2,030,194
Small packs:	$9.86/order x 494,927 orders	=	$4,879,980
Total logistics costs			**$6,910,174**

Production costs:

Large packs:	$190/order x 205,902 orders=		$39,121,380
Small packs:	$98/order x 494,927 orders	=	$48,502,846
Total production costs			**$87,624,226**

Display costs:

Large packs:	$35/display x 22,140 initial orders	=	$774,900
Small packs:	$18/display x 27,060 initial orders	=	$487,080
Total display costs			**$1,261,980**

Total costs	**$95,796,380**
Profits	**$3,330,135**

The profit derived from the network with four distribution centers ($3,330,135) is greater than that of the network with three distribution centers ($3,154,928).

It is interesting to note that the differentiating cost factor, logistics cost, was actually lower for the network with four distribution centers. Class discussion might explore situations in which utilization of more facility locations results in lower costs. Situations may include favorable negotiations with transportation providers and labor organizations, or preferred government involvement (subsidization or zoning preference).

There are a host of factors aside from cost/profit that might affect the decision, including:

Customer service and responsiveness: The network of four distribution centers would likely provide quicker service response and reduces the number of outlying areas that receive slowest service levels.

Sugar Sweets must also consider the potential negative impact on the candy and tobacco jobbers to reassure them that this strategy is not designed to reduce or eliminate their business. Rather, the strategy should have little impact because of the impulse-buying nature of snack food purchases.

Case 5

Westminster Company: A System Design Assessment

Overview

As its name implies, this case finds the Westminster Company assessing the efficiency and effectiveness of its logistics system design. A number of internal and external influences have made the firm reconsider its current system. As it stands, Westminster operates three separate distribution systems, one for each domestic sales division. It may seem obvious that consolidation of the systems can significantly improve efficiency, but there are a number of constraints placed on the company to make the determination a complicated one.

Students are encouraged to consider the various pieces of cost information as well as numerous qualitative factors in order to reach conclusions for this case. As with all case questions, answers are not necessarily clear-cut though all responses should be adequately justified.

Solutions to Questions

1.   System consolidation would make it easier for transportation economies to be gained. Truckload volumes would be more easily gathered to and from distribution centers, lowering transfer and customer freight costs.

The effect of using third party warehousing and transportation on transfer and customer freight costs is less apparent. It is likely that these costs would be higher in this scenario though inventory costs should be lower without the fixed investments and overhead expenses of the warehouse. Third party warehousing and transportation is often a good idea considering that specialists can often provide better service at a lower total cost.

2.   Warehouse consolidation is likely to have the following effects:

> **Inventory carrying costs** would be reduced with better utilization of facilities and less duplication of effort. The company operates two warehouses in Newark, NJ (one for Division A and one for Division C) and Los Angeles, CA (one for Division B and one for Division C). These are clear candidates for consolidation. Regardless of any changes in product volume, the reduction in facilities alone represent significant savings.

The effect on **customer service levels** is less clear. Should all products still have to go through a distribution center prior to final delivery to customers (perhaps for light processing or packaging) the effect may be minimal. Customers generally feel more comfortable when product is stored nearby. Without more details of the planned consolidation, however, this is difficult to tell. The possibility of mixed product shipments would likely be embraced.

Order fill rates could improve with inventory dispersed across fewer storage locations. It is likely that fewer freight transfers will be required to meet customer demand. Pending on the distance from new warehouse locations to customer locations, delivery time may be a concern though.

3.   Public warehousing generally involves higher variable costs than private warehousing, though fixed investment is usually not required. Storage and handling costs are usually greater for high volume products distributed through public warehouses, though the quality of performance may make up for this difference. Fixed facility costs are definitely more of a concern with private warehousing. Outsourcing warehouse functions is often a good idea when the product in question has a seasonal, cyclical, or uncertain sales nature. We can assume that this is not the case, however, for Westminster's line of health products.

4.   There is certainly greater opportunities for truckload shipping volumes with consolidated distribution centers and mixed product shipments. This would require fewer outbound shipments, with each in greater quantities for better transportation economies. The potentially longer distances from distribution centers to customer locations might be the only detriment to transportation cost in this scenario (and we cannot tell from the information provided).

5.   There are several possible factors. An incomplete list includes:

- Fixed costs associated with each facility
- Customer Service (customers prefer several well-stocked facilities nearby)
- Size and dispersion of sales markets
- Efficient interface with manufacturing facilities
- Transportation costs (inbound, outbound, and transfer)
- Handling costs (a product handled more frequently is more likely to be damage)
- More warehouses generally result in higher average inventory
- Labor availability and costs (Table 5 depicts the variability in costs)
- Environmental factors (legislation, zoning, and public opinion)

6.   As with any logistics decision, there are inherent cost/service criteria to be evaluated.

<u>With regard to costs</u>: Can we do it cheaper ourselves?

Will the **total cost** of transfer and outbound transportation, product handling, storage, labor, facility maintenance, taxes, and interest as well as opportunity costs (investment that could be directed elsewhere) be lower than we can accomplish with our own resources?

<u>With regard to service</u>: Can we do it better ourselves?

In particular, will **fill rates** be higher? **deliver time** quicker? **order accuracy** higher? **product damage** lower? **customer satisfaction** higher?

Case 6

Michigan Liquor Control Commission

Overview

A central issue in this case is the unique role that the Michigan Liquor Control Commission finds itself. The state agency is asked to simultaneously regulate sales of liquor in Michigan while taking an active position in the distribution of products. It may be argued that a conflict of interest is apparent in this situation. A number of other governmental bodies experience similar circumstances, however.

The Federal Aviation Administration (FAA), for instance, must balance its responsibility of ensuring the safety of every passenger that boards an aircraft in the United States while also trying to maintain the vitality of the industry. One similar example from the private sector is the hospital that promotes a certain brand of medication. Students should readily identify and consider the social and ethical responsibilities that the agency faces in addition to cutting costs and generating profits.

Solutions to Questions

1.   Answers to this question will vary though all positions should be supported adequately. Responses should consider the social, ethical, and competitive issues faced by the Commission. As the text notes, changes should reflect key operational issues. Possible solutions might include:

Downsizing and consolidation of facilities: It might be worthwhile to investigate the possibility of reducing the number of warehouse locations and state stores. Also, direct shipping from the warehouses to retailers might reduce some unnecessary storage at the state stores. It could be more damaging to "put people out of work" though than to let the system's inefficiencies go uncorrected. Union membership by a vast majority of MLCC employees would be extremely resistant to downsizing efforts.

Privatization: Eliminate the state's competitive involvement in the industry altogether. Considering that the state generates considerable amounts of revenue from liquor distribution, it would not be likely to take this course of action. The moneys gathered from distribution and taxation of liquor are directed toward several worthwhile programs in Michigan. Taxation alone would fall short of maintaining current returns.

Investment in management information systems (MIS): The MLCC may find that investment in information systems provides for better assessment of customer needs and logistical control within the system. By sharing information with distillers and retailers, service could be improved with minimal levels of inventory required at all levels of the channel, reducing costs significantly.

Reevaluate relations with channel participants: The state could try to negotiate new, more favorable agreements with distillers, retailers, and transportation providers. Currently, distillers assume ownership of inventory until time of shipment to state stores, but the expense is passed along in the form of higher selling prices. The MLCC could make an effort to reduce distillers' needs for inventory (see "Investment in MIS" above). The markup price that the state charges retailers might be altered to generate higher margins. The state might also limit the number of retail licensees that it should serve. In addition, transportation should be reviewed to ensure that expected service levels are met at the lowest possible cost.

2.   This question is a supplement to Question 1. The student should acknowledge the risks and potential disadvantages of a chosen design alternative as well as its benefits. Pending upon the desired changes in the distribution system and policy, any number of considerations might exert strong influences. A brief description of influences that might exert stronger influences include:

Political: The political system truly serves as the means toward policy change and enactment. Though it is the right and responsibility of citizens to elect and voice opinions to political leaders, it is ultimately these leaders that effect change. As the vehicle of change, political considerations can never be overlooked.

Economic: Along with social considerations, economics will be a major driver in policy change. The revenues that the state generates from liquor control and distribution are sizable. The commission employs a number of people and reinvests returns in the state. The MLCC is directed toward policy that maximizes these returns. Evaluating the social costs of making liquor readily available for responsible public consumption should be a consideration as well.

Geographic: This case has implications for people throughout Michigan. Not only are customers dispersed throughout the state but so are facilities and employees. Geography is significant in determinations of facility location and transportation alternatives. Though the analysis of MLCC's distribution is limited to Michigan, the state's proximity to Canada adds an international dimension of influence to the case as well.

Special-interest groups (SIGs): These are typically well-organized assemblies of citizens. Though they may not represent majority opinions, SIGs' skills and success in gaining awareness of their positions on issues often make them very influential. There are a number of special-interest groups at work on both sides of this issue with religious groups and MADD mostly making up one side and affiliations representing distillers, retailers, and state employees on the other.

3. A number of considerations may still be important. First and foremost, the state learned from its prohibition policy that despite its efforts to prevent bootlegging, liquor would be produced and distributed in Michigan. It was determined that the state could best benefit from active participation in the industry and derive significant revenues in the process. It appears that the state has come to rely on these hefty monetary returns and wishes to maintain its involvement in the business.

Though "druggists" may not be the political force that they were at the time of the state's original control of the industry, small retailers of all kinds still benefit from the uniform pricing policy that treats them as equals to the large retailers.

Whether the government is any more efficient than private middlemen is questionable. Competitive pressures would most likely prevent private enterprises from charging "excessively" high prices that were feared originally.

In addition, as noted in previous questions, the state's extensive network employs many people. Should state involvement in liquor distribution cease, many citizens would lose the relatively high-paying jobs that they have relied upon.

4. This is a question of opinion. Some may feel that it is unjust to participate and derive moneys from what may be considered a "vice" in the first place. The state finds itself in a unique position in that it does participate in product placement and makes money from the sale of alcohol yet it cannot actively promote the product's consumption. Others may feel that so long as the products are being traded, the state should derive some benefit from the trade and put the money to work for the state. Opinions are likely to vary across these two general extremes.

5. This question addresses the student's ability to not only determine the content of the report but its presentation as well. As the case illustrates, the issue of state-controlled distribution of liquor is a sensitive subject and source of much debate in Michigan. The report must at least address the following key areas:

A clear explanation of how each of Joseph's stated general and specific objectives will be achieved under the new policy.

Justification of the new policy as being best for the state, considering all stakeholders in the issue (distillers, retailers, MLCC employees, consumers, state programs that are recipients of the revenues, and the general public).

OBJECTIVES

1. To allow students to use various analytical tools when making distribution structure decisions.
2. To demonstrate that a firm can reduce total costs while actually improving customer service performance.

SOLUTION QUESTIONS

1. What is the total distribution cost for W-G-P Chemical Company? What is the cost per pound, cubic foot, case, line, and order? How can these measures contribute to the distribution review process?

    Table 4 data include average inventory of $90 million. Applying the 18% carrying cost, annual inventory carrying cost is $16.2 million. When added to the remaining costs in Table 4, total distribution costs are $33.2 million or slightly over 6.3% of sales.

    It is interesting to note that total transportation cost in the system is $9.1 million. Thus inventory carrying cost in W-G-P's system is far greater than transportation cost and accounts for almost half of W-G-P's total distribution cost (as the text discusses, in aggregate for the U. S., transportation is more than half of total distribution cost).

    Using data from Table 1, other cost measures are:
    Cost/pound = $33,200,000/242,717,768 = 13.68 cents/pound
    Cost/cuFt = $33,200,000/26,887,513 = $1.235/cubic foot
    Cost/case = $33,200,000/2,912,753 = $11.40/case
    Cost/line = $33,200,000/25,392 = $1307.68/line
    Cost/order = $33,200,000/19139 = $1734.68/order

    It is possible to also calculate unit costs for each of the individual functions. For example, transportation to customers cost $5,600,000/19,919 orders or $292.60 per order. Storage cost $3,100,000/2,912,753 cases or $1.06 per case. Similar calculation can be made for other functions.

To be most useful these metrics should be compared against previous years' performance and/or against industry benchmarks. While such data is not available in the case itself, the abnormally high inventory carrying cost can be used as one example. This might also indicate that W-G-P's storage costs are most likely high due to the large inventory being held.

2.   On a map, plot the distribution facilities and network for W-G-P Chemical Company. What product and market characteristics can help explain this distribution structure?

-   In plotting the distribution facilities and network for W-G-P Chemical Company it can be easily seen that the locations center in agricultural areas along major highways, waterways and railways. Since the product is sold in bulk to farmers, who buy during a relatively short time period during the year (which is difficult to forecast, the distribution structure must be structured to respond quickly with short lead times when demand occurs.

3.   What alternative methods of distribution should W-G-P consider for Prevention and Support?

-   Open this question up for class discussion to generate alternative distribution structures.

-   One clear area for discussion concerns the number of warehouse locations. To some extent the large number of warehouses may be justified due to the nature of the market and the customer service requirements of short lead times. A drastic reduction in number of warehouses, which would most likely reduce inventory levels and carrying costs significantly, would probably be difficult to justify given the service requirements.

   Nevertheless, from the plotting of locations, there are some clear candidates for consolidation. Decatur and Rockville, Illinois provide one example. The Indiana, Michigan, and Ohio warehouses (a total of four) could probably be consolidated in to two facilities and maintain customer service levels. Of course, the impact on transportation cost would also have to be investigated.

4.   Discuss the rationale for: (a) the early order program, (b) customer pickup policies, and (c) use of public versus private warehouse facilities.

-   The rational behind the early order program is to better plan and distribute the products to meet demand. If distribution is planned in advance, more cost efficient methods can be used. In addition, the program reduces W-G-P's inventory by shifting some of the burden on to dealers. The customer pickup policy is most likely considered a service to dealers who want to utilize their own equipment as fully as possible. It also relieves W-G-P of the need to schedule common carriers for pickup at the warehouse and delivery to dealers. Public warehouses seem to make sense in this structure given the highly seasonal demand. W-G-P avoids considerable fixed costs associated with private warehousing and the need to maintain fulltime labor and supervision which a private facility would require

133

Case 8

Western Pharmaceuticals (A)

Overview

Western Pharmaceuticals (A) is a supply chain network design case placed in the setting of a merger of two firms, Western Pharmaceutical and Atlantic Medical. While their product lines don't overlap, there is definite overlap in their distribution systems. Both the demand and cost data is provided in spreadsheets to facilitate a total cost analysis. This case provides students with a comprehensive and realistic distribution center location problem that can be solved using a spreadsheet analysis.

While the analysis can be completed using a supply chain design planning tool such as CAPS, Supply Chain Planner, Supply Chain Navigator, or Logic*Net, it is often useful to have the students completed the analysis using a spreadsheet so they develop some insight regarding the logic and dynamics of such planning tools. This case can also be used to illustrate and apply the Logistics Planning Process discussed in Chapter 16.

This case is an effective tool for students understand the process of developing a total cost model and then using it to determine relevant total cost curves includes the major logistics cost components.

Solution

The *first* step in solving the case is to define the critical assumptions for completing analysis. Specific assumptions include:

1. All demand is assigned to a single point within each state. A representative point is the capitol or the largest city;
2. All demand is shipped to customers in either less-than-truckload (LTL) or truckload (TL) volumes and each state receives a combination of both;
3. Service level is measured as the percent of volume within 750 miles of distribution centers. In effect the demand point in each state for 95 percent of the total volume must be within 750 miles of the servicing distribution center;
4. The analysis scope includes movements from plants to distribution centers to markets;
5. Analysis costs include fixed costs of distribution centers, variable costs at distribution centers, inbound transportation cost (plants to distribution centers), outbound transportation cost (distribution centers to markets), and inventory carrying cost
6. Market demand is assigned to the distribution center with the lowest total cost of service;
7. Projections regarding changes in inventory carrying costs are estimated using the "Square Root of N" approach;

8. All products in a state are served from a common distribution center so it is not necessary to consider alternate sources for each product. This is a common practical assumption to minimize complexity and provide consistency for customers
9. The product mix for all states is the same as provided in Table 3 from the case
10. For determining service distances, the student either look up miles such a by using Mapquest (rather tedious) or use a disk that equates to a 750 mile scale for the map they are using; and
11. The fixed and variable distribution center rates are independent of throughput volume.

The *second* step is to develop a total cost model in concept and then apply it to a spreadsheet. In concept the objective is to minimize

$$TC = \Sigma\, F_i + \Sigma(\, \Sigma_j \,((C_{i,j,tl} + H_i) * D_{j,tl}) + \Sigma_j \,((C_{i,j,ltl} + H_i) * D_{j,ltl})) + \Sigma\, (P_{k,i} * (D_{j,tl} + D_{j,ltl}))$$

Where:
TC = Total logistics cost;
Fi = Fixed cost for facility i;
$C_{i,j,tl}$ = Per pound transportation cost for truckload movement from distribution center i to state j;
H_i = Per pound handling or variable cost for distribution center i;
$D_{j,tl}$ = Truckload demand for market j;
$C\ i,j,ltl$ = Per pound transportation cost for LTL movement from distribution center i to state j;
$D\ j,ltl$ = LTL demand form market j; and
$P_{k,i}$ = Per pound transportation cost from plant k to distribution center i.

The *third* step is to determine the inventory carrying cost implications for the varying number of distribution center locations. Although there are currently eight distribution centers, there is an obvious redundancy in Atlanta that would be removed when the systems are combined. So there are currently seven distribution centers from an inventory perspective. "Case 8 – Inventory Calculator for Western Pharmaceuticals" provides the details of the inventory analysis concerning the impact of the number of stocking locations. This applies the "Square Root of N" approach discussed in Chapter Fifteen. Row 2 of the spreadsheet contains the dollar sales for each company (Total Pounds * $5/pound * Percent of Sales for division). Row 3 calculates the inventory for each company based on annual turns. Row 4 contains the number of current distribution centers. Row 5 contains the typical replenishment cycle for each company (bi-weekly from the case). The cycle and safety stock factors are calculated for each company based on the values of Rows 2-5. The factors are different because the turn rates are different. The lower part of the spreadsheet contains the aggregate inventory levels for a range in the number of distribution centers. Column B contains the number of distribution center locations. Column D contains the projected inventory for Western Pharmaceuticals for the corresponding number of locations in Column B. Column D is calculated using the cycle and safety stock factors and the number of stocking locations. Column F contains the Western Pharmaceutical inventory turns based on the annual sales and projected inventory level. Columns H and J contain the projected inventory level and turn rates for Atlantic Medical using the Atlantic Medical factors and number of stocking locations. Columns L and M contain the combined inventory and turn rates for both systems if there were aggregated into a common distribution system assuming current inventory management practices.

The *fourth* step is to cost out each combination of each distribution system scenario. While there are numerous combinations that could be considered, there are a relatively few that are logical and feasible. Table 8-1 summarizes the feasible scenarios tested. Table 8-2 summarizes the results of these scenarios. Scenario 1 represents the base case using all seven current locations. Scenarios 2 through 7 are the six distribution center scenarios without considering the closing of Atlanta. Atlanta is not considered for closures since it really doesn't have an alternative site that can service the major populations in the Southeast within the 750-mile limit. Scenarios 8 and 9 consider five and four distribution center scenarios by closing Mechanicsburg, Sparks, and then Indianapolis. While there are other combinations of four and five distribution centers, the combinations considered are the most logical due to service and demand densities. While one could consider fewer than four distribution centers, it is not possible to meet management's service objective with any fewer locations.

Once the minimum cost number of distribution centers is determined, the *final* step is to complete some sensitivity analyses by consolidating production of key products. Since A and F represent the highest volume products and they are produced on the geographic extremes of the U.S., the sensitivity analysis considers the relocation of production to a more centralized plant location such a Omaha. While there would likely be some reduction in annual operating costs, there is a substantial one-time cost to shift the volume.

Table 8-2 summarizes the results of each scenario. The base case with the existing assignments has a total cost of $80.197 million with 98.14 percent of demand within 750 miles of a distribution center. The total cost of the six DC scenarios ranges from $75.9 to $77.0 million. They all meet the service objective except the scenario without Omaha. The five and four DC scenarios continue to reduce cost as the increases in transportation costs are more than overcome by decreases in fixed and inventory carrying cost. The minimum operational cost scenario (transportation, variable, and fixed costs) is five distribution centers while the minimum total cost scenario (including inventory carrying cost) is four DCs (Atlanta, Los Angeles, New Brunswick, and Omaha). The total cost for the minimum total cost four DC scenario is $68.053 million which represents a savings of $12.144 million from the base.

The sensitivity analyses (Scenarios 10 and 11) shift production of one or two product groups to the more central facility in Omaha. This reduces backhaul from the respective plants. This results in substantial additional savings with no impact on service. The shift of product A results in an annual savings of $5.2 million for a one-time cost of movement of $500 thousand. The shift of product F yields an additional $1.367 million for an additional one-time cost of $500 thousand.

Table 8-1
Supply Chain Scenarios Tested

Scenario	Description	Atlanta	Indianapolis	Los Angeles	Mechanicsburg	New Brunswick	Omaha	Sparks
1	Current 7 DCs, 6 Plants	X	X	X	X	X	X	X
2	6 DCs (no NB)	X	X	X	X		X	X
3	6 DCs (no Mech)	X	X	X		X	X	X
4	6 DCs (no Sparks)	X	X	X	X	X	X	
5	6 DCs (no LA)	X	X		X	X	X	X
6	6 DCs (no Omaha)	X	X	X	X	X		X
7	6 DCs (no Indianapolis)	X		X	X	X	X	X
8	5 DCs (no Mech, Sparks)	X	X	X		X	X	
9	4 DCs (no Mech, Sparks, Indy)	X		X		X	X	
10	4 DCs (No Mech, Sparks, Indy), Product A to Omaha	X		X		X	X	
11	4 DCs (No Mech, Sparks, Indy), Product A and F to Omaha	X		X		X	X	

Table 8-2
Western Pharmaceuticals (A)
Scenario Total Cost Analysis
($000)

Scenario Number	Scenario	Fixed	Variable	Inbound Trans.	Outbound Trans.	Total Less Inventory	Inventory Carrying	Total Cost	Capacity Shift Cost	Service Level	Savings
	No Capacity Shifts										
1	Current 7 DCs, 6 Plants	2,100	1,369	12,786	10,448	26,703	53,453	80,197	0	98.14%	
2	6 DCs (no NB)	1,800	1,369	12,984	10,609	26,762	49,696	76,496	0	98.14%	$3,701
3	6 DCs (no Mech)	1,800	1,369	12,571	10,472	26,212	49,734	75,946	0	98.14%	$4,251
4	6 DCs (no Sparks)	1,800	1,369	12,772	10,462	26,403	49,734	76,137	0	96.36%	$4,060
5	6 DCs (no LA)	1,800	1,369	12,824	10,874	26,867	49,734	76,601	0	98.14%	$3,596
6	6 DCs (no Omaha)	1,800	1,369	13,002	10,333	26,504	49,734	76,238	0	87.99%	$3,959
7	6 DCs (no Indy)	1,800	1,369	13,166	10,958	27,293	49,734	77,027	0	98.14%	$3,170
8	5 DCs (no Mech, Sparks)	1,500	1,369	12,557	10,486	25,912	45,645	71,557	0	96.36%	$8,640
9	4 DCs (no Mech, Sparks, Indy)	1,500	1,369	12,950	11,111	26,930	41,123	68,053	0	96.36%	$12,144
	Capacity Shifts										
10	4 DCs (No Mech, Sparks, Indy) Product A to Omaha	1,200	1,369	7,965	11,111	21,645	41,123	62,768	500	96.36%	$17,429
11	4 DCs (No Mech, Sparks, Indy) Products A and F to Omaha	1,200	1,369	6,598	11,111	20,278	41,123	61,401	1,000	96.36%	$18,796

	2 Week Review	4 Week Review
Annual Sales	$146,291	$4,557
Average Inventory	$7,017	$492
Number of stocking locations	3	3
Typical replenishment cycle (days)	15	30
Cycle factor	0.020547945	0.04109589
Safety stock factor	0.015829845	0.038607341

Number of Stocking Locations	2 Week Review Total Inventory	2 Week Review Inventory Turns	4 Week Review Total Inventory	4 Week Review Inventory Turns	Total Inventory	Total Turns	Inventory Carrying Cost (20%)
1	$5,322	27.49	$363	12.55	$5,685	26.53	1,137
2	$6,281	23.29	$436	10.45	$6,717	22.46	1,343
3	$7,017	20.85	$492	9.26	$7,509	20.09	1,502
4	$7,638	19.15	$539	8.45	$8,177	18.45	1,635
5	$8,184	17.87	$581	7.85	$8,765	17.21	1,753
6	$8,678	16.86	$618	7.37	$9,297	16.23	1,859
7	$9,133	16.02	$653	6.98	$9,786	15.42	1,957
8	$9,556	15.31	$685	6.65	$10,241	14.73	2,048
9	$9,953	14.70	$715	6.37	$10,668	14.14	2,134
10	$10,329	14.16	$744	6.13	$11,073	13.62	2,215
11	$10,686	13.69	$771	5.91	$11,457	13.17	2,291
12	$11,028	13.27	$797	5.72	$11,825	12.76	2,365
13	$11,356	12.88	$822	5.55	$12,177	12.39	2,435
14	$11,671	12.53	$846	5.39	$12,516	12.05	2,503
15	$11,975	12.22	$869	5.25	$12,844	11.75	2,569
16	$12,269	11.92	$891	5.11	$13,160	11.46	2,632
17	$12,554	11.65	$913	4.99	$13,467	11.20	2,693
18	$12,831	11.40	$934	4.88	$13,765	10.96	2,753
19	$13,100	11.17	$954	4.78	$14,054	10.73	2,811
20	$13,362	10.95	$974	4.68	$14,336	10.52	2,867

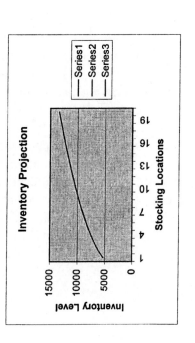

Inventory Projection

Inventory Level (15000, 10000, 5000, 0) vs. Stocking Locations (1, 4, 7, 10, 13, 16, 19)

— Series1 — Series2 — Series3

Case 9

Western Pharmaceuticals (B)

Overview

Western Pharmaceuticals (B) is a loose extension of the Western Pharmaceuticals (A) case as it requires an inventory analysis focusing on determining inventory requirements based on desired service level and applying the "Square Root of N" approach to determine the aggregate inventory. It applies the material from Chapter Ten including both the idea of a comprehensive inventory analysis and the setting of safety stock.

The data includes sales and inventory history for 100 sample products at three different distribution centers (Atlanta, GA; New Brunswick, NJ; and Los Angeles, CA). Using the sample data, students are asked to determine the service, safety stock, and inventory characteristics of a number of alternatives.

This case is an effective tool for students understand the process of developing an inventory cost model and then using it to determine relevant inventory related cost and service curves. It also demonstrates the trade-off between inventory service objectives and marginal profitability. It is suggested that students use and justify their own inventory carrying cost although this case analysis uses a figure of 20 percent annually.

Solution

Columns A through Q are given in the case data spreadsheet. Column A is the item name (Product 1 = P 001). Columns C, D, and E are the weekly unit demand for the three distribution centers while column B is the total weekly unit demand for the three distribution centers combined. Column F is the unit standard cost for each item. This can be used to calculate inventory carrying cost. Columns H, I, and J are the average unit inventory for each distribution center. Column G is the sum of the average inventory for the three distribution centers combined. Columns K, L, and M are the weekly standard deviation in sales for each distribution center. In effect, this becomes the σ_D for each DC-product combination. Column N is the order replenishment or lead time for each DC-product combination. The majority of products are reviewed and replenished every two weeks while some are reviewed and replenished every four weeks. The above items are provided on the basic student spreadsheet while the remaining columns are calculated as part of the solution.

Columns O, P, and Q represent the order quantity for each DC-product combination. The order quantity is the average weekly demand multiplied by the replenishment period which is either two or four weeks. This analysis is assuming that the replenishment order quantity is the same as the review cycle.

Columns S, T, and U represent the current safety stock based on existing inventory. The imputed DC-product safety stocks are calculated as the existing average inventory level less the replenishment order quantity divided by 2.

Columns W, X, and Y are the calculated σ_C using a combination of average weekly demand, σ_D, average replenishment lead time, and a default value 1 for σ_T. The computation uses formula from page 304 of the text. This becomes the combined demand and performance cycle uncertainty (σ_C) for each DC-product combination.

Columns AA, AB, and AC represent the current k values based on current safety stock and σ_C. In effect, this is the k value that would provide the current level of safety stock. Columns AE, AF, and AG are adjusted k values to bring the values within ±3 standard deviations. If k is greater than 3.0, it is adjusted to 3.0.

Columns AI, AJ, and AK is the calculated service level based on existing safety stock and order quantities. These columns use a lookup table to find the f(k) values for the Normal Loss Function.

Question 1.

In order to determine a weighted service level, the demand quantity must be multiplied by the calculated service level to estimate resulting sales as opposed to demand (The sales figure assumes that the non-filled orders are stocked-out). Columns AM, AN, and AO is the weighted sales for each DC-product combination. Column AQ is the sum of the sales for all the DCs while column AR is the sum of the demand for all the DCs. Column AS is the average service percentage (Column AQ/Column AR). Columns AU, AV, and AW complete a similar service analysis by value instead of units. This demonstrates the difference between a unit and a standard cost analysis and how it impacts total results across products and DCs. Column AX is the current inventory value based on standard cost. The results illustrate a 96.10 percent fill rate in terms of units and a 96.31 percent fill rate by value. By looking at individual products, students can see that some items are significantly overstocked while others are dramatically overstocked.

Question 2.

Columns AZ through BK develop the answer for question 2. Columns AZ, BA, and BB provide the calculated f(k) value for each DC-product combination based on the 95 percent fill rate, σ_C, and the order quantity. Columns BD, BE, and BF calculate the required safety stock level based on a looked-up value of k and σ_C. Columns BH, BI, and BJ provide the DC-product inventory averages necessary to provide a 95 percent service level. Column BK converts the aggregate average inventory units into average inventory dollars based on standard cost. Students should see that the analytical inventory approach requires $7.5 million to achieve a 95 percent fill rate while the existing situation only yields a 96+ percent service with twice the inventory.

Question 3.

Columns BM through BX develop the answer for question 3. These columns go through the same process as described in Question 2 only at the 99 percent fill rate level. Comparing columns BK and BX illustrates how much additional inventory is necessary to provide the increase in service. Students should note that the additional 4 percent in service requires $2.5 million in average inventory.

Columns BZ through CD complete the marginal contribution analysis. In effect, it compares the marginal contribution of additional sales with the cost of additional inventory.

Column BZ is the sales value at 95 percent service level (assuming no backorders). It is computed as the weekly unit sales multiplied by standard cost multiplied by 52 multiplied by 95 percent fill rate. Column CA is the comparable sales level at 99 percent service. Column CB is the incremental margin between the two service levels. In effect, the incremental profit for the additional sales is 25 percent of the difference between columns CA and BZ. Column CC is the carrying cost for the incremental inventory necessary to increase the service level from 95 to 99 percent. Column CD represents the incremental contribution. A positive value indicates that the additional inventory is justified while a negative value indicates that the additional inventory is not justified. On the basis, of the generally positive results, the service level for most items should be increased.

Question 4.

Columns CF through CU provide the analysis to support question 4. The objective of the question is for students to compare the results of a detailed item based inventory analysis with an aggregate approach such as "Square Root of N." Spreadsheet "Case 9 – Inventory_Calculator for Western Pharm (B) provides the aggregate analysis for the two and four week review cycle items.

Column CF is the review cycle for each product. Columns CG and CI are the annual sales volume for two and four week review products respectively. Columns CH and CJ are the average inventory value for two and four week review products respectively. These must be separated because they have different review cycles as is required for the "Square Root of N" analysis. The sum of the sales and inventory values for the two and four week review products are entered into the Inventory Calculator. The first step is to determine the combined σ_C for the combination of DCs into a single DC. While this should technically be weighted, this solution uses the simplified formula provided with the case. Column CL is the combined demand σ_D. Column CM is the combined σ_C calculated using the combination formula from the case. Column CN is the combined replenishment order quantity which is the sum of the individual order quantities. Column CO is the calculated $f(k)$ for a 95 percent fill rate based on the service objective, the combined replenishment order quantity, and σ_C. Column CP is the calculated safety stock based on the k value and the σ_C. Column CQ is the resulting inventory in units based on one-half the replenishment order quantity plus the safety stock. Column CR is the inventory value at standard cost.

Column CT is the corresponding sum of the inventory value for the three DCs. This can be compared with the inventory value for the combined volume in a single DC which is illustrated in Column CR. These results demonstrate two analytical approaches ("Square Root of N" and Individual safety stock) calculations can be used to determine the inventory impact of different supply chain alternatives. A comparison of the results for a single and three DCs illustrates that the aggregate inventory values are reasonably close.

	Western Pharmaceuticals	Atlantic Medical
Annual Sales	$443,495	$238,805
Average Inventory	$126,713	$79,602
Number of stocking locations	5	3
Typical replenishment cycle (days)	15	15
Cycle factor	0.020547945	0.020547945
Safety stock factor	0.118585993	0.180586728

	Western Pharmaceuticals		Atlantic Medical				
Number of Stocking Locations	WP Total Inventory	WP Inventory Turns	AM Total Inventory	AM Inventory Turns	Total Inventory	Total Turns	Inventory Carrying Cost (20%)
1	$61,705	7.19	$48,032	4.97	$109,737	6.22	21,947
2	$83,490	5.31	$65,895	3.62	$149,385	4.57	29,877
3	$100,205	4.43	$79,602	3.00	$179,807	3.79	35,961
4	$114,298	3.88	$91,157	2.62	$205,454	3.32	41,091
5	$126,713	3.50	$101,337	2.36	$228,050	2.99	45,610
6	$137,937	3.22	$110,541	2.16	$248,478	2.75	49,696
7	$148,259	2.99	$119,005	2.01	$267,264	2.55	53,453
8	$157,866	2.81	$126,883	1.88	$284,749	2.40	56,950
9	$166,890	2.66	$134,282	1.78	$301,172	2.27	60,234
10	$175,424	2.53	$141,280	1.69	$316,705	2.15	63,341
11	$183,542	2.42	$147,936	1.61	$331,478	2.06	66,296
12	$191,298	2.32	$154,296	1.55	$345,594	1.97	69,119
13	$198,737	2.23	$160,396	1.49	$359,134	1.90	71,827
14	$205,895	2.15	$166,266	1.44	$372,161	1.83	74,432
15	$212,802	2.08	$171,929	1.39	$384,731	1.77	76,946
16	$219,482	2.02	$177,407	1.35	$396,889	1.72	79,378
17	$225,956	1.96	$182,716	1.31	$408,672	1.67	81,734
18	$232,243	1.91	$187,871	1.27	$420,114	1.62	84,023
19	$238,357	1.86	$192,885	1.24	$431,242	1.58	86,248
20	$244,313	1.82	$197,768	1.21	$442,081	1.54	88,416

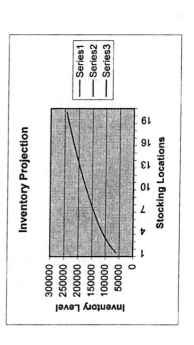

Inventory Projection

Inventory Level — 0, 50000, 100000, 150000, 200000, 250000, 300000

Stocking Locations — 1, 4, 7, 10, 13, 16, 19

Series1, Series2, Series3

Western Pharm B Data.xls

	A	B	C	D	E	F	G	H	I	J	K	L	M	N	O	P	Q
1	Product	Total Demand (Weekly)	ATL Dmd (Weekly)	NB Dmd (Weekly)	LA Dmd (Weekly)	Standard Cost	Total Inventory	Atl Inven (Average)	NB Inven (Average)	LA Inv (Average)	Atl Std	NB Std	LA Std	OCT	Atl OQ	NB OQ	LA OQ
3	P 001	452.9	210.1	55.3	187.6	423.761	1,487	764	337	387	182.7	41.3	126.1	2	420	111	375
4	P 002	1937.8	797.0	330.7	810.0	43.818	8,370	3,945	1,505	2,919	408.0	150.1	361.6	2	1,594	661	1,620
5	P 003	272.4	29.1	16.2	227.1	80.927	3,828	1,716	1,058	1,053	52.5	33.6	390.1	2	58	32	454
6	P 004	1651.9	659.9	274.1	717.9	47.489	7,221	2,942	1,096	3,184	279.6	116.2	237.2	2	1,320	548	1,436
7	P 005	3630.0	1234.2	665.0	1730.8	8.165	37,304	13,019	5,819	18,466	1,082.9	421.6	1,231.4	2	2,468	1,330	3,462
8	P 006	1767.2	719.6	308.6	739.0	35.222	8,956	3,416	1,838	3,701	289.5	137.6	288.0	2	1,439	617	1,478
9	P 007	153.2	53.4	29.7	70.0	31.382	8,169	2,392	1,448	4,329	126.1	64.3	154.9	4	214	119	280
10	P 008	452.8	167.3	82.9	202.5	13.505	19,036	6,612	4,066	8,358	478.5	136.0	320.3	4	669	332	810
11	P 009	1489.5	643.2	285.9	560.4	52.817	6,077	2,770	936	2,370	589.2	213.4	441.9	2	1,286	572	1,121
12	P 010	1413.6	504.6	246.0	663.0	14.446	17,296	7,926	3,751	5,619	447.2	217.8	590.5	2	1,009	492	1,326
13	P 011	379.2	63.5	29.4	286.3	74.637	3,591	2,145	582	863	101.4	53.6	373.2	2	127	59	573
14	P 012	3390.5	1314.2	628.0	1448.3	8.605	29,394	9,837	5,329	14,228	755.1	371.1	927.5	2	2,628	1,256	2,897
15	P 013	1467.5	617.0	252.8	597.6	32.464	8,139	3,753	1,705	2,681	307.9	99.0	237.7	2	1,234	506	1,195
16	P 014	200.8	61.6	35.1	104.1	35.021	6,326	2,374	1,028	2,925	111.2	62.8	187.9	4	246	141	416
17	P 015	440.5	186.8	65.7	187.9	34.406	6,577	2,774	1,087	2,716	92.8	32.6	78.7	2	374	131	376
18	P 016	1654.6	655.5	277.7	721.3	38.319	6,609	2,910	1,280	2,418	276.7	110.0	258.1	2	1,311	555	1,443
19	P 017	9022.5	3120.3	1902.5	3999.7	7.600	33,457	12,896	6,674	13,886	1,173.2	605.3	1,273.8	2	6,241	3,805	7,999
20	P 018	969.7	405.6	194.5	369.7	43.115	5,041	983	569	3,488	160.5	95.4	198.9	2	811	389	739
21	P 019	704.5	255.5	134.7	314.3	19.727	10,097	4,475	1,669	3,953	263.3	150.6	317.6	2	511	269	629
22	P 020	339.5	85.2	93.1	161.3	144.076	1,579	477	201	901	61.3	90.8	90.2	2	170	186	323
23	P 021	1472.6	487.1	234.7	750.9	23.741	8,906	2,616	1,062	5,228	206.7	103.0	496.7	2	974	469	1,502
24	P 022	313.8	69.6	85.8	158.4	99.547	2,106	589	234	1,283	49.5	63.4	88.3	2	139	172	317
25	P 023	920.7	349.8	196.1	374.8	76.076	3,089	1,106	642	1,341	168.8	69.8	135.6	2	700	392	750
26	P 024	5753.3	2186.7	1477.7	2108.9	5.054	34,529	12,227	5,461	16,842	1,018.1	731.5	747.7	2	4,333	2,955	4,218
27	P 025	2488.9	1035.5	409.2	1044.2	19.853	10,031	4,306	1,783	3,942	377.3	130.0	335.9	2	2,071	818	2,088
28	P 026	1625.8	628.0	281.4	716.4	28.826	6,885	3,086	1,278	2,521	290.9	147.0	307.4	2	1,256	563	1,433
29	P 027	2932.1	818.7	895.2	1218.3	13.219	13,650	3,839	4,299	5,513	292.9	305.1	393.6	2	1,637	1,790	2,437
30	P 028	350.4	160.3	41.2	148.9	48.025	3,299	1,835	300	1,164	91.5	23.0	63.1	2	321	82	298
31	P 029	2841.7	1025.2	355.9	1260.6	13.786	12,319	4,628	1,470	6,220	424.7	128.1	540.2	2	2,050	712	2,521
32	P 030	814.7	292.4	140.2	382.2	19.727	7,390	3,128	1,807	2,456	290.1	140.6	342.9	2	585	280	764
33	P 031	2221.6	559.0	733.3	929.2	14.530	10,798	4,994	2,841	2,962	245.8	278.4	343.1	2	1,118	1,467	1,858
34	P 032	5749.8	2439.1	895.8	2414.8	8.709	16,491	6,778	2,950	6,762	1,539.4	517.7	1,560.1	2	4,878	1,792	4,830
35	P 033	1304.6	525.5	197.3	581.8	14.172	9,261	4,024	1,823	3,415	538.6	194.2	585.2	2	1,051	395	1,164
36	P 034	365.1	146.5	63.7	154.9	35.106	3,817	1,146	700	1,971	141.1	54.7	131.0	2	293	127	310
37	P 035	721.2	281.2	144.8	295.3	44.870	2,978	618	437	1,922	150.8	101.6	150.2	2	562	290	591
38	P 036	1037.9	415.6	201.9	420.4	22.063	5,867	1,771	2,204	1,892	201.2	99.0	202.1	2	831	404	841
39	P 037	2046.5	851.0	275.2	920.3	21.171	7,043	3,325	1,147	2,571	302.1	96.8	262.5	2	1,702	550	1,841
40	P 038	466.9	154.3	75.0	237.6	43.667	2,819	1,031	400	1,388	112.2	52.7	132.0	2	309	150	475

	A	B	C	D	E	F	G	H	I	J	K	L	M	N	O	P	Q
1	Product	Total Demand (Weekly)	ATL Dmd (Weekly)	NB Dmd (Weekly)	LA Dmd (Weekly)	Standard Cost	Total Inventory	Atl Inven (Average)	NB Inven (Average)	LA Inv (Average)	Atl Std	NB Std	LA Std	OCT	Atl OQ	NB OQ	LA OQ
41	P 039	478.0	179.7	102.6	195.7	47.834	2,589	927	490	1,173	117.8	60.0	156.5	2	359	205	391
42	P 040	572.0	80.7	34.6	456.7	17.451	7,105	4,121	1,347	1,637	136.6	80.2	641.8	2	161	69	913
43	P 041	5892.2	2091.7	1428.7	2371.8	16.350	9,030	1,643	216	7,170	2,239.1	1,430.7	2,920.6	2	4,183	2,857	4,744
44	P 042	1055.3	363.3	227.7	464.3	16.045	7,078	3,318	722	3,038	188.9	100.5	208.1	2	727	455	929
45	P 043	1731.3	368.3	646.1	716.9	13.629	9,084	1,839	3,454	3,791	212.2	265.3	271.2	2	737	1,292	1,434
46	P 044	2423.8	669.7	647.5	1106.6	13.644	9,510	3,653	3,067	2,790	295.2	239.2	391.3	2	1,339	1,295	2,213
47	P 045	289.5	132.1	60.9	96.5	41.253	2,712	1,724	560	428	71.0	47.9	56.3	2	264	122	193
48	P 046	252.5	75.7	77.4	99.2	22.902	4,526	1,623	1,459	1,444	241.8	163.6	223.6	4	303	310	397
49	P 047	1108.1	404.1	277.9	426.1	15.470	7,314	3,753	1,120	2,441	404.3	203.8	440.0	2	808	556	852
50	P 048	5928.3	1924.0	1669.1	2335.2	10.204	11,306	2,913	1,889	6,504	705.3	623.8	930.1	2	3,848	3,338	4,670
51	P 049	3385.2	1183.7	752.8	1448.6	8.002	12,965	2,652	2,285	8,028	1,135.5	564.1	1,201.3	2	2,367	1,506	2,897
52	P 050	1249.0	461.6	192.7	594.7	19.323	5,803	2,180	1,089	2,534	239.7	76.9	286.6	2	923	385	1,189
53	P 051	1710.2	661.4	325.2	723.5	11.703	9,391	1,724	2,153	5,513	620.5	237.9	499.4	2	1,323	650	1,447
54	P 052	3867.2	1381.1	687.2	1799.0	10.915	11,361	1,793	1,926	7,643	794.1	271.8	903.1	2	2,762	1,374	3,598
55	P 053	257.8	70.8	43.9	143.1	9.155	10,157	6,053	1,051	3,053	84.0	119.2	167.9	4	283	176	572
56	P 054	863.3	347.8	109.7	405.8	18.713	5,210	2,228	657	2,325	169.1	57.1	198.4	2	696	219	812
57	P 055	1063.6	383.6	204.8	475.3	24.755	4,183	1,173	783	2,227	164.5	97.1	216.2	2	767	410	951
58	P 056	1105.9	456.6	209.8	439.5	22.957	4,480	1,621	776	2,084	226.1	80.6	154.2	2	913	420	879
59	P 057	1464.8	654.8	218.3	591.7	15.777	6,231	2,053	759	3,419	285.0	88.7	230.6	2	1,310	437	1,183
60	P 058	2943.6	1066.0	557.1	1320.5	9.114	9,883	3,562	2,177	4,144	811.0	340.6	1,131.6	2	2,132	1,114	2,641
61	P 059	496.4	120.8	210.7	164.9	13.303	6,282	2,177	2,102	2,003	307.2	415.3	359.0	4	483	843	660
62	P 060	163.1	64.3	34.7	64.2	20.885	3,879	1,481	700	1,698	46.0	21.9	36.0	4	257	139	257
63	P 061	910.7	36.4	392.9	481.4	16.275	5,099	231	1,955	2,913	89.1	511.0	413.7	2	73	786	963
64	P 062	644.2	227.3	130.6	286.2	18.032	4,800	1,003	609	3,188	129.0	56.8	114.0	2	455	261	572
65	P 063	720.3	217.1	99.8	403.4	23.675	3,774	1,014	517	2,243	86.4	44.5	400.3	2	434	200	807
66	P 064	3581.2	1205.6	976.5	1399.1	8.464	10,351	2,907	2,530	4,914	746.7	588.0	767.4	2	2,411	1,953	2,798
67	P 065	10673.1	3723.3	1996.9	4952.9	10.302	15,015	5,044	2,470	7,501	1,459.3	643.6	1,530.6	2	7,447	3,994	9,906
68	P 066	572.1	236.3	110.3	225.5	42.151	2,226	632	374	1,220	102.7	52.6	89.7	2	473	221	451
69	P 067	289.5	108.7	52.3	128.5	45.832	1,759	594	381	785	73.5	38.5	68.7	2	217	105	257
70	P 068	833.8	322.4	177.5	333.9	16.045	4,976	1,548	719	2,709	175.6	79.9	136.8	2	645	355	668
71	P 069	392.3	166.8	70.6	155.0	39.000	2,206	798	540	868	67.0	34.5	53.6	2	334	141	310
72	P 070	306.5	99.8	62.0	144.7	22.063	3,603	1,097	289	1,349	48.4	36.8	93.7	4	399	248	579
73	P 071	185.4	43.4	55.4	86.5	78.846	1,081	289	143	650	31.5	24.9	40.0	4	87	111	173
74	P 072	410.1	131.6	99.4	179.1	20.885	3,783	952	565	2,266	100.9	60.8	151.8	2	527	398	716
75	P 073	1021.5	379.2	228.9	413.5	10.805	7,092	2,709	1,838	2,545	334.6	155.8	335.0	2	758	458	827
76	P 074	753.4	304.3	128.2	320.9	21.175	3,989	1,282	483	2,224	316.8	122.4	264.6	2	609	256	642
77	P 075	2510.1	795.9	672.3	1041.9	11.821	6,756	2,794	772	3,190	354.4	260.6	555.2	2	1,592	1,345	2,084
78	P 076	901.9	339.5	180.2	382.2	12.319	6,313	2,002	1,201	3,110	168.9	89.2	236.9	2	679	360	764

	A	B	C	D	E	F	G	H	I	J	K	L	M	N	O	P	Q
1	Product	Total Demand (Weekly)	ATL Dmd (Weekly)	NB Dmd (Weekly)	LA Dmd (Weekly)	Standard Cost	Total Inventory	Atl Inven (Average)	NB Inven (Average)	LA Inv (Average)	Atl Std	NB Std	LA Std	OCT	Atl OQ	NB OQ	LA OQ
79	P 077	3079.0	1181.0	531.9	1366.1	11.020	8,567	3,625	1,147	3,796	573.3	221.9	538.1	2	2,362	1,064	2,732
80	P 078	1040.3	409.9	261.7	368.7	15.823	4,726	1,853	988	1,884	226.8	119.5	156.6	2	820	523	737
81	P 079	83.1	68.0	0.2	14.9	21.910	3,466	3,466	0	0	234.0	1.2	66.1	4	272	1	59
82	P 080	2355.2	943.5	397.8	1013.9	9.916	7,676	2,883	1,315	3,479	718.6	262.2	721.1	2	1,887	796	2,028
83	P 081	1457.4	546.1	305.3	606.0	12.724	5,762	1,778	975	3,008	210.4	98.7	158.3	2	1,092	611	1,212
84	P 082	373.2	1.0	1.0	371.2	42.900	1,803	0	0	1,802			533.5	2	1	1	742
85	P 083	3370.0	1183.8	688.0	1498.2	8.818	8,601	2,675	2,118	3,808	438.6	261.4	531.4	2	2,368	1,376	2,996
86	P 084	3743.8	1540.0	697.0	1506.8	11.967	6,741	1,496	1,238	4,007	645.4	248.0	552.6	2	3,080	1,394	3,014
87	P 085	1994.8	925.4	309.4	760.0	48.255	2,940	1,567	394	979	626.9	204.2	491.5	2	1,851	619	1,520
88	P 086	830.7	285.1	166.5	379.2	12.409	5,799	2,067	1,054	2,678	128.3	76.4	361.9	2	570	333	758
89	P 087	855.6	384.1	146.3	325.3	9.018	7,692	3,346	1,311	3,036	290.6	132.8	272.8	4	1,536	585	1,301
90	P 088	13.7	5.8	3.2	4.7	39.836	1,589	335	37	1,218	22.4	11.9	17.0	4	23	13	19
91	P 089	554.4	277.1	102.0	175.3	38.030	1,838	993	343	502	112.8	32.5	68.9	2	554	204	351
92	P 090	1670.7	690.4	358.9	621.3	5.057	13,479	6,403	2,453	4,622	560.4	229.8	396.3	4	2,762	1,436	2,485
93	P 091	555.8	135.7	87.9	332.2	43.741	1,594	730	0	864	250.6	139.5	397.8	2	271	176	664
94	P 092	137.1	41.6	34.4	61.2	32.133	2,052	534	564	955	27.0	23.2	42.4	4	166	137	245
95	P 093	2038.4	746.0	359.5	932.9	8.822	7,631	2,880	1,711	3,041	749.9	319.3	876.3	2	1,492	719	1,866
96	P 094	1936.0	764.5	359.8	811.7	11.658	5,905	1,985	1,345	2,575	364.9	174.0	357.8	2	1,529	720	1,623
97	P 095	745.7	242.7	78.1	424.9	18.356	3,988	1,175	568	2,244	216.1	160.1	474.0	2	485	156	850
98	P 096	1109.2	380.8	155.1	573.3	17.112	4,656	1,492	640	2,524	416.6	299.0	682.9	2	762	310	1,147
99	P 097	416.6	136.4	91.3	188.8	16.024	4,057	1,325	1,349	1,383	216.9	131.0	242.0	4	546	365	755
100	P 098	398.4	196.3	54.2	147.9	6.031	10,165	3,690	1,240	5,236	231.6	67.0	208.3	4	785	217	592
101	P 099	130.3	48.9	31.9	49.4	32.133	2,013	655	168	1,189	42.8	26.8	36.5	4	196	128	198
102	P 100	658.6	289.9	116.0	252.7	33.381	2,278	1,173	472	632	142.8	52.7	105.3	2	580	232	505
103																	
104																	

	A	S	T	U	V	W	X	Y	Z	AA	AB	AC	AD	AE	AF
1	Product	Atl Calc	NB Calc	LA Calc		Atl	NB	LA		Atl	NB	LA		Atl	NB
2		SS	SS	SS		Sigma C	Sigma C	Sigma C		k	k	k		Adj k	Adj k
3	P 001	553	282	199		333	80	259		1.6619	3.5007	0.7701		1.66	3.00
4	P 002	3,148	1,175	2,109		984	393	958		3.1993	2.9893	2.2019		3.00	2.99
5	P 003	1,687	1,042	826		80	50	597		21.1490	20.7628	1.3848		3.00	3.00
6	P 004	2,282	821	2,466		769	320	792		2.9659	2.5707	3.1117		2.97	2.57
7	P 005	11,785	5,154	16,736		1,967	893	2,455		5.9918	5.7704	6.8162		3.00	3.00
8	P 006	2,697	1,530	2,962		828	365	844		3.2574	4.1934	3.5103		3.00	3.00
9	P 007	2,285	1,389	4,189		258	132	318		8.8643	10.5180	13.1873		3.00	3.00
10	P 008	6,278	3,900	7,953		972	284	672		6.4618	13.7149	11.8352		3.00	3.00
11	P 009	2,127	650	1,810		1,053	416	839		2.0202	1.5648	2.1564		2.02	1.56
12	P 010	7,421	3,505	4,956		809	394	1,066		9.1725	8.8929	4.6478		3.00	3.00
13	P 011	2,082	553	577		157	81	600		13.2790	6.7967	0.9605		3.00	3.00
14	P 012	8,523	4,700	12,780		1,693	818	1,954		5.0333	5.7432	6.5404		3.00	3.00
15	P 013	3,136	1,452	2,083		755	289	686		4.1531	5.0239	3.0381		3.00	3.00
16	P 014	2,250	957	2,717		231	130	390		9.7506	7.3363	6.9670		3.00	3.00
17	P 015	2,587	1,021	2,528		228	80	218		11.3305	12.7182	11.5738		3.00	3.00
18	P 016	2,255	1,003	1,697		763	318	808		2.9536	3.1499	2.0988		2.95	3.00
19	P 017	9,775	4,772	9,887		3,534	2,086	4,387		2.7661	2.2874	2.2538		2.77	2.29
20	P 018	578	375	3,119		465	237	465		1.2431	1.5841	6.7138		1.24	1.58
21	P 019	4,219	1,535	3,638		452	252	548		9.3420	6.0895	6.6374		3.00	3.00
22	P 020	392	108	740		122	159	206		3.2257	0.6805	3.5984		3.00	0.68
23	P 021	2,129	828	4,477		568	276	1,028		3.7473	2.9963	4.3539		3.00	3.00
24	P 022	519	148	1,125		99	124	202		5.2604	1.1926	5.5761		3.00	1.19
25	P 023	756	446	966		423	220	421		1.7852	2.0335	2.2955		1.79	2.03
26	P 024	10,060	3,983	14,733		2,601	1,804	2,359		3.8671	2.2080	6.2450		3.00	2.21
27	P 025	3,271	1,373	2,898		1,165	449	1,147		2.8076	3.0614	2.5264		2.81	3.00
28	P 026	2,458	996	1,805		751	350	838		3.2736	2.8476	2.1542		3.00	2.85
29	P 027	3,020	3,404	4,294		918	994	1,339		3.2913	3.4252	3.2063		3.00	3.00
30	P 028	1,674	259	1,015		206	52	174		8.1272	4.9413	5.8489		3.00	3.00
31	P 029	3,603	1,115	4,960		1,188	399	1,474		3.0325	2.7908	3.3646		3.00	2.79
32	P 030	2,835	1,666	2,074		504	243	617		5.6282	6.8500	3.3586		3.00	3.00
33	P 031	4,435	2,108	2,033		658	832	1,048		6.7382	2.5329	1.9396		3.00	2.53
34	P 032	4,339	2,055	4,347		3,269	1,157	3,271		1.3271	1.7761	1.3291		1.33	1.78
35	P 033	3,498	1,625	2,833		925	338	1,012		3.7803	4.8077	2.8004		3.00	3.00
36	P 034	999	636	1,816		248	100	241		4.0357	6.3531	7.5203		3.00	3.00
37	P 035	337	292	1,627		353	204	364		0.9557	1.4325	4.4729		0.96	1.43
38	P 036	1,356	2,002	1,472		504	246	508		2.6917	8.1473	2.8947		2.69	3.00
39	P 037	2,474	872	1,650		952	307	992		2.5984	2.8369	1.6631		2.60	2.84
40	P 038	876	325	1,151		221	106	302		3.9594	3.0697	3.8082		3.00	3.00

	A	R	S	T	U	V	W	X	Y	Z	AA	AB	AC	AD	AE	AF
1	Product		Atl Calc SS	NB Calc SS	LA Calc SS		Atl Sigma C	NB Sigma C	LA Sigma C		Atl k	NB k	LA k		Atl Adj k	NB Adj k
41	P 039		747	387	977		245	133	295		3.0487	2.9070	3.3068		3.00	2.91
42	P 040		4,040	1,313	1,180		209	119	1,016		19.3003	11.0736	1.1615		3.00	3.00
43	P 041		-448	-1,212	4,798		3,795	2,477	4,763		-0.1182	-0.4894	1.0074		-0.12	-0.49
44	P 042		2,955	494	2,574		451	268	550		6.5527	1.8418	4.6824		3.00	1.84
45	P 043		1,471	2,808	3,074		475	747	813		3.0961	3.7576	3.7812		3.00	3.00
46	P 044		2,984	2,420	1,683		789	731	1,237		3.7807	3.3122	1.3603		3.00	3.00
47	P 045		1,592	500	331		166	91	125		9.5937	5.4858	2.6472		3.00	3.00
48	P 046		1,471	1,305	1,245		490	336	458		3.0053	3.8804	2.7190		3.00	3.00
49	P 047		3,349	842	2,015		700	400	754		4.7826	2.1039	2.6721		3.00	2.10
50	P 048		989	220	4,168		2,167	1,888	2,680		0.4564	0.1166	1.5553		0.46	0.12
51	P 049		1,468	1,532	6,580		1,995	1,097	2,233		0.7361	1.3966	2.9470		0.74	1.40
52	P 050		1,719	896	1,939		573	221	720		3.0010	4.0505	2.6941		3.00	3.00
53	P 051		1,062	1,828	4,790		1,099	468	1,011		0.9669	3.9071	4.7375		0.97	3.00
54	P 052		411	1,239	5,844		1,780	787	2,206		0.2311	1.5733	2.6487		0.23	1.57
55	P 053		5,911	963	2,767		182	242	365		32.4303	3.9730	7.5816		3.00	3.00
56	P 054		1,880	547	1,919		422	136	493		4.4551	4.0172	3.8907		3.00	3.00
57	P 055		790	578	1,752		449	247	565		1.7606	2.3438	3.0994		1.76	2.34
58	P 056		1,164	566	1,644		557	239	491		2.0888	2.3695	3.3509		2.09	2.37
59	P 057		1,398	541	2,827		769	252	676		1.8185	2.1486	4.1842		1.82	2.15
60	P 058		2,496	1,620	2,824		1,566	736	2,075		1.5938	2.2001	1.3610		1.59	2.20
61	P 059		1,936	1,680	1,673		626	857	737		3.0916	1.9605	2.2708		3.00	1.96
62	P 060		1,353	631	1,569		112	56	96		12.0497	11.2882	16.2645		3.00	3.00
63	P 061		195	1,562	2,432		131	822	758		1.4848	1.8990	3.2099		1.48	1.90
64	P 062		776	479	2,902		292	153	329		2.6605	3.1207	8.8325		2.66	3.00
65	P 063		797	417	1,840		249	118	695		3.1986	3.5316	2.6467		3.00	3.00
66	P 064		1,702	1,554	3,515		1,603	1,283	1,771		1.0618	1.2114	1.9849		1.06	1.21
67	P 065		1,321	473	2,548		4,257	2,195	5,405		0.3103	0.2154	0.4715		0.31	0.22
68	P 066		396	263	995		277	133	259		1.4273	1.9783	3.8432		1.43	1.98
69	P 067		485	328	656		150	76	161		3.2261	4.3462	4.0734		3.00	3.00
70	P 068		1,226	541	2,375		407	210	386		3.0122	2.5719	6.1534		3.00	2.57
71	P 069		631	470	713		192	86	173		3.2917	5.4733	4.1321		3.00	3.00
72	P 070		897	1,033	1,059		139	96	237		6.4548	10.7345	4.4744		3.00	3.00
73	P 071		245	88	563		62	66	103		3.9447	1.3340	5.4495		3.00	1.33
74	P 072		689	366	1,907		241	157	352		2.8584	2.3337	5.4119		2.86	2.33
75	P 073		2,330	1,609	2,132		606	318	629		3.8419	5.0645	3.3905		3.00	3.00
76	P 074		978	354	1,903		542	215	493		1.8060	1.6458	3.8613		1.81	1.65
77	P 075		1,999	100	2,148		941	767	1,305		2.1248	0.1302	1.6465		2.12	0.13
78	P 076		1,662	1,021	2,727		415	220	508		4.0047	4.6421	5.3655		3.00	3.00

	A	R	S	T	U	V	W	X	Y	Z	AA	AB	AC	AD	AE	AF
1	Product		Atl Calc SS	NB Calc SS	LA Calc SS		Atl Sigma C	NB Sigma C	LA Sigma C		Atl k	NB k	LA k		Atl Adj k	NB Adj k
79	P 077		2,444	615	2,430		1,432	618	1,564		1.7060	0.9953	1.5537		1.71	1.00
80	P 078		1,443	726	1,515		520	311	430		2.7730	2.3322	3.5231		2.77	2.33
81	P 079		3,330	0	-30		473	2	133		7.0394	-0.1867	-0.2235		3.00	-0.19
82	P 080		1,939	917	2,465		1,387	544	1,438		1.3983	1.6861	1.7140		1.40	1.69
83	P 081		1,232	670	2,402		622	336	646		1.9810	1.9967	3.7186		1.98	2.00
84	P 082		0	0	1,431		1	1	841		-0.0100	-0.0100	1.7017		-0.01	-0.01
85	P 083		1,491	1,430	2,309		1,337	781	1,676		1.1158	1.8314	1.3779		1.12	1.83
86	P 084		-44	541	2,500		1,790	780	1,697		-0.0247	0.6933	1.4731		-0.02	0.69
87	P 085		641	85	219		1,282	423	1,030		0.5005	0.2010	0.2122		0.50	0.20
88	P 086		1,782	888	2,299		338	198	637		5.2729	4.4713	3.6088		3.00	3.00
89	P 087		2,578	1,018	2,385		697	303	635		3.7017	3.3568	3.7551		3.00	3.00
90	P 088		323	31	1,208		45	24	34		7.1442	1.2728	35.1978		3.00	1.27
91	P 089		716	241	327		320	112	201		2.2381	2.1567	1.6299		2.24	2.16
92	P 090		5,023	1,735	3,379		1,316	583	1,007		3.8154	2.9760	3.3554		3.00	2.98
93	P 091		594	-88	532		380	216	653		1.5656	-0.4070	0.8146		1.57	-0.41
94	P 092		451	495	832		68	58	105		6.6160	8.5813	7.9617		3.00	3.00
95	P 093		2,134	1,351	2,108		1,297	577	1,551		1.6456	2.3408	1.3591		1.65	2.34
96	P 094		1,221	985	1,764		922	436	957		1.3235	2.2595	1.8437		1.32	2.26
97	P 095		932	490	1,819		390	240	794		2.3896	2.0443	2.2924		2.39	2.04
98	P 096		1,111	485	1,951		701	450	1,123		1.5836	1.0768	1.7372		1.58	1.08
99	P 097		1,053	1,166	1,005		455	277	520		2.3142	4.2038	1.9350		2.31	1.08
100	P 098		3,297	1,131	4,940		503	144	442		6.5545	7.8305	11.1755		3.00	3.00
101	P 099		557	105	1,090		99	62	88		5.6507	1.6775	12.3652		3.00	1.68
102	P 100		883	356	380		353	138	293		2.4998	2.5819	1.2945		2.50	2.58
103																
104																

Product	LA Adj k	Atl Service	NB Service	LA Service	Atl Avg Service	NB Avg Service	LA Avg Service	Serviced	Demand	Average Service	$ Serviced
P 001	0.77	0.98	1.00	0.90	206	55	169	431	453	95.07%	182,463
P 002	2.20	1.00	1.00	1.00	797	331	808	1,935	1,938	99.87%	84,803
P 003	1.38	1.00	1.00	0.94	29	16	214	259	272	95.02%	20,943
P 004	3.00	1.00	1.00	1.00	660	274	718	1,651	1,652	99.96%	78,420
P 005	3.00	1.00	1.00	1.00	1,234	665	1,731	3,630	3,630	100.00%	29,638
P 006	3.00	1.00	1.00	1.00	720	309	739	1,767	1,767	100.00%	62,242
P 007	3.00	1.00	1.00	1.00	53	30	70	153	153	100.00%	4,806
P 008	3.00	1.00	1.00	1.00	167	83	203	453	453	100.00%	6,114
P 009	2.16	0.99	0.98	1.00	639	280	558	1,477	1,489	99.15%	78,000
P 010	3.00	1.00	1.00	1.00	505	246	663	1,414	1,414	100.00%	20,420
P 011	0.96	1.00	1.00	0.89	64	29	256	349	379	92.05%	26,054
P 012	3.00	1.00	1.00	1.00	1,314	628	1,448	3,391	3,391	100.00%	29,177
P 013	3.00	1.00	1.00	1.00	617	253	598	1,467	1,467	100.00%	47,640
P 014	3.00	1.00	1.00	1.00	62	35	104	201	201	100.00%	7,032
P 015	3.00	1.00	1.00	1.00	187	66	188	440	440	100.00%	15,155
P 016	2.10	1.00	1.00	1.00	655	278	718	1,651	1,655	99.80%	63,276
P 017	2.25	0.97	1.00	1.00	3,119	1,897	3,989	9,005	9,022	99.81%	68,441
P 018	3.00	1.00	0.98	1.00	393	191	370	953	970	98.30%	41,096
P 019	3.00	1.00	1.00	1.00	256	135	314	705	705	100.00%	13,898
P 020	3.00	1.00	0.86	1.00	85	80	161	326	340	96.06%	46,990
P 021	3.00	1.00	1.00	1.00	487	235	751	1,472	1,473	99.99%	34,959
P 022	3.00	1.00	0.95	1.00	70	82	158	310	314	98.64%	30,811
P 023	2.30	0.99	1.00	1.00	347	195	374	916	921	99.48%	69,672
P 024	3.00	1.00	1.00	1.00	2,167	1,473	2,109	5,749	5,753	99.92%	29,056
P 025	2.53	1.00	1.00	1.00	1,035	409	1,043	2,487	2,489	99.94%	49,381
P 026	2.15	1.00	1.00	1.00	628	281	714	1,623	1,626	99.83%	46,784
P 027	3.00	1.00	1.00	1.00	819	895	1,218	2,932	2,932	100.00%	38,758
P 028	3.00	1.00	1.00	1.00	160	41	149	350	350	100.00%	16,830
P 029	3.00	1.00	1.00	1.00	1,025	356	1,261	2,641	2,642	99.99%	36,415
P 030	3.00	1.00	1.00	1.00	292	140	382	815	815	100.00%	16,071
P 031	1.94	1.00	1.00	1.00	559	732	925	2,216	2,222	99.76%	32,203
P 032	1.33	0.97	0.99	0.97	2,365	888	2,340	5,593	5,750	97.27%	48,709
P 033	2.80	1.00	1.00	1.00	526	197	581	1,304	1,305	99.97%	18,484
P 034	3.00	1.00	1.00	1.00	146	64	155	365	365	100.00%	12,818
P 035	3.00	0.94	0.97	1.00	263	141	295	700	721	97.03%	31,398
P 036	2.89	1.00	1.00	1.00	415	202	420	1,037	1,038	99.95%	22,888
P 037	1.66	1.00	1.00	0.99	850	275	909	2,034	2,047	99.39%	43,060
P 038	3.00	1.00	1.00	1.00	154	75	238	467	467	100.00%	20,389

	A	AG	AH	AI	AJ	AK	AL	AM	AN	AO	AP	AQ	AR	AS	AT	AU
1	Product	LA Adj k		Atl Service	NB Service	LA Service		Atl Avg Service	NB Avg Service	LA Avg Service		Serviced	Demand	Average Service		$ Serviced
41	P 039	3.00		1.00	1.00	1.00		180	103	196		478	478	99.99%		22,864
42	P 040	1.16		1.00	1.00	0.92		81	35	422		537	572	93.91%		9,373
43	P 041	1.01		0.64	0.65	0.92		1,335	935	2,173		4,443	5,892	75.40%		72,639
44	P 042	3.00		1.00	0.99	1.00		363	226	464		1,054	1,055	99.86%		16,908
45	P 043	3.00		1.00	1.00	1.00		368	646	717		1,731	1,731	100.00%		23,596
46	P 044	1.36		1.00	1.00	0.97		670	647	1,078		2,396	2,424	98.84%		32,686
47	P 045	2.65		1.00	1.00	1.00		132	61	96		289	289	99.97%		11,938
48	P 046	2.72		1.00	1.00	1.00		76	77	99		252	252	99.95%		5,776
49	P 047	2.67		1.00	1.00	1.00		404	277	426		1,106	1,108	99.84%		17,114
50	P 048	1.56		0.87	0.80	0.98		1,674	1,338	2,296		5,308	5,928	89.54%		54,164
51	P 049	2.95		0.88	0.97	1.00		1,041	728	1,448		3,217	3,385	95.03%		25,741
52	P 050	2.69		1.00	1.00	1.00		462	193	594		1,248	1,249	99.96%		24,124
53	P 051	3.00		0.92	1.00	1.00		606	325	724		1,655	1,710	96.77%		19,368
54	P 052	2.65		0.80	0.98	1.00		1,108	676	1,797		3,581	3,867	92.60%		39,088
55	P 053	3.00		1.00	1.00	1.00		71	44	143		258	258	100.00%		2,360
56	P 054	3.00		1.00	1.00	1.00		348	110	406		863	863	100.00%		16,156
57	P 055	3.00		0.99	1.00	1.00		380	204	475		1,060	1,064	99.66%		26,239
58	P 056	3.00		1.00	1.00	1.00		455	209	440		1,103	1,106	99.77%		25,331
59	P 057	3.00		0.99	1.00	1.00		651	218	592		1,460	1,465	99.66%		23,031
60	P 058	1.36		0.98	1.00	0.96		1,043	555	1,273		2,872	2,944	97.56%		26,173
61	P 059	2.27		1.00	0.99	0.99		121	209	164		494	496	99.46%		6,568
62	P 060	3.00		1.00	1.00	1.00		64	35	64		163	163	100.00%		3,407
63	P 061	3.00		0.93	0.99	1.00		34	388	481		904	911	99.24%		14,708
64	P 062	3.00		1.00	1.00	1.00		227	131	286		644	644	99.97%		11,612
65	P 063	2.65		1.00	1.00	1.00		217	100	403		720	720	99.93%		17,042
66	P 064	1.98		0.94	0.96	0.99		1,139	941	1,392		3,471	3,581	96.92%		29,380
67	P 065	0.47		0.85	0.83	0.87		3,156	1,660	4,330		9,146	10,673	85.69%		94,221
68	P 066	3.00		0.98	0.99	1.00		231	110	226		566	572	99.02%		23,878
69	P 067	3.00		1.00	1.00	1.00		109	52	129		290	290	100.00%		13,269
70	P 068	3.00		1.00	1.00	1.00		322	177	334		834	834	99.97%		13,375
71	P 069	3.00		1.00	1.00	1.00		167	71	155		392	392	100.00%		15,302
72	P 070	3.00		1.00	1.00	1.00		100	62	145		307	307	100.00%		6,762
73	P 071	3.00		1.00	0.97	1.00		43	54	87		184	185	99.19%		14,497
74	P 072	3.00		1.00	1.00	1.00		132	99	179		410	410	99.96%		8,561
75	P 073	3.00		1.00	1.00	1.00		379	229	414		1,022	1,022	100.00%		11,038
76	P 074	3.00		0.99	0.98	1.00		301	126	321		748	753	99.27%		15,837
77	P 075	1.65		1.00	0.80	0.99		793	538	1,027		2,357	2,510	93.92%		27,867
78	P 076	3.00		1.00	1.00	1.00		340	180	382		902	902	100.00%		11,111

Western Pharm B Data.xls

	A	AG	AH	AI	AJ	AK	AL	AM	AN	AO	AP	AQ	AR	AS	AT	AU
1		LA		Atl	NB	LA		Atl Avg	NB Avg	LA Avg				Average		$
2	Product	Adj k		Service	Service	Service		Service	Service	Service		Serviced	Demand	Service		Serviced
79	P 077	1.55		0.99	0.94	0.98		1,171	501	1,343		3,015	3,079	97.92%		33,224
80	P 078	3.00		1.00	1.00	1.00		410	261	369		1,040	1,040	99.92%		16,448
81	P 079	-0.22		1.00	-0.07	0.11		68	0	2		70	83	83.74%		1,525
82	P 080	1.71		0.97	0.98	0.99		912	391	1,004		2,307	2,355	97.96%		22,877
83	P 081	3.00		1.00	1.00	1.00		544	304	606		1,453	1,457	99.72%		18,492
84	P 082	1.70		0.60	0.60	0.98		1	1	365		366	373	98.19%		15,721
85	P 083	1.38		0.96	0.99	0.97		1,138	684	1,460		3,282	3,370	97.38%		28,939
86	P 084	1.47		0.77	0.91	0.98		1,183	631	1,476		3,290	3,744	87.88%		39,371
87	P 085	0.21		0.86	0.79	0.79		799	244	602		1,645	1,995	82.47%		79,389
88	P 086	3.00		1.00	1.00	1.00		285	166	379		831	831	100.00%		10,308
89	P 087	3.00		1.00	1.00	1.00		384	146	325		856	856	100.00%		7,715
90	P 088	3.00		1.00	0.89	1.00		6	3	5		13	14	97.53%		530
91	P 089	1.63		1.00	1.00	0.99		276	102	173		551	554	99.38%		20,952
92	P 090	3.00		1.00	1.00	1.00		690	359	621		1,671	1,671	99.99%		8,448
93	P 091	0.81		0.96	0.51	0.88		130	45	293		468	556	84.18%		20,464
94	P 092	3.00		1.00	1.00	1.00		42	34	61		137	137	100.00%		4,406
95	P 093	1.36		0.98	1.00	0.96		731	358	898		1,987	2,038	97.48%		17,530
96	P 094	1.84		0.97	1.00	0.99		744	359	806		1,909	1,936	98.59%		22,252
97	P 095	2.29		0.97	0.99	1.00		242	77	423		742	746	99.53%		13,623
98	P 096	1.74		0.97	0.88	0.99		371	136	565		1,072	1,109	96.66%		18,348
99	P 097	1.94		1.00	1.00	0.99		136	91	188		415	417	99.64%		6,651
100	P 098	3.00		1.00	1.00	1.00		196	54	148		398	398	100.00%		2,403
101	P 099	3.00		1.00	0.99	1.00		49	32	49		130	130	99.72%		4,174
102	P 100	1.29		1.00	1.00	0.97		289	116	245		650	659	98.66%		21,691
103																
104												151,432	157,573	96.10%		2,793,884

Western Pharm B Data.xls

	A	AV	AW	AX	AY	AZ	BA	BB	BC	BD	BE	BF	BG	BH	BI
1															
2	Product	$ Demand	Average Service	Current Inv $		Atl f(k) @ 95	NB f(k) @ 95	LA f(k) @ 95		Atl SS@95	NB SS@95	LA SS@95		Atl Avg@95	NB Avg@95
3	P 001	191,931	95.07%	630,238		0.0631	0.0687	0.0725		400	88	285		610	144
4	P 002	84,910	99.87%	366,754		0.0810	0.0842	0.0846		1,082	393	958		1,879	724
5	P 003	22,042	95.02%	309,751		0.0364	0.0323	0.0381		120	75	835		149	91
6	P 004	78,448	99.96%	342,912		0.0858	0.0858	0.0906		769	320	792		1,429	594
7	P 005	29,638	100.00%	304,578		0.0627	0.0745	0.0705		2,360	982	2,701		3,594	1,647
8	P 006	62,242	100.00%	315,435		0.0869	0.0846	0.0876		828	365	844		1,547	673
9	P 007	4,806	100.00%	256,345		0.0415	0.0450	0.0441		361	185	445		468	244
10	P 008	6,114	100.00%	257,080		0.0344	0.0583	0.0603		1,457	341	806		1,792	507
11	P 009	78,670	99.15%	320,946		0.0611	0.0688	0.0668		1,263	457	1,007		1,906	743
12	P 010	20,420	100.00%	249,861		0.0624	0.0624	0.0622		971	473	1,280		1,475	719
13	P 011	28,303	92.05%	267,987		0.0405	0.0362	0.0477		219	122	781		283	151
14	P 012	29,177	100.00%	252,950		0.0776	0.0767	0.0741		1,863	900	2,149		3,177	1,528
15	P 013	47,640	100.00%	264,225		0.0817	0.0875	0.0872		831	289	686		1,448	542
16	P 014	7,032	100.00%	221,552		0.0534	0.0538	0.0534		300	170	507		423	240
17	P 015	15,155	100.00%	226,278		0.0818	0.0819	0.0860		251	88	218		438	154
18	P 016	63,401	99.80%	253,246		0.0859	0.0872	0.0892		763	318	808		1,419	596
19	P 017	68,573	99.81%	254,278		0.0883	0.0912	0.0912		3,534	2,086	4,387		6,654	3,989
20	P 018	41,808	98.30%	217,345		0.0873	0.0822	0.0796		465	260	511		870	455
21	P 019	13,898	100.00%	199,177		0.0566	0.0534	0.0573		542	328	658		798	462
22	P 020	48,916	96.06%	227,520		0.0701	0.0587	0.0784		134	190	226		219	283
23	P 021	34,961	99.99%	211,432		0.0857	0.0850	0.0730		568	276	1,131		1,055	511
24	P 022	31,235	98.64%	209,613		0.0705	0.0691	0.0785		109	137	222		178	222
25	P 023	70,040	99.48%	235,029		0.0826	0.0893	0.0890		466	220	421		816	416
26	P 024	29,077	99.92%	174,510		0.0833	0.0819	0.0894		2,862	1,984	2,359		5,028	3,462
27	P 025	49,412	99.94%	199,146		0.0889	0.0912	0.0910		1,165	449	1,147		2,200	858
28	P 026	46,865	99.83%	198,462		0.0836	0.0804	0.0855		751	385	838		1,379	666
29	P 027	38,758	100.00%	180,436		0.0892	0.0901	0.0910		918	994	1,339		1,736	1,889
30	P 028	16,830	100.00%	158,450		0.0778	0.0785	0.0858		227	58	174		387	99
31	P 029	36,417	99.99%	169,828		0.0863	0.0891	0.0855		1,188	399	1,474		2,213	755
32	P 030	16,071	100.00%	145,785		0.0580	0.0576	0.0619		605	292	741		897	432
33	P 031	32,280	99.76%	156,901		0.0849	0.0881	0.0886		658	832	1,048		1,217	1,566
34	P 032	50,076	97.27%	143,623		0.0746	0.0774	0.0738		3,596	1,273	3,598		6,035	2,168
35	P 033	18,489	99.97%	131,256		0.0568	0.0583	0.0575		1,110	406	1,214		1,636	603
36	P 034	12,818	100.00%	133,984		0.0592	0.0636	0.0642		297	120	290		444	184
37	P 035	32,360	97.03%	133,605		0.0797	0.0710	0.0812		388	224	400		669	369
38	P 036	22,899	99.95%	129,443		0.0825	0.0822	0.0827		554	270	559		970	472
39	P 037	43,327	99.39%	149,108		0.0894	0.0895	0.0927		952	307	992		1,803	582
40	P 038	20,389	100.00%	123,086		0.0697	0.0709	0.0786		243	116	332		398	191

Western Pharm B Data.xls

	A	AV	AW	AX	AY	AZ	BA	BB	BC	BD	BE	BF	BG	BH	BI
1	Product	$ Demand	Average Service	Current Inv $		Atl f(k) @ 95	NB f(k) @ 95	LA f(k) @ 95		Atl SS@95	NB SS@95	LA SS@95		Atl Avg@95	NB Avg@95
41	P 039	22,867	99.99%	123,858		0.0733	0.0771	0.0662		270	147	355		449	249
42	P 040	9,981	93.91%	123,994		0.0385	0.0292	0.0449		293	190	1,422		374	224
43	P 041	96,335	75.40%	147,633		0.0551	0.0577	0.0498		4,934	2,972	6,192		7,025	4,401
44	P 042	16,932	99.86%	113,570		0.0806	0.0848	0.0845		496	268	550		859	496
45	P 043	23,596	100.00%	123,806		0.0775	0.0865	0.0882		523	747	813		891	1,393
46	P 044	33,071	98.84%	129,758		0.0849	0.0886	0.0894		789	731	1,237		1,459	1,378
47	P 045	11,942	99.97%	111,883		0.0796	0.0669	0.0771		183	109	138		315	170
48	P 046	5,779	99.95%	103,651		0.0309	0.0460	0.0433		734	437	641		886	592
49	P 047	17,142	99.84%	113,148		0.0577	0.0694	0.0565		840	440	905		1,244	718
50	P 048	60,492	89.54%	115,365		0.0888	0.0884	0.0871		2,167	1,888	2,680		4,091	3,557
51	P 049	27,087	95.03%	103,742		0.0593	0.0686	0.0649		2,394	1,207	2,679		3,578	1,959
52	P 050	24,133	99.96%	112,121		0.0806	0.0871	0.0826		630	221	792		1,091	414
53	P 051	20,014	96.77%	109,897		0.0602	0.0695	0.0716		1,319	515	1,112		1,980	840
54	P 052	42,211	92.60%	124,009		0.0776	0.0873	0.0815		1,958	787	2,427		3,339	1,475
55	P 053	2,360	100.00%	92,986		0.0777	0.0362	0.0784		200	364	401		342	452
56	P 054	16,156	100.00%	97,500		0.0824	0.0806	0.0823		464	150	543		812	260
57	P 055	26,329	99.66%	103,546		0.0855	0.0830	0.0841		449	271	565		832	476
58	P 056	25,389	99.77%	102,855		0.0819	0.0879	0.0896		613	239	491		1,070	449
59	P 057	23,110	99.66%	98,305		0.0852	0.0867	0.0876		769	252	676		1,424	470
60	P 058	26,828	97.56%	90,075		0.0681	0.0756	0.0636		1,879	810	2,490		2,945	1,367
61	P 059	6,604	99.46%	83,566		0.0386	0.0492	0.0448		877	1,114	1,031		1,118	1,536
62	P 060	3,407	100.00%	81,012		0.1145	0.1241	0.1330		101	45	77		230	114
63	P 061	14,821	99.24%	82,991		0.0277	0.0478	0.0635		210	1,069	909		246	1,462
64	P 062	11,615	99.97%	86,553		0.0780	0.0852	0.0871		321	153	329		548	284
65	P 063	17,053	99.93%	89,341		0.0871	0.0846	0.0580		249	118	834		466	218
66	P 064	30,312	96.92%	87,617		0.0752	0.0761	0.0790		1,763	1,411	1,948		2,968	2,387
67	P 065	109,952	85.69%	154,683		0.0875	0.0910	0.0916		4,257	2,195	5,405		7,980	4,191
68	P 066	24,115	99.02%	93,817		0.0852	0.0829	0.0871		277	146	259		514	257
69	P 067	13,269	100.00%	80,629		0.0723	0.0693	0.0798		165	83	177		274	135
70	P 068	13,379	99.97%	79,833		0.0792	0.0844	0.0865		448	210	386		770	388
71	P 069	15,302	100.00%	86,041		0.0869	0.0823	0.0898		192	94	173		359	165
72	P 070	6,762	100.00%	79,489		0.1435	0.1289	0.1222		97	77	189		297	201
73	P 071	14,615	99.19%	85,270		0.0698	0.0844	0.0837		68	66	103		112	121
74	P 072	8,565	99.96%	79,006		0.1092	0.1266	0.1016		217	126	317		480	324
75	P 073	11,038	100.00%	76,628		0.0625	0.0720	0.0658		728	349	755		1,107	578
76	P 074	15,953	99.27%	84,476		0.0562	0.0595	0.0651		650	258	592		954	387
77	P 075	29,671	93.92%	79,868		0.0846	0.0877	0.0799		941	767	1,435		1,736	1,439
78	P 076	11,111	100.00%	77,766		0.0818	0.0819	0.0752		457	242	559		796	422

Western Pharm B Data.xls

	A	AV	AW	AX	AY	AZ	BA	BB	BC	BD	BE	BF	BG	BH	BI
1		$	Average	Current		Atl	NB	LA		Atl	NB	LA		Atl	NB
2	Product	Demand	Service	Inv $		f(k) @ 95	f(k) @ 95	f(k) @ 95		SS@95	SS@95	SS@95		Avg@95	Avg@95
79	P 077	33,930	97.92%	94,410		0.0824	0.0861	0.0874		1,576	618	1,564		2,757	1,150
80	P 078	16,461	99.92%	74,773		0.0788	0.0840	0.0857		573	311	430		982	573
81	P 079	1,821	83.74%	75,934		0.0288	0.0187	0.0223		757	4	226		893	5
82	P 080	23,354	97.96%	76,115		0.0680	0.0731	0.0705		1,664	598	1,582		2,608	996
83	P 081	18,543	99.72%	73,314		0.0878	0.0909	0.0938		622	336	646		1,168	641
84	P 082	16,012	98.19%	77,354		0.0500	0.0500	0.0441		1	1	1,177		2	2
85	P 083	29,717	97.38%	75,845		0.0886	0.0881	0.0894		1,337	781	1,676		2,520	1,469
86	P 084	44,803	87.88%	80,670		0.0860	0.0893	0.0888		1,790	780	1,697		3,330	1,477
87	P 085	96,259	82.47%	141,861		0.0722	0.0731	0.0738		1,410	466	1,133		2,335	775
88	P 086	10,308	100.00%	71,955		0.0844	0.0839	0.0595		338	198	764		623	365
89	P 087	7,715	100.00%	69,368		0.1102	0.0965	0.1024		627	303	572		1,395	596
90	P 088	544	97.53%	63,318		0.0254	0.0265	0.0275		72	39	55		84	45
91	P 089	21,083	99.38%	69,905		0.0867	0.0912	0.0874		320	112	201		597	214
92	P 090	8,449	99.99%	68,162		0.1049	0.1231	0.1234		1,185	466	806		2,566	1,184
93	P 091	24,309	84.18%	69,734		0.0358	0.0407	0.0508		569	302	849		705	390
94	P 092	4,406	100.00%	65,942		0.1220	0.1192	0.1170		55	52	94		138	121
95	P 093	17,983	97.48%	67,326		0.0575	0.0623	0.0601		1,556	693	1,861		2,302	1,052
96	P 094	22,570	98.59%	68,842		0.0829	0.0825	0.0849		1,015	479	957		1,779	839
97	P 095	13,687	99.53%	73,197		0.0622	0.0326	0.0535		468	360	1,032		711	438
98	P 096	18,981	96.66%	79,678		0.0543	0.0344	0.0510		912	676	1,460		1,293	831
99	P 097	6,675	99.64%	65,009		0.0600	0.0659	0.0727		546	333	571		819	516
100	P 098	2,403	100.00%	61,306		0.0780	0.0750	0.0669		553	159	530		946	267
101	P 099	4,185	99.72%	64,674		0.0992	0.1024	0.1121		99	56	79		196	120
102	P 100	21,986	98.66%	76,026		0.0821	0.0841	0.0861		389	138	293		679	254
103															
104		2,900,913	96.31%	14,337,162										147,029	80,202

	BJ	BK	BL	BM	BN	BO	BP	BQ	BR	BS	BT	BU	BV	BW
	LA	Total $		Atl	NB	LA		Atl	NB	LA		Atl	NB	LA
Product	Avg@95	Avg@95		f(k) @ 99	f(k) @ 99	f(k) @ 99		SS @99	SS @99	SS @99		Avg @99	Avg @99	Avg @99
P 001	472	519,417		0.0126	0.0137	0.0145		599	145	440		810	200	628
P 002	1,768	191,533		0.0162	0.0168	0.0169		1,673	668	1,628		2,470	999	2,438
P 003	1,062	105,415		0.0073	0.0065	0.0076		168	105	1,193		197	122	1,420
P 004	1,510	167,788		0.0172	0.0172	0.0181		1,308	543	1,347		1,968	817	2,065
P 005	4,432	78,981		0.0125	0.0149	0.0141		3,540	1,518	4,419		4,774	2,183	6,150
P 006	1,583	133,971		0.0174	0.0169	0.0175		1,407	620	1,434		2,127	929	2,173
P 007	585	40,693		0.0083	0.0090	0.0088		516	251	604		622	310	743
P 008	1,211	47,407		0.0069	0.0117	0.0121		2,040	512	1,209		2,375	678	1,614
P 009	1,568	222,737		0.0122	0.0138	0.0134		1,895	748	1,511		2,538	1,034	2,071
P 010	1,943	59,764		0.0125	0.0125	0.0124		1,456	710	1,919		1,961	955	2,582
P 011	1,067	112,049		0.0081	0.0072	0.0095		314	171	1,141		377	200	1,427
P 012	3,598	71,450		0.0155	0.0153	0.0148		2,879	1,391	3,322		4,193	2,019	4,770
P 013	1,283	106,251		0.0163	0.0175	0.0174		1,284	491	1,166		1,901	744	1,763
P 014	715	48,268		0.0107	0.0108	0.0107		439	248	741		562	318	949
P 015	406	34,350		0.0164	0.0164	0.0172		388	137	371		575	202	559
P 016	1,530	135,831		0.0172	0.0174	0.0178		1,298	541	1,374		1,953	819	2,096
P 017	8,386	144,627		0.0177	0.0182	0.0182		6,008	3,546	7,457		9,128	5,449	11,457
P 018	881	95,103		0.0175	0.0164	0.0159		790	402	790		1,196	597	1,159
P 019	972	44,028		0.0113	0.0107	0.0115		813	479	987		1,068	614	1,301
P 020	387	128,179		0.0140	0.0117	0.0157		219	286	350		304	379	511
P 021	1,882	81,857		0.0171	0.0170	0.0146		966	470	1,748		1,453	704	2,499
P 022	380	77,724		0.0141	0.0138	0.0157		178	224	343		247	309	501
P 023	796	154,205		0.0165	0.0179	0.0178		720	373	716		1,070	569	1,090
P 024	4,468	65,491		0.0167	0.0164	0.0179		4,422	3,066	4,011		6,589	4,544	6,120
P 025	2,191	104,220		0.0178	0.0182	0.0182		1,980	763	1,950		3,016	1,172	2,994
P 026	1,554	103,755		0.0167	0.0161	0.0171		1,276	595	1,424		1,904	876	2,141
P 027	2,558	81,728		0.0178	0.0180	0.0182		1,560	1,689	2,277		2,378	2,584	3,495
P 028	322	38,821		0.0156	0.0157	0.0172		350	89	295		511	130	444
P 029	2,735	78,624		0.0173	0.0178	0.0171		2,020	679	2,506		3,045	1,035	3,767
P 030	1,123	48,371		0.0116	0.0115	0.0124		907	438	1,111		1,199	578	1,494
P 031	1,977	69,169		0.0170	0.0176	0.0177		1,119	1,415	1,782		1,678	2,148	2,711
P 032	6,013	123,818		0.0149	0.0155	0.0148		5,558	1,967	5,561		7,997	2,862	7,976
P 033	1,796	57,183		0.0114	0.0117	0.0115		1,666	609	1,821		2,191	806	2,403
P 034	445	37,640		0.0118	0.0127	0.0128		446	180	435		592	244	590
P 035	695	77,799		0.0159	0.0142	0.0162		600	367	618		881	512	914
P 036	980	53,423		0.0165	0.0164	0.0165		856	418	864		1,272	620	1,285
P 037	1,913	91,002		0.0179	0.0179	0.0185		1,619	522	1,687		2,470	798	2,607
P 038	570	50,616		0.0139	0.0142	0.0157		398	190	514		553	265	751

	A	BJ	BK	BL	BM	BN	BO	BP	BQ	BR	BS	BT	BU	BV	BW
		LA	Total $		Atl	NB	LA		Atl	NB	LA		Atl	NB	LA
1	Product	Avg@95	Avg@95		f(k) @ 99	f(k) @ 99	f(k) @ 99		SS @99	SS @99	SS @99		Avg @99	Avg @99	Avg @99
41	P 039	550	59,728		0.0147	0.0154	0.0132		417	226	532		596	329	728
42	P 040	1,879	43,228		0.0077	0.0058	0.0090		419	261	1,930		499	295	2,387
43	P 041	8,564	326,824		0.0110	0.0115	0.0100		6,831	4,458	9,050		8,923	5,887	11,421
44	P 042	1,014	38,017		0.0161	0.0170	0.0169		767	456	935		1,130	684	1,399
45	P 043	1,530	51,982		0.0155	0.0173	0.0176		808	1,270	1,382		1,176	1,916	2,099
46	P 044	2,344	70,687		0.0170	0.0177	0.0179		1,342	1,242	2,103		2,011	1,889	3,210
47	P 045	234	29,657		0.0159	0.0134	0.0154		282	164	213		414	225	309
48	P 046	840	53,069		0.0062	0.0092	0.0087		1,077	639	870		1,228	794	1,069
49	P 047	1,331	50,952		0.0115	0.0139	0.0113		1,260	721	1,357		1,664	999	1,783
50	P 048	5,015	129,218		0.0178	0.0177	0.0174		3,684	3,209	4,556		5,608	4,879	6,891
51	P 049	4,128	77,335		0.0119	0.0137	0.0130		3,591	1,974	4,019		4,775	2,727	5,467
52	P 050	1,386	55,877		0.0120	0.0174	0.0165		974	376	1,224		1,435	569	1,818
53	P 051	1,836	54,484		0.0155	0.0139	0.0143		1,978	842	1,719		2,639	1,167	2,442
54	P 052	4,226	98,668		0.0155	0.0175	0.0163		3,026	1,338	3,751		4,407	2,026	5,550
55	P 053	688	13,561		0.0165	0.0072	0.0157		310	509	620		451	597	907
56	P 054	948	37,803		0.0171	0.0161	0.0165		717	232	839		1,065	341	1,244
57	P 055	1,040	58,138		0.0164	0.0166	0.0168		763	419	961		1,146	624	1,436
58	P 056	930	56,212		0.0170	0.0176	0.0179		948	406	834		1,404	616	1,274
59	P 057	1,267	49,872		0.0136	0.0173	0.0175		1,307	428	1,149		1,962	646	1,740
60	P 058	3,810	74,028		0.0077	0.0151	0.0127		2,819	1,252	3,735		3,885	1,809	5,055
61	P 059	1,361	53,411		0.0229	0.0098	0.0090		1,252	1,628	1,400		1,494	2,050	1,730
62	P 060	205	11,469		0.0055	0.0248	0.0266		191	89	154		319	159	283
63	P 061	1,391	50,436		0.0156	0.0096	0.0127		289	1,563	1,364		325	1,956	1,845
64	P 062	615	26,087		0.0174	0.0170	0.0174		496	261	558		723	391	845
65	P 063	1,238	45,493		0.0150	0.0169	0.0116		423	201	1,251		641	300	1,655
66	P 064	3,347	73,663		0.0150	0.0152	0.0158		2,724	2,180	3,010		3,930	3,157	4,409
67	P 065	10,358	232,099		0.0175	0.0182	0.0183		7,237	3,731	9,189		10,960	5,728	14,142
68	P 066	484	52,883		0.0170	0.0166	0.0174		471	226	440		708	336	665
69	P 067	306	32,781		0.0145	0.0139	0.0160		256	136	274		364	188	402
70	P 068	720	30,130		0.0158	0.0169	0.0173		692	358	656		1,014	535	990
71	P 069	327	33,191		0.0174	0.0165	0.0180		326	146	293		493	216	448
72	P 070	479	21,549		0.0287	0.0258	0.0244		222	154	379		422	278	668
73	P 071	190	33,335		0.0140	0.0169	0.0167		112	112	176		155	167	262
74	P 072	675	30,909		0.0218	0.0253	0.0203		410	251	599		673	450	957
75	P 073	1,168	30,828		0.0125	0.0144	0.0132		1,091	540	1,132		1,471	769	1,545
76	P 074	912	47,713		0.0112	0.0119	0.0130		975	388	887		1,279	516	1,208
77	P 075	2,477	66,816		0.0169	0.0175	0.0160		1,599	1,303	2,218		2,395	1,976	3,260
78	P 076	941	26,605		0.0164	0.0164	0.0150		706	374	864		1,045	554	1,246

	A	BJ	BK	BL	BM	BN	BO	BP	BQ	BR	BS	BT	BU	BV	BW
1	Product	LA	Total $		Atl	NB	LA		Atl	NB	LA		Atl	NB	LA
2		Avg@95	Avg@95		f(k) @ 99	f(k) @ 99	f(k) @ 99		SS @99	SS @99	SS @99		Avg @99	Avg @99	Avg @99
79	P 077	2,930	75,334		0.0165	0.0172	0.0175		2,435	1,050	2,658		3,616	1,582	4,024
80	P 078	799	37,255		0.0158	0.0168	0.0171		885	530	731		1,295	791	1,100
81	P 079	256	25,271		0.0058	0.0037	0.0045		1,041	6	306		1,177	6	336
82	P 080	2,596	61,472		0.0136	0.0146	0.0141		2,496	925	2,588		3,440	1,322	3,602
83	P 081	1,252	38,947		0.0176	0.0182	0.0188		1,057	571	1,098		1,603	876	1,704
84	P 082	1,548	66,584		0.0100	0.0100	0.0088		2		1,598		2	2	1,969
85	P 083	3,174	63,170		0.0177	0.0176	0.0179		2,272	1,328	2,849		3,456	2,016	4,348
86	P 084	3,204	95,877		0.0172	0.0179	0.0178		3,043	1,326	2,886		4,583	2,023	4,392
87	P 085	1,893	241,420		0.0144	0.0146	0.0148		2,179	720	1,751		3,104	1,029	2,511
88	P 086	1,144	26,449		0.0169	0.0168	0.0119		574	337	1,147		860	504	1,526
89	P 087	1,222	28,973		0.0220	0.0193	0.0205		1,184	516	1,080		1,952	808	1,730
90	P 088	64	7,695		0.0051	0.0053	0.0055		100	53	76		111	59	85
91	P 089	376	45,125		0.0173	0.0182	0.0175		544	190	341		821	292	516
92	P 090	2,048	29,322		0.0210	0.0246	0.0247		2,238	933	1,611		3,619	1,651	2,854
93	P 091	1,182	99,587		0.0072	0.0081	0.0102		797	432	1,241		933	520	1,574
94	P 092	216	15,254		0.0244	0.0238	0.0234		109	92	167		192	161	290
95	P 093	2,794	54,242		0.0115	0.0125	0.0120		2,334	1,039	2,792		3,080	1,398	3,725
96	P 094	1,768	51,139		0.0166	0.0165	0.0170		1,568	741	1,626		2,333	1,101	2,438
97	P 095	1,457	47,823		0.0124	0.0065	0.0107		702	504	1,508		945	582	1,933
98	P 096	2,033	71,131		0.0109	0.0069	0.0102		1,333	946	2,134		1,714	1,101	2,707
99	P 097	949	36,586		0.0120	0.0132	0.0145		819	499	883		1,091	682	1,261
100	P 098	826	12,300		0.0156	0.0150	0.0134		855	246	796		1,248	354	1,092
101	P 099	178	15,893		0.0198	0.0205	0.0224		168	106	150		265	170	249
102	P 100	546	49,354		0.0164	0.0168	0.0172		601	234	499		891	350	751
103															
104		172,970	7,508,227						197,306				197,306	108,453	233,168

Western Pharm B Data.xls

	A	BX	BY	BZ	CA	CB	CC	CD	CE	CF	CG	CH	CI
1	Product	Total $ Avg @99		Sales @95	Sales @99	Incremental Margin	Incremental ICC @ 20	Contribution		OCT	Sales for 2 wk	Inv for 2 wk	Sales for 4 wk
3	P 001	693,757		9,481,407	9,880,624	99,804	34,868	64,936		2	9,980,429	519,417	
4	P 002	258,840		4,194,545	4,371,157	44,153	13,461	30,692		2	4,415,310	191,533	
5	P 003	140,696		1,088,862	1,134,709	11,462	7,056	4,406		2	1,146,170	105,415	
6	P 004	230,326		3,875,318	4,038,489	40,793	12,508	28,285		2	4,079,282	167,788	
7	P 005	107,024		1,464,099	1,525,745	15,412	5,609	9,803		2	1,541,157	78,981	
8	P 006	184,181		3,074,753	3,204,217	32,366	10,042	22,324		2	3,236,583	133,971	
9	P 007	52,602		237,429	247,426	2,499	2,382	117		4			249,926
10	P 008	63,028		302,047	314,765	3,179	3,124	55		4			317,944
11	P 009	298,065		3,886,279	4,049,912	40,908	15,065	25,843		2	4,090,820	222,737	
12	P 010	79,436		1,008,766	1,051,241	10,619	3,934	6,684		2	1,061,859	59,764	
13	P 011	149,600		1,398,183	1,457,054	14,718	7,510	7,207		2	1,471,772	112,049	
14	P 012	94,509		1,441,354	1,502,043	15,172	4,612	10,561		2	1,517,215	71,450	
15	P 013	143,111		2,353,426	2,452,517	24,773	7,372	17,401		2	2,477,290	106,251	
16	P 014	64,053		347,403	362,030	3,657	3,157	500		4			365,687
17	P 015	45,982		748,668	780,191	7,881	2,326	5,554		2	788,072	34,350	
18	P 016	186,532		3,132,025	3,263,899	32,969	10,140	22,829		2	3,296,868	135,831	
19	P 017	197,865		3,387,495	3,530,126	35,658	10,648	25,010		2	3,565,784	144,627	
20	P 018	127,270		2,065,320	2,152,280	21,740	6,433	15,307		2	2,174,021	95,103	
21	P 019	58,845		686,548	715,456	7,227	2,963	4,263		2	722,683	44,028	
22	P 020	171,917		2,416,471	2,518,217	25,437	8,748	16,689		2	2,543,654	128,179	
23	P 021	110,535		1,727,071	1,799,789	18,180	5,736	12,444		2	1,817,969	81,857	
24	P 022	105,299		1,542,993	1,607,961	16,242	5,515	10,727		2	1,624,203	77,724	
25	P 023	207,644		3,459,959	3,605,642	36,421	10,688	25,733		2	3,642,062	154,205	
26	P 024	87,196		1,436,424	1,496,905	15,120	4,341	10,779		2	1,512,025	65,491	
27	P 025	142,585		2,440,957	2,543,734	25,694	7,673	18,021		2	2,569,428	104,220	
28	P 026	141,863		2,315,142	2,412,622	24,370	7,622	16,748		2	2,436,992	103,755	
29	P 027	111,806		1,914,665	1,995,283	20,154	6,016	14,139		2	2,015,437	81,728	
30	P 028	52,105		831,404	866,411	8,752	2,657	6,095		2	875,162	38,821	
31	P 029	108,169		1,799,021	1,874,769	18,937	5,909	13,028		2	1,893,706	78,624	
32	P 030	64,521		793,911	827,339	8,357	3,230	5,127		2	835,696	48,371	
33	P 031	94,991		1,594,609	1,661,750	16,785	5,165	11,621		2	1,678,536	69,169	
34	P 032	164,041		2,473,768	2,577,927	26,040	8,045	17,995		2	2,603,966	123,818	
35	P 033	76,529		913,375	951,832	9,614	3,869	5,745		2	961,447	57,183	
36	P 034	50,051		633,196	659,857	6,665	2,482	4,183		2	666,522	37,640	
37	P 035	103,499		1,598,593	1,665,902	16,827	5,140	11,687		2	1,682,730	77,799	
38	P 036	70,073		1,131,235	1,178,866	11,908	3,330	8,578		2	1,190,773	53,423	
39	P 037	124,374		2,140,330	2,230,449	22,530	6,675	15,855		2	2,252,979	91,002	
40	P 038	68,531		1,007,213	1,049,622	10,602	3,583	7,019		2	1,060,224	50,616	

	A	BX	BY	BZ	CA	CB	CC	CD	CE	CF	CG	CH	CI
1													
2	Product	Total $ Avg @99		Sales @95	Sales @99	Incremental Margin	Incremental ICC @ 20	Contribution		OCT	Sales for 2 wk	Inv for 2 wk	Sales for 4 wk
41	P 039	79,064		1,129,614	1,177,177	11,891	3,867	8,024		2	1,189,068	59,728	
42	P 040	55,527		493,078	513,839	5,190	2,460	2,731		2	519,029	43,228	
43	P 041	428,869		4,758,935	4,959,311	50,094	20,409	29,685		2	5,009,405	326,824	
44	P 042	51,546		836,422	871,639	8,804	2,706	6,099		2	880,444	38,017	
45	P 043	70,752		1,165,629	1,214,709	12,270	3,754	8,516		2	1,226,978	51,982	
46	P 044	97,018		1,633,683	1,702,470	17,197	5,266	11,930		2	1,719,666	70,687	
47	P 045	39,115		589,938	614,778	6,210	1,892	4,318		2	620,988	29,657	
48	P 046	70,782		285,470	297,490	3,005	3,543	-538		4			300,495
49	P 047	68,785		846,831	882,487	8,914	3,567	5,347		2	891,401	50,952	
50	P 048	177,327		2,998,321	3,114,145	31,456	9,622	21,834		2	3,145,601	129,218	
51	P 049	103,775		1,338,098	1,394,439	14,085	5,288	8,797		2	1,408,524	77,335	
52	P 050	73,852		1,192,185	1,242,382	12,549	3,595	8,954		2	1,254,932	55,877	
53	P 051	73,133		988,670	1,030,298	10,407	3,730	6,677		2	1,040,705	54,484	
54	P 052	130,790		2,085,238	2,173,037	21,950	6,425	15,525		2	2,194,987	98,668	
55	P 053	17,899		116,600	121,509	1,227	868	360		4			122,736
56	P 054	49,610		798,099	831,703	8,401	2,361	6,040		2	840,104	37,803	
57	P 055	79,367		1,300,646	1,355,410	13,691	4,246	9,445		2	1,369,101	58,138	
58	P 056	75,613		1,254,192	1,307,000	13,202	3,880	9,322		2	1,320,202	56,212	
59	P 057	68,605		1,141,636	1,189,705	12,017	3,747	8,271		2	1,201,722	49,872	
60	P 058	97,963		1,325,299	1,381,102	13,951	4,787	9,163		2	1,395,052	74,028	
61	P 059	70,149		326,222	339,957	3,434	3,348	86		4			343,391
62	P 060	15,890		168,288	175,373	1,771	884	887		4			177,145
63	P 061	67,147		732,167	762,995	7,707	3,342	4,365		2	770,702	50,436	
64	P 062	35,323		573,802	597,962	6,040	1,847	4,193		2	604,002	26,087	
65	P 063	61,452		842,441	877,912	8,868	3,192	5,676		2	886,780	45,493	
66	P 064	97,308		1,497,430	1,560,480	15,762	4,729	11,033		2	1,576,242	73,663	
67	P 065	317,601		5,431,644	5,660,344	57,175	17,101	40,075		2	5,717,520	232,099	
68	P 066	72,066		1,191,302	1,241,463	12,540	3,837	8,703		2	1,254,003	52,883	
69	P 067	43,770		655,496	683,096	6,900	2,198	4,702		2	689,995	32,781	
70	P 068	40,745		660,915	688,743	6,957	2,123	4,834		2	695,700	30,130	
71	P 069	45,144		755,894	787,721	7,957	2,391	5,566		2	795,678	33,191	
72	P 070	30,187		334,055	348,121	3,516	1,728	1,789		4			351,637
73	P 071	46,095		721,992	752,392	7,600	2,552	5,048		2	759,992	33,335	
74	P 072	43,447		423,120	440,935	4,454	2,508	1,946		4			445,389
75	P 073	40,895		545,263	568,222	5,740	2,013	3,726		2	573,961	30,828	
76	P 074	63,594		788,073	821,255	8,296	3,176	5,119		2	829,551	47,713	
77	P 075	90,196		1,465,772	1,527,488	15,429	4,676	10,753		2	1,542,918	66,816	
78	P 076	35,056		548,886	571,997	5,778	1,690	4,088		2	577,775	26,605	

Western Pharm B Data.xls

	A	BX	BY	BZ	CA	CB	CC	CD	CE	CF	CG	CH	CI
1	Product	Total $		Sales	Sales	Incremental	Incremental	Contribution		OCT	Sales	Inv	Sales
2		Avg @99		@95	@99	Margin	ICC @ 20				for 2 wk	for 2 wk	for 4 wk
79	P 077	101,632		1,676,160	1,746,735	17,644	5,260	12,384		2	1,764,379	75,334	
80	P 078	50,411		813,188	847,428	8,560	2,631	5,929		2	855,988	37,255	
81	P 079	33,271		89,941	93,728	947	1,600	-653		4			94,675
82	P 080	82,939		1,153,667	1,202,242	12,144	4,294	7,850		2	1,214,386	61,472	
83	P 081	53,230		916,046	954,617	9,643	2,857	6,786		2	964,259	38,947	
84	P 082	84,672		790,982	824,286	8,326	3,618	4,708		2	832,613	66,584	
85	P 083	86,587		1,468,024	1,529,836	15,453	4,683	10,770		2	1,545,289	63,170	
86	P 084	131,629		2,213,247	2,306,436	23,297	7,150	16,147		2	2,329,733	95,877	
87	P 085	320,599		4,755,178	4,955,396	50,055	15,836	34,219		2	5,005,450	241,420	
88	P 086	35,851		509,228	530,670	5,360	1,880	3,480		2	536,030	26,449	
89	P 087	40,494		381,143	397,191	4,012	2,304	1,708		4			401,203
90	P 088	10,173		26,869	28,001	283	496	-213		4			28,284
91	P 089	61,953		1,041,523	1,085,377	10,963	3,366	7,598		2	1,096,340	45,125	
92	P 090	41,082		417,365	434,939	4,393	2,352	2,041		4			439,332
93	P 091	132,363		1,200,854	1,251,416	12,641	6,555	6,085		2	1,264,057	99,587	
94	P 092	20,654		217,652	226,816	2,291	1,080	1,211		4			229,107
95	P 093	72,372		888,365	925,770	9,351	3,626	5,725		2	935,121	54,242	
96	P 094	68,445		1,114,951	1,161,896	11,736	3,461	8,275		2	1,173,632	51,139	
97	P 095	63,502		676,149	704,618	7,117	3,136	3,982		2	711,735	47,823	
98	P 096	94,489		937,678	977,159	9,870	4,672	5,199		2	987,029	71,131	
99	P 097	48,621		329,738	343,621	3,471	2,407	1,064		4			347,092
100	P 098	16,243		118,691	123,688	1,249	789	461		4			124,938
101	P 099	21,980		206,754	215,459	2,176	1,218	959		4			217,635
102	P 100	66,506		1,086,103	1,131,834	11,433	3,431	8,002		2	1,143,267	49,354	
103													
104		10,096,607		143,305,106	149,339,005	1,508,475	517,676	990,799			146,290,863	7,016,597	4,556,617

	A	CJ	CK	CL	CM	CN	CO	CP	CQ	CR	CS	CT	CU
1	Product	Inv		Combined	Combined	Combined	Comb	Comb	Comb	Comb		Sum of	Inventory $
2		for 4 wk		Dmd Sigma	Sigma	OQ	f(k) @ 95	SS @ 95	Inv	Inv $		Inv $	Difference
3	P 001			226	554	906	0.0817	610	1,063	450,258		519,417	-69,159
4	P 002			565	2,096	3,876	0.0924	2,096	4,034	176,766		191,533	-14,767
5	P 003			395	622	545	0.0438	870	1,143	92,466		105,415	-12,949
6	P 004			385	1,739	3,304	0.0950	1,739	3,391	161,039		167,788	-6,749
7	P 005			1,693	4,349	7,260	0.0835	4,349	7,979	65,142		78,981	-13,838
8	P 006			431	1,869	3,534	0.0945	1,869	3,636	128,081		133,971	-5,890
9	P 007	40,693		210	447	613	0.0686	536	842	26,436		40,693	-14,257
10	P 008	47,407		592	1,267	1,811	0.0715	1,394	2,299	31,050		47,407	-16,356
11	P 009			767	1,842	2,979	0.0808	2,027	3,516	185,711		222,737	-37,027
12	P 010			772	1,786	2,827	0.0791	1,965	3,378	48,804		59,764	-10,960
13	P 011			390	670	758	0.0566	804	1,183	88,296		112,049	-23,753
14	P 012			1,252	3,825	6,781	0.0886	3,825	7,216	62,095		71,450	-9,356
15	P 013			401	1,573	2,935	0.0933	1,573	3,041	98,721		106,251	-7,530
16	P 014	48,268		227	497	803	0.0808	547	948	33,204		48,268	-15,064
17	P 015			126	475	881	0.0927	475	916	31,503		34,350	-2,847
18	P 016			394	1,746	3,309	0.0948	1,746	3,400	130,302		135,831	-5,529
19	P 017			1,834	9,388	18,045	0.0961	9,388	18,411	139,924		144,627	-4,703
20	P 018			273	1,044	1,939	0.0929	1,044	2,013	86,804		95,103	-8,298
21	P 019			439	939	1,409	0.0750	1,033	1,738	34,278		44,028	-9,751
22	P 020			142	394	679	0.0861	394	734	105,738		128,179	-22,442
23	P 021			548	1,664	2,945	0.0885	1,664	3,136	74,465		81,857	-7,393
24	P 022			119	356	628	0.0880	356	670	66,711		77,724	-11,013
25	P 023			227	975	1,841	0.0944	975	1,896	144,232		154,205	-9,973
26	P 024			1,460	6,112	11,507	0.0941	6,112	11,866	59,970		65,491	-5,521
27	P 025			522	2,596	4,978	0.0959	2,596	5,085	100,949		104,220	-3,271
28	P 026			448	1,745	3,252	0.0932	1,745	3,371	97,163		103,755	-6,591
29	P 027			578	3,044	5,864	0.0963	3,044	5,976	78,994		81,728	-2,734
30	P 028			113	385	701	0.0909	385	736	35,341		38,821	-3,481
31	P 029			699	2,821	5,283	0.0937	2,821	5,462	75,302		78,624	-3,323
32	P 030			471	1,052	1,629	0.0774	1,157	1,972	38,899		48,371	-9,472
33	P 031			506	2,334	4,443	0.0952	2,334	4,555	66,190		69,169	-2,979
34	P 032			2,252	6,573	11,500	0.0875	6,573	12,323	107,322		123,818	-16,496
35	P 033			819	1,744	2,609	0.0748	1,919	3,223	45,682		57,183	-11,501
36	P 034			200	462	730	0.0790	508	873	30,658		37,640	-6,982
37	P 035			236	795	1,442	0.0908	795	1,516	68,014		77,799	-9,785
38	P 036			302	1,122	2,076	0.0925	1,122	2,160	47,660		53,423	-5,763
39	P 037			412	2,128	4,093	0.0962	2,128	4,174	88,373		91,002	-2,629
40	P 038			181	533	934	0.0877	533	999	43,644		50,616	-6,972

	A	CJ	CK	CL	CM	CN	CO	CP	CQ	CR	CS	CT	CU
1	Product	Inv for 4 wk		Combined Dmd Sigma	Combined Sigma	Combined OQ	Comb f(k) @ 95	Comb SS @ 95	Comb Inv	Comb Inv $		Sum of Inv $	Inventory Difference
41	P 039			205	559	956	0.0855	559	1,037	49,606		59,728	-10,122
42	P 040			661	1,096	1,144	0.0522	1,425	1,997	34,844		43,228	-8,385
43	P 041			3,948	8,118	11,784	0.0726	8,930	14,822	242,329		326,824	-84,495
44	P 042			298	1,137	2,111	0.0928	1,137	2,192	35,168		38,017	-2,849
45	P 043			435	1,837	3,463	0.0942	1,837	3,568	48,635		51,982	-3,347
46	P 044			545	2,544	4,848	0.0953	2,544	4,967	67,775		70,687	-2,912
47	P 045			102	324	579	0.0894	324	613	25,298		29,657	-4,360
48	P 046	53,069		368	778	1,009	0.0649	933	1,438	32,926		53,069	-20,143
49	P 047			631	1,423	2,216	0.0779	1,565	2,673	41,358		50,952	-9,594
50	P 048			1,323	6,217	11,857	0.0954	6,217	12,145	123,928		129,218	-5,291
51	P 049			1,747	4,191	6,770	0.0808	4,610	7,995	63,971		77,335	-13,363
52	P 050			381	1,360	2,498	0.0918	1,360	2,609	50,421		55,877	-5,456
53	P 051			831	2,075	3,420	0.0824	2,283	3,993	46,728		54,484	-7,756
54	P 052			1,233	4,242	7,734	0.0912	4,242	8,109	88,515		98,668	-10,153
55	P 053	13,561		222	514	1,031	0.1003	514	1,030	9,427		13,561	-4,135
56	P 054			267	942	1,727	0.0916	942	1,806	33,787		37,803	-4,015
57	P 055			289	1,139	2,127	0.0934	1,139	2,203	54,529		58,138	-3,609
58	P 056			285	1,177	2,212	0.0939	1,177	2,283	52,415		56,212	-3,797
59	P 057			377	1,559	2,930	0.0940	1,559	3,024	47,705		49,872	-2,168
60	P 058			1,433	3,574	5,887	0.0824	3,931	6,875	62,658		74,028	-11,369
61	P 059	53,411		629	1,353	1,986	0.0734	1,488	2,481	33,000		53,411	-20,410
62	P 060	11,469		62	205	652	0.1588	144	470	9,816		11,469	-1,653
63	P 061			663	1,308	1,821	0.0696	1,438	2,349	38,229		50,436	-12,207
64	P 062			181	693	1,288	0.0929	693	1,337	24,118		26,087	-1,969
65	P 063			412	926	1,441	0.0778	1,019	1,739	41,180		45,493	-4,314
66	P 064			1,222	3,976	7,162	0.0901	3,976	7,557	63,967		73,663	-9,695
67	P 065			2,211	11,122	21,346	0.0960	11,122	21,795	224,524		232,099	-7,575
68	P 066			146	608	1,144	0.0940	608	1,180	49,757		52,883	-3,126
69	P 067			108	327	579	0.0885	327	617	28,263		32,781	-4,518
70	P 068			236	898	1,668	0.0928	898	1,732	27,794		30,130	-2,336
71	P 069			92	414	785	0.0949	414	806	31,431		33,191	-1,760
72	P 070	21,549		112	379	1,226	0.1616	265	878	19,382		21,549	-2,167
73	P 071			57	202	371	0.0918	202	387	30,537		33,335	-2,798
74	P 072	30,909		192	562	1,640	0.1459	393	1,214	25,347		30,909	-5,562
75	P 073			498	1,241	2,043	0.0823	1,365	2,387	25,789		30,828	-5,039
76	P 074			431	969	1,507	0.0778	1,066	1,819	38,515		47,713	-9,198
77	P 075			708	2,703	5,020	0.0929	2,703	5,213	61,619		66,816	-5,198
78	P 076			304	999	1,804	0.0903	999	1,901	23,422		26,605	-3,182

Western Pharm B Data.xls

	A	CJ	CK	CL	CM	CN	CO	CP	CQ	CR	CS	CT	CU
1	Product	Inv		Combined	Combined	Combined	Comb	Comb	Comb	Comb		Sum of	Inventory $
2		for 4 wk		Dmd Sigma	Sigma	OQ	f(k) @ 95	SS @ 95	Inv	Inv $		Inv $	Difference
79	P 077			817	3,289	6,158	0.0936	3,289	6,368	70,171		75,334	-5,163
80	P 078			300	1,124	2,081	0.0926	1,124	2,164	34,242		37,255	-3,013
81	P 079	25,271		243	493	332	0.0337	740	906	19,859		25,271	-5,412
82	P 080			1,051	2,785	4,710	0.0846	2,785	5,140	50,971		61,472	-10,501
83	P 081			281	1,511	2,915	0.0965	1,511	2,968	37,765		38,947	-1,183
84	P 082			534	842	744	0.0442	1,178	1,551	66,525		66,584	-58
85	P 083			737	3,527	6,740	0.0955	3,527	6,897	60,823		63,170	-2,347
86	P 084			885	3,948	7,488	0.0948	3,948	7,691	92,043		95,877	-3,834
87	P 085			822	2,309	3,990	0.0864	2,309	4,304	207,682		241,420	-33,737
88	P 086			391	998	1,661	0.0832	1,098	1,929	23,935		26,449	-2,514
89	P 087	28,973		420	1,199	3,422	0.1427	959	2,670	24,081		28,973	-4,892
90	P 088	7,695		31	63	55	0.0436	88	115	4,583		7,695	-3,112
91	P 089			136	587	1,109	0.0945	587	1,141	43,402		45,125	-1,723
92	P 090	29,322		724	2,211	6,683	0.1511	1,547	4,889	24,723		29,322	-4,600
93	P 091			490	889	1,112	0.0625	1,067	1,622	70,960		99,587	-28,627
94	P 092	15,254		55	176	548	0.1556	123	398	12,775		15,254	-2,479
95	P 093			1,197	2,649	4,077	0.0769	2,914	4,953	43,694		54,242	-10,548
96	P 094			540	2,081	3,872	0.0930	2,081	4,017	46,831		51,139	-4,307
97	P 095			545	1,072	1,491	0.0695	1,180	1,925	35,341		47,823	-12,482
98	P 096			854	1,640	2,218	0.0676	1,968	3,077	52,654		71,131	-18,477
99	P 097	36,586		350	815	1,666	0.1022	734	1,567	25,107		36,586	-11,479
100	P 098	12,300		319	751	1,594	0.1060	676	1,473	8,884		12,300	-3,416
101	P 099	15,893		62	180	521	0.1445	126	387	12,426		15,893	-3,467
102	P 100			185	709	1,317	0.0929	709	1,367	45,644		49,354	-3,709
103													
104		491,630							351,637	6,570,018		7,508,227	-938,209

Case 10

Woodson Chemical Company

Overview

In a market where products are commodity-like, customer service offers a prime way to set yourself apart. The case indicates that differentiation can be achieved through quick and accurate performance of order cycles. To shorten and improve order cycles, availability of timely information is a necessity. this case illustrates the advantage of having smooth, consistent information flows to complement inventory flows, and even supplant inventory in many cases.

To successfully implement the integration strategy, information availability throughout the supply chain and perhaps across divisions will be necessary. Students should be able to address key issues confronting Woodson Chemical and identify potential opportunities.

Solutions to Questions

1. Critical issues may include but are not limited to the following:

    • Sales across most divisions are leveling off or falling

    • The company is trying to reverse downward sales trend by improving customer service -- how is this to be accomplished?

    • Management and communications bottlenecks with expanded operations

    • The company believes that efficiency and effectiveness improvements can be achieved through integration -- which is only possible with information technology

    • Woodson Chemical might serve "common" customers by merging resources

2. The text of the case cites that competitive advantage in the industry is gained "from a focused market position, good raw materials supply..., and a lean efficient organizational structure." Students are encouraged to consider a number of possible changes or provide explanation why the current approach is acceptable. Reasonable options may include integration within WCC divisions and across the supply chain. Joining forces with other divisions as well as

with supply chain partners might develop synergism and greater efficiency in resource utilization. Alliances with suppliers and/or transportation providers would ensure that the stream of inputs and delivery of goods meet demands. Locking into long-term, trusting relationships with customers would allow for better planning and smoother operations. Any of these close relationships will rely on improved communications and information technology among participants.

3.   The perceived risks and benefits depend on the specific changes students determined in question 2 above, but a short list of general risks and benefits among the parties might include:

a) WCC North America corporate management:

Risks	Benefits
•Loss associated with failure: loss of investment, competitive position, employee faith	• Potential competitive advantage • Improved worker morale and support • Better relationships across divisions and supply chain

b) WCC North America line distribution management:

Risks	Benefits
• Having to "correct" operations and regain workers' confidence if the plan fails given that people are generally adverse to change	• Greater certainty in demand with closer relationships with customers and better information technologies • Less uncertainty with regard to supply given closer relationships with suppliers and transportation providers

c) WCC North America customers:

Risks	Benefits
• Close relationships often entail disclosing "trade secrets" or availability, information that would be very valuable to competitors	• Better service through trusting relationship with less uncertainty in product quicker response, and higher fill rates

4.   Briefly, under ideal circumstances, costs would lower while service improves. Lower cost would lead to higher margins. Better service should generate greater sales -- improving the bottom line.

5.   Basically, all cooperative participants must be "on the same page" with regard to information capabilities and willingness to share information -- that is, participants must be able to effectively communicate across functions and channel levels to better serve one another. Suppliers may need to "see" the inventory status and sales data of customers. Likewise, customers would like to check materials availability and shipment progress. Again, before any of this information can be transferred and shared, all parties must agree to cooperate given the risks and benefits of close supply chain arrangements.

6.   Ms. Sanders is not the foremost authority of the company's problems though she should have an idea of current issues. As her brief biography notes, she has held a number of positions with the company over the past six years -- many of which allow for immediate contact with the customer. It is from this customer contact that makes identifying problems easy. Good customers not only inform you when you are doing your job well but also when there is need for improvement. Her only limitation might be that her current perspective is from only one of Woodson's three North American divisions. So long as she is aware of issues and concerns from other divisions, Melinda should be able to contribute to any corporate-wide discussions for improvement.

7.   WCC may be experiencing similar problems outside of North America. The case text cites that one-third of the corporation's business is conducted overseas. Though the exact dispersion of international sales is not described, it is likely that the operations span national boundaries, creating a need for sound communications with suppliers and customers as well as among the various processing facilities. There are a number of issues that must be considered when communications cross national boundaries. There are cultural differences that must be observed and adhered to. Also, there is the possibility that channel partners in many countries do not have the ability to monitor the status of their own processes, thereby not making information sharing even a possibility. When information is available, it may not be in an acceptable, transferable form. Therefore, it is easy to see that conducting business across global regions creates several additional dimensions to the problem.

Case 11
Performance Control

Overview

This case illustrates a very good point: It is important to know where your costs and profits come from. Products and customers that are unprofitable will not overcome the problem through greater volume! In the Happy Chips, Inc. case, Wendell Worthman has been prompted to examine the contributions of its three primary customer types as a result of the latest demands of Buy 4 Less. Though a crisis is often necessary to initiate reexamination of the business, determining whom you should serve and at what expense provides crucial insight. Gathering information and regularly assessing products, services, and customers should become common practice in the successful firm.

A lack of accurate, timely information is the most significant barrier to performing activity-based costing or segment profitability analysis. For this case, information is provided to develop the segment analysis. Students are encouraged to utilize a computer spreadsheet application (such as Microsoft Excel) to perform the analysis.

Solutions to Questions

1.   **Activity-based costing** allocates operational costs by the processes that create them. **Segment profitability analysis** breaks down costs according to customers that demand the good or service. Only costs relevant to a particular customer or customer type should serve as input in segment analysis. The best alternative is to perform both activity-based costing and segment profitability analysis.

Segment profitability analysis clarifies which customers are profitable (attractive) and which ones are unprofitable (unattractive).

The segment profitability report on the next page helps to illuminate Happy Chips' attractive segments.

Happy Chips, Inc.
Segment Profitability Report

Retail Accounts:	GROCERY	DRUG	MASS MERCHANDISE
Unit Sales	40,000	18000	22000
Trade Price	$1.90	$2.30	$1.50
Revenue	**$ 76,000.00**	**$ 41,400.00**	**$ 33,000.00**
Total COGS	$84,000.00	$84,000.00	$84,000.00
COGS/unit	$ 1.05	$1.05	$1.05
Unit Sales/segment	40,000	18,000	22,000
Labeling cost	0	0	5,660.00
COGS/segment	**$ 42,000.00**	**$ 18,900.00**	**$ 23,100.00**
Net Margin	**$ 34,000.00**	**$ 22,500.00**	**$ 4,240.00**
Controllable Fixed Costs:			
Stocking Cost	$ 6,739.20	$ 2,433.60	$ 1,310.40
Information Cost	$ 1,000.00	$ 8,000.00	$ 1,000.00
Delivery Cost	$ 18,720.00	$ 10,140.00	$ 2,808.00
Total Controllable Fixed Costs:	**$ 26,459.20**	**$ 20,573.60**	**$ 5,118.40**
Profit/segment	**$ 7,540.80**	**$ 1,926.40**	**$ (878.40)**

* Stocking Cost and Delivery Cost for each segment is the product of :

Cost/delivery x deliveries/year x number of retail locations served

Grocery's Stocking Cost example:

$1.80 x 2 deliveries/week x 52 weeks x 36 grocery locations = $6,739.20

Grocery's Delivery Cost example:

$5.00 x 2 deliveries/week x 52 weeks x 36 grocery locations = $18,720.00

2.   As the segment profitability report indicates, Happy Chips is already losing money on the Buy 4 Less (mass merchandise) business. Given that Buy 4 Less' new demands require higher levels of service (more frequent delivery and automated order inquiry) at lower product prices, Happy Chips should not accept the changes. It would only make an unprofitable segment more costly. Happy Chips should perhaps consider improving its service but at a price that covers costs.

3.   The segment profitability report shows that the grocery and drug segments are profitable and should continue. Unless profits can be managed with the mass merchandise business it should be eliminated.

4.   First, look at the effect of higher price on revenues for the mass merchandise segment:

Current trade price: $1.50/unit
New trade price: $1.50/unit x 1.20 = $1.80

Revenue at current volume: 22,000 units x $1.80/unit   = $39,600.00
Total cost of serving segment: $23,100 + $5,660 + $5,118.40 = $33,878.40
Segment profit: $ 5,721.60

Assuming that sales volume remains unchanged, raising the price by 20% makes serving the mass merchandiser profitable. Rather than incurring a loss of $878.40, Happy Chips earns a profit of $5,721.60. Therefore, the response to question 4 is different than that of question 3.

5.   There are a number of potential considerations aside from segment profitability. The following are a just a few possible considerations. It may be that selling an unprofitable product or serving an unprofitable segment promotes sales to other areas where profits can be made. Refusing to serve a customer may have negative implications on other customers that Happy Chips serves. It may be that third parties can provide logistics services at a lower cost. Most importantly, however, Happy Chips should determine how it can make mass merchandise sales profitable.

Case 12

Managing Change in Wholesaling:
The Case of Wilmont Drug Company

Overview

Change is essential for a firm to maintain or achieve market leadership in any industry. However, effort towards change is perhaps the most difficult mission for any organization to accomplish. Unfortunately, the initiator of change is often viewed in a villainous light. In fact, many organizations seek outside sources to introduce the change movement so that "blame" is placed outside the firm.

In the Wilmont Drug Company case, Charlie Smith has the responsibility of introducing and developing the model for change, promoting a strategy of customer segmentation. Students are encouraged to critically evaluate the model, identify issues of concern, and determine how a chosen plan can best be implemented.

Solutions to Questions

1. Internal and external influences may include but are not limited to the following:

Internal Influences

- The cost of providing high service to all customers has become too great

- Wilmont's disjointed network design fails to efficiently allow for uniform service throughout the national market

- Firms often find themselves complacent despite consistent signs of decline

External Influences

- The competitive environment changed dramatically out of events such as transportation deregulation and technological advancements, creating a favorable cost/service relationship for "companies with both efficient and effective customer service strategies"

- All customers apparently do not value the high level service package offered by Wilmont enough to pay for it

- The idea that if Wilmont fails to assume leadership in the new environment a competitor is sure to do so

2.   The model is sound in that it seeks to gain control of internal operations before implementing the customer segmentation strategy. However, there is little mention of how the new basic service will be defined during the cost effectiveness stage -- that is, it might be wise to seek customer input before determining exactly which services should be offered to which customers. In addition, a clearer time line with specific micro-management issues might be reasonably requested upon initial approval. Otherwise, there seems to be a natural transition with regard to developing close relations with a set of customers and working toward systems integration. Again, students are encouraged to identify any deficient or unclear areas.

3.   It would be important for management to realized the cultural differences across Though change is important in most business cultures the means of achieving change can vary substantially. In addition, Charlie Smith's drive for customer segmentation may not be feasible in localities outside the U.S. Wilmont would have to identify possible limitations toward achieving change in each foreign market.

4.   Students must first determine a way to sell the idea to upper management. It is imperative for any change effort to have support at the top. Upon gaining upper management's confidence, leaders must figure out how to make change happen on the operational level. Students should provide clear guidelines for implementation with arguments for how and why the strategy will work.

Case 13

Dream Beauty

Overview

Dream Beauty is a case setting to apply the concepts of segmental costing and margin, activity based costing, and the strategic profit model. The case provides revenue and cost data for three distribution channels and limited individual accounts. The specific answers are provided in the accompanying Powerpoint presentation. This is the used as a basis for class discussion to illustrate segmental costing and profitability analysis.

Solutions to Questions

Slide 2 provides a segmental profitability summary for Retail, Convenience stores (C-Stores), and Mass Merchants. All costs are assigned based on percent of revenue thus resulting in an equal contribution of all segments. This is clearly inappropriate as the activities to serve each segment are quite different.

Slide 3 uses more appropriate drivers for assigning costs. COGS are assigned based on percentage of revenue. Ordering and delivery costs are assigned based on the number of orders. Packaging costs are assigned based on the number of packages. Labeling cost is assigned only to the mass merchants since that is the only segment that uses it. The resulting segmental contribution reveals a very different story as the C-Store segment is clearly loosing money while the retail and mass merchant segment is very profitable. The major reason is that C-Stores require substantially more orders and resulting deliveries. Another cost category that could be included is inventory carrying cost. However, it has not been included here since it is difficult to assign specific products to segments.

Since the C-Store segment is not profitable, there obviously needs to be some action taken to remedy the situation. The alternatives could include dropping the segment from service, increasing the price, or investigating the segment further to determine if it is a generic problem or if it can be isolated to specific accounts. Slide 4 summarizes the gross margin (Sales – COGS) for each C-Store. At the gross margin level, all the stores appear to be profitable. However, when the ordering, packaging, and delivery costs are assigned based on the number of orders and packages (Slide 5), it becomes clear that there are four profitable accounts and nine accounts that have a negative contribution (Slide 6). This demonstrates how logistics cost can influence account profitability. This obvious point is that there needs to be some action with the unprofitable accounts in the C-Store segment to either increase their revenue, decrease the cost of serving them, or stop serving them. Slide 7 summarizes these options.

While Slide 3 provides an accurate assessment of segmental profitability, it does not reflect the differences in the asset requirements to achieve such profitability. Slides 8-10 provide a strategic profit model summary for each of the segments. The operating costs are taken from the previous analyses. The strategic profit model (discussed in Chapter Eighteen) includes the relevant assets for each segment. The specific assets include the inventory (based on the turns for each segment), accounts receivable (based on days of receivables), and other fixed assets such as the labeler. Since the labeler is only used for the mass merchant segment, it is only included as an asset for the segment. The strategic profit analysis has also assigned inventory carrying cost (at 20% annually) to the operating costs for each segment. The point needs to be made that these return-on-assets appear to be extremely high because there is no overhead assigned to each segment. A review of the return-on-assets demonstrates that while the mass merchants had the highest profit contribution, it does not provide the highest return-on-assets due to the labeler. This illustrates how logistics assets including inventory, accounts receivable, and equipment can impact the return-on-assets for key segments.

Dream Beauty
Case Solution

DREAM BEAUTY

(2)

Current Assignment of Costs
(000')

Segment	Retail	C-Stores	Mass Merchants	Total
Sales	$65,000	$39,000	$26,000	$130,000
COGS	$26,000	$15,600	$10,400	$52,000
Gross Margin	$39,000	$23,400	$15,600	$78,000
Ordering Costs	$5,000	$3,000	$2,000	$10,000
Packaging Costs	$4,000	$2,400	$1,600	$8,000
Labeling Costs	$1,000	$600	$400	$2,000
Delivery Costs	$15,000	$9,000	$6,000	$30,000
Total Logistics Cost	$25,000	$15,000	$10,000	$50,000
Segment Profit	$14,000	$8,400	$5,600	$28,000
% Contribution	22%	22%	22%	22%

Dream Beauty–Activity Based Analysis (3)

(000') Segment	Retail	C-Stores	Mass Merchants	Total
Sales	$65,000	$39,000	$26,000	$130,000
COGS	$26,000	$15,600	$10,400	$52,000
Gross Margin	$39,000	$23,400	$15,600	$78,000
Ordering Costs	$2,777	$6,944	$277	$10,000
Packaging Costs	$3,200	$4,400	$400	$8,000
Labeling Costs	$0	$0	$2,000	$2,000
Delivery Costs	$8,333	$20,833	$833	$30,000
Total Logistics Cost	$14,311	$32,177	$3,511	$50,000
Segment Profit	$24,688	($8,777)	$12,089	$28,000
% Contribution	38%	-23%	46%	22%

Customer Analysis

C-Stores
(000')

Store Name	Sales	COGS	G. Margin	T. Cost	Profit/Store
Cosmo Naturelle	$3,500	$1,400	$2,100		
La Belle Femme	$5,000	$2,000	$3,000		
Beautyss Bliss	$10,000	$4,000	$6,000		
Looking Good	$1,500	$600	$900		
Love Your Style	$5,000	$2,000	$3,000		
Nuttin Homely	$1,000	$400	$600		
Make-up Galore	$2,000	$800	$1,200		
Wild by Nature	$3,000	$1,200	$1,800		
Beautee Fatale	$1,000	$400	$600		
Fruity Beauty	$1,500	$600	$900		
L'Air Du Jour	$1,000	$400	$600		
Tuti Fruity	$2,000	$800	$1,200		
Le Beau Monsieur	$2,500	$1,000	$1,500		
Totals	$39,000	$15,600	$23,400		

Customer Analysis

C-Stores

Order Cost:	$6,944
Packaging Cost:	$4,400
Delivery Cost:	$20,833

Store Name	Orders	Pcking	Dlvry	(000') Orders $	Pcking $	Dlvry $	T. Cost
Love Your Style	300	50	300	$833	$200	$2,499	$3,533
Looking Good	75	10	75	$208	$40	$624	$873
Wild by Nature	200	100	200	$555	$400	$1,666	$2,622
Beautyss Bliss	450	150	450	$1,249	$600	$3,749	$5,599
Cosmo Naturelle	60	30	60	$166	$120	$499	$786
Beautee Fatale	100	100	100	$277	$400	$833	$1,511
La Belle Femme	200	20	200	$555	$80	$1,666	$2,302
Le Beau Monsieur	320	200	320	$888	$800	$2,666	$4,355
Fruity Beauty	120	120	120	$333	$480	$999	$1,813
Tuti Fruity	250	200	250	$694	$800	$2,083	$3,577
L'Air Du Jour	150	75	150	$416	$300	$1,249	$1,966
Make-up Galore	175	10	175	$486	$40	$1,458	$1,984
Nuttin Homely	100	35	100	$277	$140	$833	$1,251
Totals	2,500	1,100	2,500	$6,944	$4,400	$20,833	$32,177

Customer Analysis

C-Stores
(000')

Store Name	Sales	COGS	G. Margin		T. Cost	Profit/Store
Cosmo Naturelle	$3,500	$1,400	$2,100		$786	**$1,313**
La Belle Femme	$5,000	$2,000	$3,000		$2,302	**$697**
Beautyss Bliss	$10,000	$4,000	$6,000		$5,599	**$400**
Looking Good	$1,500	$600	$900		$873	**$26**
Love Your Style	$5,000	$2,000	$3,000		$3,533	($533)
Nuttin Homely	$1,000	$400	$600		$1,251	($651)
Make-up Galore	$2,000	$800	$1,200		$1,984	($784)
Wild by Nature	$3,000	$1,200	$1,800		$2,622	($822)
Beautee Fatale	$1,000	$400	$600		$1,511	($911)
Fruity Beauty	$1,500	$600	$900		$1,813	($913)
L'Air Du Jour	$1,000	$400	$600		$1,966	($1,366)
Tuti Fruity	$2,000	$800	$1,200		$3,577	($2,377)
Le Beau Monsieur	$2,500	$1,000	$1,500		$4,355	($2,855)
Totals	$39,000	$15,600	$23,400		$32,172	($8,776)

Pareto Results

- Keep as Customers:
  - Looking Good
  - Beautyss Bliss
  - Cosmo Naturelle
  - La Belle Femme
- Get rid of the rest, or increase Ordering, Packaging, and Delivery charges.

Profitability Analysis -- Retail (8)

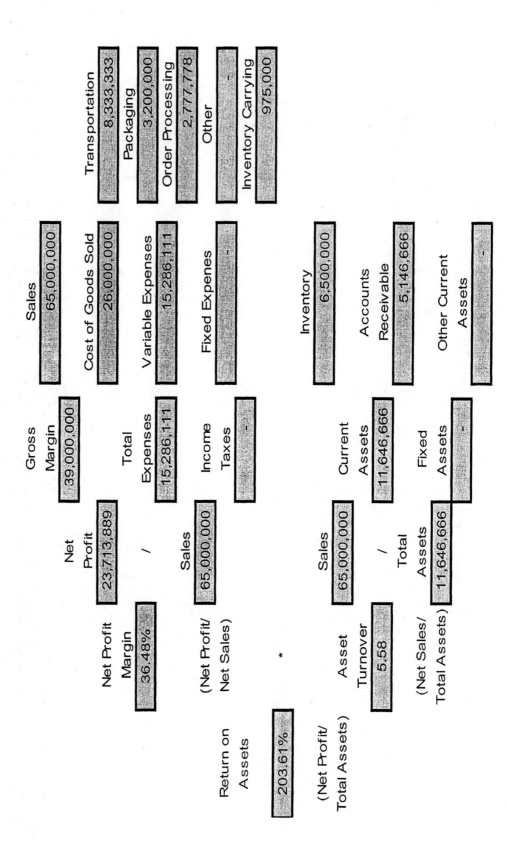

Profitability Analysis -- C-Stores (9)

Sales	39,000,000
Cost of Goods Sold	15,600,000
Gross Margin	23,400,000
Variable Expenses	32,567,778
Fixed Expenes	-
Total Expenses	32,567,778
Net Profit	(9,167,778)
Income Taxes	-

Transportation 20,833,333
Packaging 4,400,000
Order Processing 6,944,444
Other -
Inventory Carrying 390,000

Net Profit Margin = -23.51%

(Net Profit/ Net Sales) = Net Profit (9,167,778) / Sales 39,000,000

Asset Turnover = 5.22

(Net Sales/ Total Assets) = Sales 39,000,000 / Total Assets 7,475,000

Return on Assets = -122.65%

Inventory	2,600,000
Accounts Receivable	4,875,000
Other Current Assets	-
Current Assets	7,475,000
Fixed Assets	-
Total Assets	7,475,000

Profitability Analysis -- Mass M. (10)

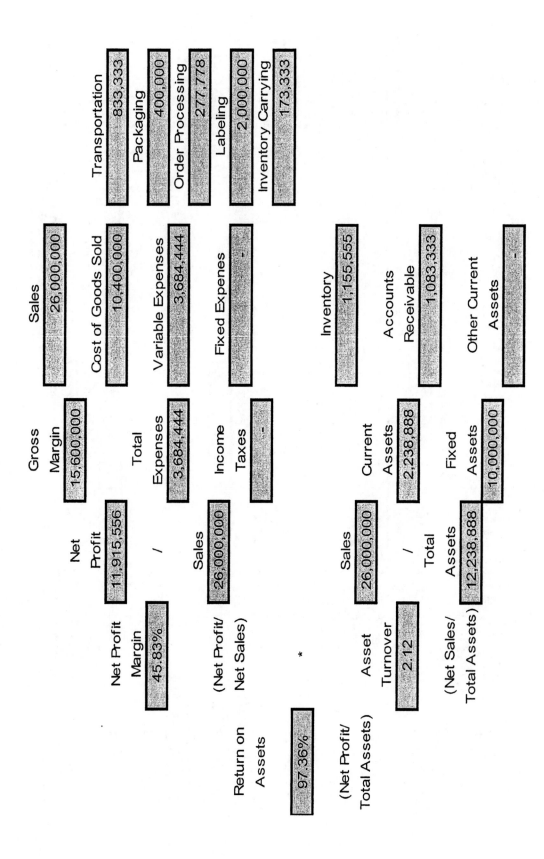

Exam 1

Customer Service

Answer **all** of the questions that appear below. Points allotted for each question are indicated. Partial credit will be given. Ensure that your answers are as specific as possible regarding implementation and application of concepts. I encourage the use of outline or bullet-point format to answer questions.

All of the exam questions are based on the following scenario:
You have just been hired as general manager of Green and White Foods (G&W's), a restaurant/bar supply business that provides a full range of wholesale products to eating and drinking establishments in mid-Michigan. The business, established 25 years ago, caters to college student-oriented bar and grills. It has traditionally offered the lowest price on the market for food service products, although the level of service offered is significantly lower than other firms. Instead, focus has been on operational efficiency to minimize costs. Growth has been steady due to the slim profit margins experienced by most of the customers the firm serves. In the last 2 years, however, a number of competitors have begun to match G&W's prices while providing higher service levels, particularly in the areas of delivery replenishment time and product availability. As a result, G&W's market share has been shrinking and the owner worries that the basis of competitive advantage – low price – will no longer sustain the company.

The owner has heard much talk of the importance of logistics lately, although she is not familiar with leading edge logistics practices. She has decided to step away from the day-to-day operation of the firm and hire you, a graduate of the MSU SCM program, to run the daily operations. She plans to move to a place where the sun shines more than 3 days per month and hopes that your ideas and expertise will reestablish G&W's competitive direction and guide the company through the next stage of its growth so she can afford to keep her condo in Antigua. She hints that if you succeed you will be given partial ownership of the firm.

1. Explain why the owner feels that logistics and supply chain management processes provide the keys to gaining advantage over competitors. List 3 factors in the business environment that have contributed to the increased importance. **(10 points)**

2. Market research indicates that customers are choosing food service firms based on the service firms' ability to deliver with shorter lead times, have greater product availability, and provide competitive prices. Given this knowledge, and the following information regarding your customers, outline a strategy to enhance competitiveness. Detail the steps you would take to implement the plan. **(25 points)**

CUSTOMER	TOTAL ANNUAL DELIVERIES	TOTAL ANNUAL REVENUE	TOTAL ANNUAL COST
Crunchy's	60	52,000	49,000
Dagwood Tavern	75	78,000	75,000
Peanut Barrel	58	55,000	50,500
Georgio's Pizza	30	30,000	27,000
Harrison Roadhouse	156	156,000	154,500
Roadhouse Pub	26	60,000	55,000
Reno's Sports Bar	104	120,000	117,000
Spartan Sports Den	72	75,000	70,500
Sparty's Coney Island	62	40,000	37,000
Landshark	114	118,000	115,000

All figures represent annual totals

3. You hired a statistics graduate student to go through last year's sales and cost figures to determine how product availability levels were related to sales and costs. Given this information, explain how you might determine the **OPTIMAL** level of product availability. **(10 points)**

4. The owner arrives in town and informs you that she won a jackpot playing Blackjack in the Bahamas. She wants to sink some of the winnings into the business to decrease the taxes she must pay. A faculty member she met on the plane back to the states tells her she should consider investing in improved information systems. Explain how you could use information systems to improve the value-added by your operation. **(25 points)**

Exam 2

Inventory

Name: _____

The second midterm exam includes three questions. All questions must be answered in a blue book or on loose leaf paper and then stapled. You may not use books, notes or conversations with classmates to complete the exam. The weight for each question is listed in terms of the number of points.

1. Your new supervisor has asked you to make a presentation that describes the inventory dynamics at a golf accessories distribution center. She wants to provide an overview of the general dynamics and then quantitatively illustrate the trade-offs. Discuss the general dynamics using the relationship between service level (SL), order quantity (OQ), combined uncertainty (σ_c), and safety stock requirements ($f(k)$). (Specifically define the formula and provide some rationale for the relationships) (20 pts.). Compute the reorder point (ROP), Safety Stock(SS), and average inventory for the following situation (20 points):

Average daily demand	10/day
Standard deviation of daily demand	2
Average cycle time	6 days
Standard deviation of cycle time	2
Order quantity	200 units

    What is the impact of reducing the order quantity to 100 units? (10 pts.)

2. Define the difference between fixed and variable data when it comes to EDI (5 pts.). Compare and contrast the use of paper based, bar code based, and electronic based (such as chips) media for communicating variable data that must accompany the contents of an order. (20 pts) Specifically define the advantages and disadvantages of each alternative.

3. The Japanese automakers are known for using interchangable parts for different cars. An interesting logistical benefit is that fewer parts must be managed, overall safety stock can be decreased and less warehouse space is required. On the manufacturing side, longer production runs are possible and economies of scale are achieved.

    In a slightly different approach, imagine you are the logistics representative for a cross-functional team evaluating development of a new retail product. The finance person is concerned about development costs and profitability prospects, the new product engineer envisions a series of "add-on features" in subsequent designs, and marketing has an exciting ad campaign that includes a retail package shaped like a pyramid. What points do you wish to stress to the team?(15 pts.) Explain the importance and implications of the points presented. (10 pts)

Exam 3

Inventory Systems

1. Answer only the three circled questions – <u>NO</u> substitutes or additions.
2. <u>Sign and return</u> this exam paper. Failure to sign and return this paper will void your examination.
3. Print your name, student ID and page number on <u>all</u> answer sheets.

1.	Compare and contrast the role and capabilities of MRP/DRP and APS.

2.	Describe the components of inventory carrying cost percentage and discuss the alternative strategies for establishing the opportunity cost component.

3.	Explain the major assumptions behind Economic Order Quantity (EOQ) model and discuss its limitations.

4.	Describe and illustrate an application of inventory stratification analysis (also called ABC or fine line analysis). Discuss how the results of stratification analysis should be used.

5.	Compare and contrast the role of time series vs. causal models for logistics forecasting applications.

6.	Compare and contrast the role of Enterprise Resource Planning (ERP) and Enterprise Extension systems. Include a discussion of the relative features and capabilities.

7.	Compare and contrast the relative impact of performance cycle uncertainty and demand uncertainty on safety stock requirements.

8.	Describe and illustrate how the convolution formula (Sigma$_c$) is related to the principle of logistics (geographic or time) postponement.

9.	Describe the forecast process model and discuss the relevant role and contribution of each of the three components.

10.	Discuss the relative trade-offs associated with single and multi-dimensional bar coding applications. Why have multiple dimensional bar coding applications not taken off in terms of popularity of use?

11.	Your firm is planning to introduce a new product line. Your task is to determine the inventory implications of the new product. The typical product will ship an average of 20 units per day from the firm's central distribution center. Historical sales patterns indicate that the standard deviation of daily sales should be approximately

3. The typical performance cycle for comparable products has been a means of 7 days and a standard deviation of 2.

    a. Assuming a replenishment quantity from the plant of 200 units, what is the safety stock and resulting average inventory for a 95 percent case fill rate?
    b. What are the inventory implications (safety stock and average inventory) of increasing the case fill rate objective to 99 percent?
    c. What would be the inventory implications for daily replenishment with a 99 percent fill rate objective assuming that the same level of demand and performance cycle uncertainty is maintained?

FORMULAE

Convolution Formula

$$\acute{o}_c = \overline{(T * \acute{o}_S^2) + (S^2 * \acute{o}_T^2)}$$

Service Level Formula

$$SL = 1 - [\, f(k) * \acute{o}_c] / OQ$$

Table of Normal Loss Integral

k	f(k)	k	f(k)	k	f(k)
0.0	0.3989	0.7	0.1428	1.4	0.0366
0.1	0.3509	0.8	0.1202	1.5	0.0293
0.2	0.3068	0.9	0.1004	1.6	0.0232
0.3	0.2667	1.0	0.0833	1.7	0.0142
0.4	0.2304	1.1	0.0686	1.8	0.0110
0.5	0.1977	1.2	0.0561	1.9	0.0084
0.6	0.1686	1.3	0.0455	2.0	0.0074

Exam 4

Warehousing/Transportation

1. Answer only the three circled questions – <u>NO</u> substitutes or additions.
2. <u>Sign and return</u> this exam paper. Failure to sign and return this paper will void your examination.
3. Print your name, student ID and page number on <u>all</u> answer sheets.
4. Each student will be assigned one question from question numbers 1-5 and one question from questions 6-10.

1. Describe the major considerations in minimizing warehousing costs. Discuss some of the specific tactics that should be employed to minimize the warehouse cost.

2. Compare and contrast a service area strategy vs. a class of trade strategy in terms of warehouse design considerations.

3. What is the future impact of transportation regulation on logistics? Your assessment should include a description of the various dimensions of transportation regulation.

4. Describe and characterize the four possible material handling technologies in terms of fixed cost, variable cost, and flexibility.

5. Compare and contract the major modes of transportation in terms of cost characteristics, service capability, accessibility, and flexibility.

6. Describe the relative cost drivers for less-than-truckload (LTL) and truckload (TL) transportation. Define a type of product (e.g., food, electronics, chemicals, etc.). For the item you defined, rank the cost drivers in terms of their relevant impact on the overall transportation cost of an item.

7. Compare and contrast the role of packaging in a marketing and supply chain environment. Identify two trends in consumer packaging being driven by marketing. Discuss how these two trends have or will impact logistics and supply chain requirements and operations.

8. Compare and contrast the cost and service benefits of warehousing. Develop a specific example illustrating the cost benefits of a warehouse. Include a specific example with appropriate cost assumptions for inbound and outbound transportation and handling costs. The example should compare the total cost of serving a market with and without a warehouse.

9. Assume that you have the responsibility to select a warehouse material handling system for a consumer goods manufacturer. Assume that the company markets over 4,000 SKUs that are small in

size and that the product line turns over about 33 percent per year. This implies that a typical product lasts about 3 years before it is outdated. They primarily ship full pallets of product to customer distribution centers for re-distribution. Justify your selection of one of the four technologies discussed in class.

10. Suppose you have responsibility for selecting a warehousing strategy for Amazing.com, an e-marketer of small consumer electronics. They market a wide range (i.e., more than 5,000 SKUs) of brand name and private label consumer electronics directly to consumers over the Internet. Consumers place the order using the Internet and the product is delivered directly to their home using one of the package delivery companies such as UPS or FedEX. The consumer can select either regular (i.e., ground) or premium (i.e., air) delivery and is charged for the corresponding freight expense. The average order size is slightly more than one line. Each of the 5,000 SKUs is stocked in only one of the company's two distribution centers (One in New Jersey and one in Los Angeles). Assuming that you keep the two existing warehouses, what is the potential role of: 1) Cross-docking; 2) Consolidation; 3) Break-bulk; 4) Processing; and 5) Mixing warehouses? Discuss how each should (or should not) be employed by Amazing. Rationalize your answer using economies of scale and service considerations. (DO NOT ASSESS THE VIABILITY OF THE ABOVE BUSINESS).

Administrator's Manual

LOGA
Michigan State
University
Logistics
Game

TABLE OF CONTENTS

Page

I. Introduction   I-3

II. Description of Program Parts and Functions   I-3

      A. Main Program   I-3
      B. Subroutine INTZE   I-5
      C. Subroutine HIST   I-5
      D. Subroutine HAND   I-5
      E. Subroutine MANUF   I-6
      F. Subroutine ALLOC   I-6
      G. Subroutine MRKET   I-8
      H. Subroutine REPRT   I-8
      I. Subroutine MKTRI   I-9
      J. Subroutine GAUSS   I-9

III. Setting up the Game   I-9

IV. Running the Game   I-11

V. Changing the Game Conditions   I-11

VI. Exhibits   I-13

INTRODUCTION

MSU LOGA is a computerized physical distribution management game. This adaptation has been designed for use on DOS based PCs. It is written in Fortran and compiled using WATFOR. There are some minor differences in the game because of the conversion, and there are additional changes that were made to improve the game. The most significant of these changes are (1) the method of calculating materials handling charges are (2) the information in (and format of) the team reports.

This write-up is intended as a guide for administrators some of whom may wish to make further adaptations to the game or to experiment with the game parameters.

DESCRIPTION OF PROGRAM PARTS AND FUNCTIONS

The MSU LOGA computer program is composed of a main program and a number of subroutines each of which serves a special purpose. The following brief descriptions explain the purpose of each part of the program.

MAIN PROGRAM

The main program controls the general execution of each round by completing the following steps: (order of actions)

1. Subroutine INTZE is called to initialize variables, read the administrator data card and read the parameter cards. A check is made to verify that parameter records were in the right sequence. If not the program is terminated.

2. Subroutine HIST (ITYPE = 0) is called to read game history. Checks are made to verify that the appropriate history records are used and that the records are in the right sequence. If not the program is terminated.

3. Team decisions records are read and checked for correct team sequence, decision record sequence, decision round number, and industry number. If any are incorrect the appropriate message is printed and the program is terminated. In addition, checks are made for obviously incorrect team decisions. The appropriate correction is made automatically and a message printed for the game administrator (the program is not terminated).

4. Raw material warehouse capacity changes are scheduled then present and future capacities are updated and the appropriate charges accumulated.

5. Company finished goods warehouse capacity changes are scheduled then present and future capacities are updated and the appropriate charges accumulated.

6. Public finished goods warehouse capacity changes are scheduled when present and future capacities are updated and the appropriate charges accumulated.

7. Raw materials are ordered then receipts and incoming shipments are updated and the appropriate charges accumulated.

8. Present and future production schedules are updated for rush, expedited and regular changes and the appropriate charges accumulated.

9. Outbound shipments are made and the appropriate charges accumulated. If insufficient inventory is available, shipments are only made until the inventory is depleted.

10. Finished goods are produced and the associated charges accumulated. If insufficient raw materials are on hand or production is scheduled is excess of the maximum, a rush schedule change is automatically made and the appropriate charges accumulated.

11. Raw materials required for production are removed from the warehouse, the inventory updated and the appropriate charges (including carrying charges on the remaining inventory) accumulated.

12. Finished goods production is received as the home warehouse (s) and the appropriate charges accumulated.

13. Finished goods shipments are received at each market, the status of intransit shipments are updated, and the appropriate charges accumulated.

14. Promotional requests are checked for errors, the allocation of each team's promotional expenditure is made, and promotional charges accumulated.

15. Each team's advertising expenditures are distributed and advertising charges accumulated.

16. Subroutine MRKET is called to determine the demand for each market.

17. Subroutine ALLOC is called to allocate sales, make sales where possible, update stockout penalties, update finished goods inventories, print administrator's sales summary, and accumulate the appropriate charges and incomes.

18. Subroutine REPRT is called to print each team's Market Research Report, Operations Planning Reports, and Financial Summary.

19. Team histories are updated and subroutine HIST (ITYPE = 1) is called to write the history file for the next decision round.

INTZE

Subroutine INTZE is used to initialize program variables with the appropriate starting values. It also reads the administrator data card and the parameter data cards. A check is made to insure that the parameter cards were in the proper sequence; if not, a message is printed and the program is terminated.

HIST

Subroutine HIST is used to read (ITYPE = 0) history cards. The industry and decision round numbers are checked with the administrator data card values. If a difference is detected, a message is printed and the program is terminated. In addition, a check is made to determine if any history cards are missing or out of order. If so, a message is printed and the program terminated.

Upon completion of the entire decision round HIST is again called to write (ITYPE = 1) the history file for the next decision round.

HAND

HAND is called each time a receipt or disbursement is made. Subroutine HAND is used to calculate company warehouse materials handling charges. All information required by HAND is passed through the subroutine argument. (ITYPE, CAP, STOCK, OPT, CAR, CHG). The variables are defined as follows:

1. ITYPE is used to designate raw material (1) or finished goods (2) warehouse.

2. CAP is the current capacity of the warehouse.

3. STOCK is the current inventory in the warehouse. (Before the receipt of disbursement)

4. OPT is the ratio of inventory to capacity (utilization) which will yield the lowest handling charge. ($0 \leq OPT \leq 1$.)

5. VAR is the unit handling charge at the optimum utilization.

6. CHG is the calculated unit handling charge.

If desired, this subroutine can be replaced with a user written subroutine (with the same argument) to calculate materials handling charges by a different method. Using the current method the unit handling charge is constant for all utilization less than optimum. As the utilization increases above optimum, the unit handling charge increases. The sensitivity of the handling charge to utilization is determined by the value of P. The values of P can easily be changed by replacing existing cards in the subroutine deck.

MANUF

Subroutine MANUF is used to calculate the penalty cost associated with over or under utilization of available production capacity. All information required by MANUF is passed through the subroutine argument. (CAP, OPT, SCHED, CHG). The variables are defined as follows:

1. CAP is the available production capacity at 100% utilization.

2. OPT is the optimum utilization which results in a zero penalty cost. $(0. \leq OPT \leq 1.)$

3. SCHED is the scheduled production level.

4. CHG is the calculated penalty cost for the current scheduled production.

If desired, this subroutine can be replaced by a user written subroutine, (with the same argument) to calculate the penalty cost by a different method.

ALLOC

Subroutine ALLOC makes a tentative allocation of demand by company and prints a summary of this allocation for the game administrator. In making the tentative allocation of demand the following relationships are used:

I. $\quad TS_{ij} = S_{ij} + PS_{ij}$

II. $\quad S_{ij} = \left[\dfrac{(D_j)(1. - SO_{ij})(4)}{(4 - TSO_j)} + DA_j \right] \qquad \left[\dfrac{SA_{ij})(F_{ij})}{(T_j)} \right]$

III. $\quad PS_{ij} = [D_j + Da_j - \underset{i=1}{4}(S_{ij})] \left[\dfrac{PA_{ij}}{TPA_j} \right] \qquad$ When $TPA_j > 0$

$\qquad PS_{ij} = \dfrac{(D_j)(1. - So_{ij})(4)(Sa_{ij})}{(4. - TSO_j)(T_j)} \qquad - S_{ij}$ When $TPA_j = 0$

WHERE:

1. TS_{ij} = total company I potential demand in market j
2. S_{ij} = company I potential safe demand in market j

3. PS_{ij} = company I potential advertising and promotional demand in market j

4. SA_{ij} = company I actual sales in market j last round.

5. T_j = total actual sales in market j last round.

6. D_j = total non-advertising market demand in this round (determined by MRKET)

7. DA_j = total advertising generated market demand this round (determined by MRKET)

8. SO_{ij} = company I stockout penalties in market j.

9. TSO_j = sum of the stockout penalties in market j for all companies.

10. PA_{ij} = company I advertising plus promotion expenditure in market j

11. TPA_j = total advertising plus promotion expenditure in market j

12. F_{ij} = company I customer loyalty factor for market j

After tentative allocation, checks are made to determine if the sales can be made. If not, the appropriate stockout penalty factors are updated using the following relationship:

$$SO_{ij} = \frac{TS_{ij} - I_{ij}}{TS_{ij}} + (\text{prior stockout penalty } SO_{ij})$$

Where I_{ij} = company i inventory in market j

Unfulfilled demand is reallocated where possible and final administrator summary printed. When making the reallocation all unfulfilled demand is placed into a pool and reallocated among the companies with additional inventory using a similar relationship as for PS_{ij} above. All goods sold are removed from inventory and the appropriate charges and income accumulated.

MRKET

Subroutine MRKET calculates the demand for each market based on the following relationships:

$$D_j = (DN_j) (RS) (RF_j) (1. - MSO_j)$$

$$Da_j = [MAD_j] [1. - (1/2) (Ta_j/Ha_j)]$$

WHERE:

D_j and DA_j are as defined earlier.

MSO_j = Market j stockout penalty

RS = Normal distributed seasonal index with mean = historical index and standard deviation = specified accuracy factor (SFLCT)

RF_j = Normally distributed random fluctuation factor for market j with mean = 1. and standard deviation = specified fluctuation factor (FLCTM)

DN_j = Normal market j demand

MAD_j = Maximum amount of demand in market j which can be generated by advertising.

Ta_j = Total advertising in market j

Ha_j = Amount of advertising in market j which will generate one-half of the maximum demand.

Additional advertising spent in the market will increase demand but at a diminishing return.

REPRT

Subroutine REPRT prints each team's Operations Planning Report and Financial Statement. (Report calls MKTRI if required.)

MKTRI

Subroutine MKTRI prints each team's market research and calculates the appropriate charges.

GAUSS

Subroutine GAUSS (IX, S, AM, V) generates normally distributed random numbers (V) with mean (AM) and standard deviation (S) using the random number seed IX. Each time GAUSS is called it automatically generates a new seed (IX).

SETTING UP THE GAME

A set of initial game conditions and parameters have been chosen. These conditions represent a deliberate suboptimal position for the teams to improve as they see fit. Each team is given an exactly identical set of starting conditions. Their actions and competitor's actions will determine the relative success or failure of each team. These initial conditions and parameters have been described in the player's manual and the week 52 Operation's Planning Report and Financial Summary. To run several groups simultaneously, assign each a different industry number complete the following for each group.

A initial file containing the administrator's record, parameter records, history records, and initial decisions is included with the instructor's material. This file represents the initial conditions to start the game. Before the game can be run, some of the values might need changing. The easiest way to edit most of the input data is using the "Edit" command from the DOS window. The most likely changes to be made are as follows:

1. ADMINISTRATOR DATA

   The number of reports to be printed for each team – usually the number of players on the largest team plus one for the administrator (ADMN columns 16-17 right justify using no decimal point). Industry number columns 5-6 right justify using no demand point.

2. PARAMETER RECORDS

   (1) The title printed at the top of each page (Parameter Card PO1 columns 11-78). The title may contain any characters desired. For neater print-outs, the title should be centered.

   (2) The industry name (Parameter Card PO2 columns 11-30). The industry name may contain any characters and should also be centered. (also printed at the top of each page.)

(3) The company names (Parameter Card PO2 columns 31-42; 43-54; 55-56; and 67-78 for Company 1-4 respectively). For neater print-outs the name should be centered.

(4) The finished product name (Parameter Card PO3 columns 9-20). For neater print-outs the name should be centered.

(5) The market names (Parameter Card PO3 columns 21-32; 33-44; 45-56; 57-68; and 69-80 for Markets 1-5 respectively No. 5 is the central market). For neater print-outs the names should be left justified.

*If any additional changes to the parameters or initial conditions are desired, read the section "Changing the Game Conditions."

3. HISTORY CARD

The industry number (history card H 001 columns 6-7 right justify using no decimal).

Check to see that (1) there are 19 parameter ("P") records and that they are in the correct order 1-19; (2) there are 97 History ("H") records and that they are in the correct order 1-97; (3) that there is an administrator ("ADMN") data record; and (4) that there are 20 team decision records and that they are in the right order – refer to the decision sheets for the decision card formats. Assemble the data in the following order:

1. Administrator Data (1)

2. Parameter Cards (19)

3. History Cards (97)

4. Team Decisions (20 or 5 for each team)

Submit the program for execution using this data set. A new history file to be used during the next round will be written automatically by the program.

RUNNING THE GAME

The player's manual and week 52 reports should be issued to the team members in advance. After they have had time to read the manuals, a brief orientation meeting should be held to answer any questions and explain the mechanics of submitting the decisions.

Upon receipt of the decisions for the round;

(1) Have entered a new administrator data record containing the following:

columns 1-4   ADMN

columns 5-6   Industry number (right justify using no decimal)

columns 7-8   Week Number (right justify using no decimal)

columns 9-15   Seasonal index for this period (place anywhere in the field but   include a decimal)

columns 16-17   The number of reports desired (right justify using no decimal)

(2) Have the team decision entered into files using the Excel data entry spreadsheet

(3) Assemble the file as follows:

    A. The administrator data card

    B. The parameter cards

    C. The history cards punched during the prior run

    D. The team decision cards

(4) Submit the program for execution.

(5) Examine the administrator reports for error listings and take the appropriate action.

CHANGING THE GAME CONDITIONS

The parameters and starting conditions for this game have been chosen carefully to give balanced emphasis on the importance of each facet of physical distribution management. However, if it is desired to shift the emphasis or to make the conditions more like those of an actual marketing situation, the game parameters and starting conditions can be changed.

In addition to changes in starting conditions or parameters the following minor program changes can be easily made:

1. Subroutine HAND can be rewritten to change the method of calculating materials handling charges.

2. Subroutine MANUF can be rewritten to change the method of calculating production penalty charges.

3. Subroutine MRKET can be rewritten to change the method of calculating market demands.

ADMINISTRATOR DATA

Variable	Input Format	Description
IND	I2	Industry number used as a check for correct history card set.
IPD	I2	Decision round (week) number used as a check for correct history card set.
NSET	I2	Number of team reports copies desired (usually the maximum number in a team plus one for the administrator).
SEAS	F7.3	Historical seasonal index for this week.

PARAMETERS

Variable	Input Format	Description
ANAME (I)	A4	Industry name printed on administrator's output only (20 characters). I=1, 5 sets of 4 characters.
CITY (I, J)	A4	Market names (12 characters). I=1, 5 Markets J=1, 3 Sets of 4 characters
CMRI (I)	F7.0	Cost of market research information, I=1, 13 Report types
CSCHD (I)	F7.3	Per Unit cost of production schedule changes. I=1, 3 1=Rush 2=Expedited 3=Regular
CSODK	F7.5	Company stockout penalty decay factor (0≤CSODK≤1) Each week the stockout penalty is reduced by multiplying by CSODK.
DKMSO (I)	F7.5	Market stockout penalty decay factor (works like CSODK above). I=1, 5, Markets
DMAND (I)	F7.0	Normal market demand. I=1, 5 Markets (Central market = 5)
FADD	F7.3	Unit charge to ass company finished goods warehouse capacity.
FBRAK(I)	F7.0	LVL – VL Shipment Quantity breakpoint (Finished goods). I=1,2 1=Regular 2=Premium
FCCHG	F7.3	Finished goods carrying charge (0≤FCCHG≤1.) (Annual interest rate/52 weeks; charged on the value of all units in inventory and intransit at week's end.

Variable	Input Format	Description
FCHNG	F7.0	Fixed charge to add or reduce company finished goods warehouse capacity.
FDD	F7.3	Finished goods D&D charge (per unit in D&D at end of week).
FFIX	F7.3	Company warehouse fixed charge per unit of capacity.
FLCTM	F7.0	Random market fluctuation parameter. The fluctuation factor is normally distributed with mean = 1. And standard deviation = FLCTM. ($0 \leq FLCTM \leq 1$.).
FNAME (I)	A4	Finished product name (12 characters) I=1, 3 Sets of 4 characters.
FOCHG	F7.0	Finished goods shipment documentation charge.
FOPT	F7.5	Optimum company finished goods warehouse utilization ($0 \leq FOPT \leq 1$.).
FRED	F7.3	Unit charge to reduce company finished goods warehouse capacity
FSHIP (I,J,K)	F7.0	Unit finished goods shipping cost (Prepaid at time of order). I=1,2 1=Regular 2=Premium J=1,3 1=Near competitive markets 2= Far competitive markets 3=Central markets K=1,2 1=VL 2=LVL
FVAR	F7.3	Company warehouse finished goods unit materials handling cost at optimum warehouse utilization.
ISEED	I5	Five digit odd integer (random number seed).
IUNT (I)	I3	Units of raw material needed to make one finished unit. I=1 Plastic I=2 Steele I=3 Aluminum

Variable	Input Format	Description
LEADF (I,J,K)	I3	Finished goods shipping lead time (Maximum = 3 weeks) (I, J, & K same as FSHIP).
LEADR (I,J,K)	I2	Lead time to receive raw material (Maximum = 8 weeks). I=1,3 Raw material types J=1,2 1=Regular 2=Premium K=1,2 1=VL 2=LVL
LFADD	I3	Lead time to reduce company finished goods warehouse capacity (Maximum = 3 weeks).
LFRED	I3	Lead time to reduce company finished goods warehouse capacity (Maximum = 3 weeks).
LPADD	I3	Lead time to add public warehouse capacity (Maximum = 3 weeks).
LPRED	I3	Lead time to add public warehouse capacity (Maximum = 3 weeks).
LRADD	I3	Lead time to add raw material warehouse capacity (Maximum = 3 weeks).
LRRED	I3	Lead time to add raw material warehouse capacity (Maximum = 3 weeks).
MPROM (I)	I3	Duration of promotion plan I=1, NPROM promotion plans (Maximum =10 weeks).
NPROM	I3	Number of promotion plans (Maximum = 5 plans).
PADD	F7.3	Unit charge to ass public warehouse capacity.
PCAPY	F7.0	Production capacity at 100% utilization (Maximum production capacity = 1.25 PCAPY)
PCHNG	F7.0	Fixed charge to change public warehouse capacity.

Variable	Input Format	Description
PRED	F7.3	Unit charge to reduce public warehouse capacity.
PRICE	F7.3	Sale price of finished goods (Physical Distribution Department's gross margin=price/5)
PRODO	F7.5	Optimum production capacity utilization ($0 \leq PROD \leq 1.$).
PROM (I, J)	F7.0	Cost by week of promotion plan. I=1, NPROM promotion plan J=1, MPROM(I) weeks
PSTOR	F7.3	Public warehousing storage charge (per unit in inventory at end of week).
PVAR	F7.3	Public warehousing materials handling charge (charged only once upon receipt of material).
RADD	F7.3	Raw material unit charge to add warehouse capacity.
RBRAK (I, J)	F7.0	LVL – VL Shipment Quantity breakpoint (raw material). I=1,3 Raw material types J=1,2 1=Regular 2=Premium
RCCHG	F7.3	Raw material carrying charge ($0 \leq RCCHG \leq 1.$) (Annual interest rate/52 weeks; charged on value of units in inventory at week's end).
RCHNG	F7.0	Fixed charge to change raw material warehouse capacity (increase or decrease).
RDD	F7.3	Raw material D&D charge (per unit in D&D at end of week).
RFIX	F7.3	Raw material warehouse fixed charge per unit of capacity.

Variable	Input Format	Description
RFLCT	F7.3	Market research accuracy parameter. The market research accuracy is normally distributed with mean = 1 and SIGMA = RFLCT ($0 \leq RFLCT \leq 1.$).
RNAME (I,J)	A4	Raw material names (12 characters). I=1,3 Types of raw material J=1,3 Sets of 4 characters
ROCHG	F7.0	Raw material order placement charge.
ROPT	F7.5	Optimum raw material warehouse utilization ($0 \leq ROPT \leq 1.$).
RRED	F7.3	Raw material unit charge to reduce warehouse capacity.
RSHIP (I, J, K)	F7.0	Unit raw material shipping cost (Prepaid at time of order). I=1,3 Raw material types J=1,2 1=Regular 2=Premium K=1,2 1=VL 2=LVL
RVAR	F7.3	Raw material handling charge (charged in and out) per unit at optimum utilization.
SAFE (I)	F7.5	Customer loyalty factor ($0 \leq SAFE (I) \leq 1.$). I=1,3 1=Home market 2=Competitor's market 3=Central market
SFLCT	F7.0	Seasonal index accuracy parameter. The seasonal index is normally distributed with mean = (normal index) and standard deviation = SFLCT ($0 \leq SFLCT \leq 1.$).
TEAM (I, J)	A4	Company names (12 characters) I=1, 4 Companies J=1,3 Sets of 4 characters
TITLE (I)	A4	Alphanumeric title printed on each page of output (68 characters). I=1, 17 sets of 4 characters.
VALUE (I)	F7.3	Value off each unit of raw materials. I=1,3 Raw material types.

Variable	Input Format	Description
COSOP (I, J)	F10.6	Company stockout Penalty by Market. I=1, 4 Teams J=1, 5 Markets
COST (I, J, K)	F10.2	Team's Cost Data. I=1, 4 Teams J=1,4 1=Current week's costs 2=Cumulative costs to date 3=Current week's unit costs 4=Cumulative unit costs to date K=1,31 1=Physical distribution gross margin 2=Production charges 3=Advertising and promotion charges 4=Marketing research charges 5=(2+3+4) 6=(1-5) 7=Order placement costs (raw material) 8=Inbound transportation costs (raw material) 9=Inventory carrying costs (raw material) 10=Warehouse capacity change costs (raw material) 11=Warehouse fixed charges (raw material) 12=Materials handling cost (raw materials) 13=(10+11+12) 14=Demurrage and detention costs (raw material) 15=(13+14) 16=(7+8+9+15) 17=Finished goods shipment documentation charges 18=Outbound finished goods transportation charges 19=Finished goods inventory carrying costs 20=Finished goods warehouse capacity charge costs 21=Finished goods warehouse fixed charges 22=Finished goods warehouse materials handling cost 23=(20+21+22) 24=Public warehouse capacity change costs 25=Public warehouse storage costs

		26=Public warehouse materials handling costs 27=(24+25+26) 28=Demurrage and detention costs 29=(23+27+28) 30=(17+18+19+29) 31=(6-16-30)
CWHSE (I, J, K)	F9.0	Company Finished Goods Warehouse Capacity Queue I=1, 4 Teams J=1, 5 Markets K=1, 4 1=Current capacity 2,3,4 = Capacity 1,2,3, weeks from now
FGINV (I, J, K)	F10.0	Finished Goods Current Inventory Status I=1, 4 Teams J=1, 5 Markets K=1,3 1=Company Warehouse 2=Public Warehouse 3= D&D

Variable	Input Format	Description
FINGD (I, J, K)	F9.0	Finished Goods Inventory Queue. I=1,4 Teams J=1,5 Markets K=1,4 1=Current Inventory 2=Inventory to be received this week. 3,4,5, = Inventory to be received 1, 2, 3 weeks from now
JND	I2	Industry Number (Used as a check to prevent errors).
IPROM (I, J)	I10	Team's Promotion Status. I=1,4 Teams J=1,5 Promotion Plans IPROM(I,J0 = 0-Plan not in effect IPROM(I,J) = "K" – Week "K" of plan
JPD	I2	Current Period Number (Used as a check to prevent errors).
PROD (I, J)	F10.0	Production Schedule Queue. I=1,4 Teams J=1,3 1= Current schedule 2,3=Schedule 1,2 weeks from now
PWHSE (I,J,K)	F9.0	Public Finished Goods Warehouse Capacity Queue I=1,4 Teams J=1,5 Markets K=1,4 1=Current capacity 2,3,4,= Capacity 1,2,3, weeks from now
RAW (I,J,K)	F10.0	Raw Material Inventory Queue I=1,4 Teams J=1,3 Raw Material Types K=1,12 1=Beginning Inventory 2=Inventory received 3=Inventory used 4=Ending inventory 5,12= Inventory to be received 1-8 weeks from now

Variable	Input Format	Description
RMINV (I,J)	F9.0	Raw Material Current Inventory Status I=1,4 Teams J=1,2 1=Company Warehouse 2==D&D
RWHSE (I,J)	F10.0	Raw Material Warehouse Capacity Queue I=1,4 Teams J=1,4 1=Current capacity 2,3,4=Capacity 1,2,3 weeks from now
SHARE (I,J)	F10.0	Company Sales Last Period by Market I=1,4 Teams J=1,5 Markets
SOPMK (I)	F10.6	Market Stockout Penalty
YTD (I)	F10.0	Year-To-Date Total Sales I=1,4 Teams

TEAM DECISION

Variable	Input Format	Description
ADV (I,J)	F6.0	Advertising expenditure I=1,4 Team number J=1,5 Market number
FWHSC (I,J)	F6.0	Finished goods warehouse capacity changes I=1,5 Markets J=1 Company warehouse J=2 Public warehouse
KPROM (I)	I1	Promotion plan number to be initiated I=1,4 Team number
LTEAM (I, J)	I1 I2 I1 I1	Used to check for correct assembly of decision card deck. I=1,5 Decision card types J=1 Team number J=2 Week number J=3 Card number J=4 Industry number
MRICK (I)		Indicates whether market research is desired (MRICK(I)>0) I=1,4 Team number
MRI (I, J, K)	I2 I1	Market research specifications. I=1,4 Team number J=1,9 Request number K=1 Market research report number K=2,6 Competitor or market number on which information is desired.
MSHIP (I,J)	I1	Finished goods shipment specifications I=1,8 Shipment number J=1 Origin market number J=2 Shipment mode J=3 Destination market number

Variable	Input Format	Description
ORDER (I,J)	F6.0	Raw material orders. I=1,3 Raw material types J=1,2 Type of transportation 1= Regular 2=Premium
QSHIP (I)	F4.0	Finished goods shipment quantity I=1,8 Shipment Number
RWHSC	F6.0	Raw material warehouse capacity changes.
SCHED (I)	F6.0	Production schedules I=1 Rush schedule changes I=2 Expedited schedule changes I=3 Regular production scheduling

INTERNAL VARIABLES

Variables	Description
APROM (I, J)	Team's promotional expenditure allocation by market I=1,4 Teams J=1,5 Markets
ASALE (I)	Calculated market demand generated be advertising. I=1,5 Markets
ICK (I)	Used to check for data set errors as follows: I. <u>Main Program and Subroutine MKTRI</u> Used to check for incorrect market research requests. I=1,13 Market research request numbers II. <u>Subroutine INTZE</u> Used to check parameter cards for missing cards or incorrect sequence. I=1,19 II. <u>Subroutine HIST</u> Used to check history cards or incorrect data sequence. I=1,97
IROUT (I,J)	Used to determine whether a shipment is being made between near, far, or central markets. I=1,5 From market number J=1,5 To marker number
ISTAR (I)	Special characters used in marking print-outs. I=1⇒b (blank) I=2⇒*
JLIST (I)	List of teams which have inventory available. This variable is used during allocation of pooled sales. I=1,4 Teams

Variable	Description
KILL	Is used to indicate that an error of sufficient magnitude to terminate the program has occurred. All remaining checks are made so that any additional errors can be detected and indicated during the run. Upon completion of all checks, the program is terminated if KILL > 0
KPD (I)	Used to print the week numbers on the Operations Planning Report. I=1,9 Week numbers
LIST (I)	List of teams which have inventory available. This variable is used during allocation of pooled sales. I=1,4 Teams
NO (I)	Used to accumulate counts during printing of market research reports. I=1,5
NPNCH	Computing system card punch device logical number
NPRNT	Computing system printer device logical number.
NREAD	Computing system card read device logical number.
PCT (I,J)	Team's percent of total market sales. I=1,4 Teams J=1,5 Markets
POOL (I)	Market demand pool. This demand is allocated to each team based on their advertising and promotional expenditures. I=1,5 Markets
PROAD (I, J)	Each team's promotional plus advertising expenditure by market. I=1,4 Teams J=1,5 Markets

Variable	Description
PSALE (I)	Calculated market demand excluding advertising generated demand. I=1,5 Markets
SALE (I, J, K)	Each team's potential allocation of sales by market. I=1,4 Teams J=1,5 Markets K=1 Safe sales due to customer loyalty K=2 Pooled sales K=3 Total safe plus pooled sales
TOTAL (I)	Used to accumulate market research information (with built-in inaccuracies) while printing market research reports. I=1,5
TOTMK (I)	Used in totaling various statistics while printing the Administrator Sales Summary. I=1,6
TPRAD (I)	Total promotional plus advertising expenditures by market I=1,5 Markets
TPROM (I)	Total team promotional expenditure I=1,5 Markets
TRAW (I)	Total raw materials – used in printing the Operations Planning Reports. I=1 Beginning Inventory 2= Receipts 3= usage 4=Ending inventory 5,12= Receipts scheduled 1-8 weeks from now
TSOP (I)	Sum of all teams stockout penalty by market. I=1,5 Markets

Variable	Description
TWHSE (I)	Total company plus public warehouse capacity. Used in printing Operations Planning Report. I=1 Current capacity I=2,3,4, Scheduled capacity 1,2, and 3 weeks from now

LOGA
Logistics Game

Participant's Manual

LOGA- A Computerized Logistics Simulator

LOGA (Logistics Game) is a simulated four-firm industry in which individual company success is measured in an interactive competitive environment. The simulator replicates a business operation in which company representatives manage all aspects of logistical operations. The management of each participating firm must make and implement decisions in an effort "to procure materials, schedule production, and deliver the right quantity of the right goods to the right place at the right time at the *least total cost*." The game is competitive in that all firms compete for industry, profits and market share.

One must remember that a simulator cannot duplicate all complexities of a competitive business world. However, you will find yourself deeply involved and highly motivated.

A tangible benefit realized from LOGA is the opportunity to manage the total logistical system. Regardless of success of failure, understanding of overall logistical management will be strengthened. LOGA requires simultaneous coordination of finished goods and raw materials, inventory management, transportation procurement, production scheduling, warehousing, sales promotion, advertising, and marketing research, while keeping in mind time lags and competitive interactions from other firms. The game places primary emphasis on decision-making and implementation of the total systems approach. However, it is not just a work exercise. A considerable amount of enjoyment results from your effort to "outsmart" competition.

FIRM AND INDUSTRY COMPETITIVE STRUCTURE

Each firm is located in a local market that is an equal distance from the central market. No firm is located in the central market. Each firm is therefore equidistant from two of the three other local markets. The remaining local market is twice as far away as the central market. The market configuration illustrated in Figure 1 illustrates distance relationships.

All firms have the same manufacturing and potential warehouse facility configuration. In the home market, each firm has a manufacturing plant, a raw-material private warehouse, and a finished-goods private warehouse. In other markets, each firm has a private finished-goods distribution center, public warehousing, and the potential to change booth. No public warehousing is available for raw materials. Table 1 illustrates the market area number and firm number for each industry.

Figure 1
Loga Market Structure

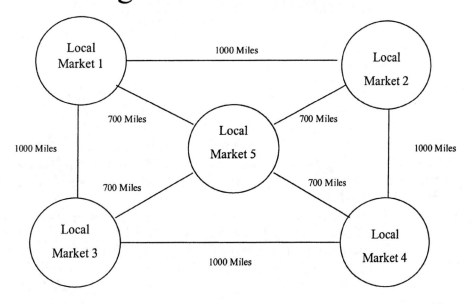

TABLE 1
FIRM LOCATION AND HOME MARKET AREA

		Industry and Team	
Market Number	East	Central	West
1	Giants	Vikings	Rams
2	Redskins	Lions	49ers
3	Eagles	Packers	Falcons
4	Colts	Bears	Cowboys
5	Super Bowl	Super Bowl	Super Bowl

All the firms produce and market a hypothetical product known as the Spartan. Spartans are manufactured from three basic raw materials: aluminum, plastic, and steel. These materials are used in fixed proportions: 4 units of aluminum, 8 units of plastic, and 12 units of steel per finished Spartan. Raw materials have varying procurement times to reach the manufacturing plant. Plastic and steel are available locally; aluminum must be purchased from a distant source.

Basic Spartan demand is approximately 9,600 units per week for all markets combined. The Central market demand is about 3,200 units per week. Each of the local markets requires approximately 1,600 units per week. When initiating the simulation, each firm has 25 per cent of the Central market, 49 per cent of its home local market, and 17 per cent of all other local markets. As the competitive strategies and tactics of each firm interact, these percentages will change.

Sales analysis and forecasting have determined an expected seasonal pattern of demand for all five markets. However, past experience has proven such estimates are accurate only to within plus or minus 5 per cent.

TABLE 2
FORECAST SPARTAN DEMAND PATTERN

Variation of Week #	Demand Index Value
1	1.00
2	.95
3	.90
4	.85
5	.90
6	1.00
7	1.05
8	1.10
9	1.15
10	1.10
11	1.00
12	1.00

Sales forecasts are also subject to unpredictable fluctuations, which randomly occur in individual markets. Table 2 reports the expected seasonal sales.

DECISION-MAKING

The logistical management task is to provide a specified level of product availability at the lowest total cost. This is achieved by having a specified amount of Spartans available for sale in each market.

To assist in decision-planning, the logistical department's tasks are discussed by functional areas. The overall decision-making responsibilities of the logistical department include the following tasks:

1. Raw-material purchasing;
2. Scheduling the number of Spartans to produce, when to produce them, and how fast to produce them, in light of probable demand and inventories on hand;
3. Determination of warehouse space is needed for raw materials at the plant and for Spartans in each of the five markets;

4. Selection of type of finished-goods warehousing to use---public and/or private;
5. Selection of transportation mode—truck and/or rail;
6. Product allocation to specific markets;
7. Selection of the number, type, and sequence of sales promotions;
8. Planning advertising for each market; and,
9. Requesting promotion, advertising, and/or demand marketing research.

For efficient operations, it is recommended that teams organize along functional areas and designate a member responsible for each decision area. Coordination of the integrated logistical system is the responsibility of the overall team.

Transportation

A significant aspect of logistical success depends upon transportation decisions. One primary transportation decision is mode selection. For fast delivery, to reduce the threat of stockouts or a production shutdown, truck transportation is available. On the other hand, lower-cost-per-unit rail transportation may be adequate. In specific situations, less-than-volume load (LVL) shipments may be desired. Charges and transit times for each mode and size of shipments are illustrated in Table 3

TABLE 3
TRANSPORTATION

Inbound Transportation of Raw Materials – Unit Rates and Transit Times

Material		Rail-VL	Rail-LVL	Truck-VL	Truck-LVL
		More than 14,000 Units	<14,000 Units	More than 6,500 Units	< 6,500 Units
Plastic	Rate:	$0.15	$0.20	$0.23	$0.30
	Transit Time:	1 week	2 weeks	Overnight	Overnight
Steel	Rate:	$0.21	$0.29	$0.31	$0.40
	Transit Time:	2 weeks	3 weeks	Overnight	Overnight
Aluminum	Rate:	$0.28	$0.28	$1.00	$1.50
	Transit Time:	8 weeks	8 weeks	1 week	1 week

Outbound Transportation of Finished Goods – Unit Rates and Transit Times

Distance		Rail-VL	Rail-LVL	Truck-VL	Truck-LVL
		More than 280 Units	<280 Units	More than 130 Units	<130 Units
700 miles	Rate:	$ 5.50	$7.50	$9.70	$11.70
	Transit Time:	1 week	1 weeks	Overnight	Overnight
1,000 miles	Rate:	$7.00	$9.00	$13.00	$15.00
	Transit Time:	1 weeks	2 weeks	Overnight	Overnight
1,400 miles	Rate:	$9.00	$11.00	$17.40	$19.40
	Transit Time:	1 weeks	2 weeks	Overnight	Overnight

An order placement charge of $75 is assessed for the documentation of each order places with suppliers. A shipment documentation charge of $75 is assessed for documenting each shipment.

For the most part, transportation transit times are dependable. However, during heavy demand periods, equipment shortages and inconsistency in transit times may be experienced.

Production Scheduling

Within the constraint of plant capacity, the logistical department is responsible for scheduling production. To support the production schedule, materials must be procured. In this regard, the sales forecast indices presented in Table 2 are helpful to guide planning. Raw-material transportation charges are assessed when the order is placed.

The per-unit manufacturing cost structure is influenced by utilization of plant capacity. Over-or underutilization results in higher per-unit costs of production. The logistical department is charged for any excess costs resulting from over-or underutilization of capacity. The standard of these excess charges is contained in Table 4.

Normal practice is to schedule production two weeks in advance. Occasions will develop wherein you may desire to increase or decrease scheduled production quantities. "Expedited" orders are adjustments with one week's delay. "At once" modifications take place during the current week. If a production schedule must be curtailed because of raw-material shortage or production schedules exceeding maximum capacity, a forced reduction penalty is charged. To initiate the game, 2,400 units have been scheduled for production.

TABLE 4
PLANT CAPACITY AND PRODUCTION CHARGES

Rated Plant Capacity	2,700 units per week		
Optimum level of weekly production	2,430 units per week (90% of rate capacity)		
Maximum level of weekly production	3,375 units per week (125% of rate capacity)		
Cost per unit of *change* for *expedited* changes	$2.00		
Cost per unit of *change* for at *once* changes	$3.50		
Cost per unit of *change* for forced reduction in production schedule	$3.50		
Examples of production charges for production above or below optimum production cost point	*% of Capacity Used*	*Units Produced*	*Production Charge*
	0%	0	$219,000
	50	1,350	43,300
	75	2,025	5,400
	90	2,430	0
	100	2,700	2,700
	115	3,110	16,200
	125	3,375	32,400

Spartans produced during a given week are transferred to the factory adjacent to the finished-goods warehouse. These Spartans are *only* available for sale in the home market during the week they are produced. Shipments cannot be made to other markets until the next week.

Inventory Planning

Inventory planning is responsible for having an adequate supply of raw materials and a strategic supply of Spartans in selected markets. Failure to plan properly may result in production shutdown or a stockout. A production shutdown may or may not be critical, depending on inventory levels. In contrast, if Spartan stockouts occur, a company is normally penalized through lost sales and may lose market share. If you stockout in a market in which a competitor has adequate Spartans available, you will lose a portion of market share. In selected instances, the inventories of all firms might be zero in a specific market. In such situations, the industry will experience a reduction in future demand in that market.

Inventory carrying charges are assessed against both raw materials and finished goods. A 15 per cent per year carrying charge is assessed against the average total weekly dollar value of all raw materials on hand. (Each unit of plastic is worth $3, steel, $4; and aluminum, $7.) Spartans are assessed at 24 per cent per year on an estimated value of $250. All goods in process, in storage, and in transit at the end of a week are assessed this charge.

For purposes of inventory planning, the following order of actions should always be kept in mind:

1. Warehouse capacity is adjusted;
2. Raw materials are received;
3. Outbound shipments from warehouses are made;[1]
4. Spartans are produced and received in the home market warehouses;[2]
5. Shipments are received at all warehouses; [2] and
6. Sales in the markets are made and deducted from inventory.

Warehousing

The logistical department is responsible for the storage of raw materials and finished goods. To facilitate this task, the company operates a raw-material and finished-goods warehouse at the factory. Finished-goods public warehouse space can also be contracted for within the home market. In the other four markets, the firm has the option of utilizing private of public warehousing.

At the start of the game, the firm has the following warehouse space (Table 5).

TABLE 5
WAREHOUSE CAPACITY

Raw-material warehouse	60,000 Units
Finished-goods warehouse—private	
a. Home market	1,700 units
b. Small non-home market	200 units
c. Central market	600 units
Finished-goods warehouse—public	
a. Home market	300 units
b. Small non-home market	100 units
c. Central market	500 units

---

1. The shipment is accumulated from inventory according to the following order: (1) demurrage and detention, (2) public warehouse, (3) company warehouse.

2. Receipts are placed in inventory according to the following order: (1) company warehouse, (2) public warehouse, (3) demurrage and detention.

In some instances, the present warehousing capacity may be inadequate. Additional private space can be obtained within three weeks for both raw materials and finished goods. Public warehouse space can be added immediately. If additional space is not added, the firm will automatically be charged demurrage and detention for storage in transport vehicles. Demurrage and detention charges are assessed only when private and public warehouse space is filled.

In markets where warehouse capacity is judged excessive, a reduction can be scheduled. For private warehouse operations, two weeks are required before becoming effective. Public warehouse capacity may be reduced instantaneously. If warehouse capacity is less than inventory at any point during the week, the overflow inventory is subject to demurrage and detention charges. Each time warehouse capacity is changed, a fixed charge of $300 is incurred.

The costs to operate private warehouses are basically of two types: space utilization and per-unit handling. Space costs are fixed and based on total available warehouse space. The per-unit handling cost is variable and based on utilization of the warehouse. The charge is assessed on warehouse receipts. The most efficient utilization rate is around 70 per cent of peak capacity. As the utilization increases, the handling costs are constant until 70 per cent of peak is reached. Storage in excess of 70 per cent of peak results in increased per-unit rates. The rate of increase is not specified to participants since labor productivity is a major problem. Participants will have to "test" the sensitivity of this cost factor. Public warehouse handling is fixed per unit and is charged upon receipt of Spartans. Table 6 provides cost schedules.

Advertising and Promotion

Advertising and promotional campaigns will be initiated when announced by the administrator. Due to the seasonal demand for finished goods, advertising and promotional expenditures normally do not start until the mid year. Once advertising and promotions are introduced, market shares are subject to alternation. Expenditures for these programs are necessary to maintain market share. The effects of advertising and promotion are somewhat different. However, each takes effect *immediately*.

Advertising causes *total demand* to increase in each market. As additional dollars are spent, demand increases at a diminishing rate. In instances where stockout has occurred and the firm has lost a portion of its demand, additional advertising will help to stimulate market-share recovery. Advertising expenditures are distributed to each market area as specified. For instance, you may allocate $100 for Market 1, $0 for Market 2, $1,000 for Market 3, $50 for Market 4, and $3,000 for Market 5.

TABLE 6
WAREHOUSE COST

Cost of Private Warehouse Operation		
	Finished Goods	Raw Material
Fixed cost per unit of capacity per week	$.40	$.02
Material handling cost per unit received[a]	$2.40	$.06
Cost of Public Warehouse Operation		
Public Warehouse	Finished Goods D&D	Raw Material D&D
Storage cost per unit in Inventory at week's end. $1.00	$6.40	$.16
Material handling cost per $3.75 Unit received	--------	

[a]At the 70 per cent warehouse utilization.

TABLE 7
SALES PROMOTION PLANS

Promotion Period	Promotion 1 Allocated Cost	Promotion 2 Allocated Cost	Promotion 3 Allocated Cost
1	$ 19,000	$24,000	$60,000
2	36,000	14,400	120,000
3	23,000	9,000	20,000
4	12,000	6,000	-----
5	7,000	3,600	-----
6	3,000	1,800	-----
7	-----	1,200	-----
	$100,000	$60,000	$200,000

Promotions help a firm maintain market share. The promotional department can initiate any one of the available three plans that it so desires. However, only one plan may be started each week, and a given plan may not be reinitiated until it has expired. If a plan was initiated and has expired, it may be repeated. If more than one plan is used, their effect is combined. The plans available are listed in Table 7.

The allocation of promotional effort to specific markets is according to per-market percentage of firm total sales. For instance, if the sales in the Central market are 50 per cent of the firm's total sales; 50 per cent of promotion charges are allocated to that market.

To accommodate competitive dynamics, customer loyalty is introduced. By having customer loyalty, a certain portion of each firm's previous week's market share is considered "safe" from competitive inroads. This is, customers will postpone purchases until succeeding weeks if a stockout occurs. The "safe" percentages are listed in Table 8.

TABLE 8
CUSTOMER LOYALTY

Market	"Safe" % of Previous Market Share
Home	60
Central	55
Non-home	40

The portions of the markets not reserved as "safe" are placed in a "pool." From the pool, demand is reallocated on the basis of relative expenditures for both advertising and promotion in the market. Thus, a firm's individual market demand can be calculated as its "safe" share of the total demand plus share of the pooled demand.

When advertising and sales promotions are in effect, one fifth of the total expenditure is charged to the logistical department. This is justified since logistics received one fifth of the revenue from sales for performances measurement. Thus, only one fifth of expenditure placed on decision sheets is allocated to logistical management.

Competitive Objectives – Performance Criteria

LOGA has two closely related competitive objectives. First, each company should attempt to earn the highest total gross profit during the competition. Second, each company should attempt to maximize its total company market share. Total gross profit is an indication of overall past performance, while market share is a long-run barometer indicative of future potential.

The winners are those teams achieving the highest performance index. This performance index is determined by multiplying "total to date" gross profit by "average to date" market share. If, for example, your team achieved a total to-date gross profit of $200,00- and a 25 per cent average total market share, your index of performance would be 50,000 (200,000 x .25).

Before reaching a final decision on who wins, game administrators will check "in transit pipelines," Spartan inventories, warehouse capacity, and raw materials on order to determine a firm's competitive posture. If a firm has attempted a "game end" strategy, its performance index may be discounted by the game administrator.

MARKETING RESEARCH INFORMATION

Confidential reports are available to each firm regarding selected competitive activities. These reports become available when advertising and promotion are initiated. The cost of such information varies according to the desired number and selection of reports. Such information can assist a firm in competing more effectively by knowing, at least in part, what is occurring in the market. The data provided are accurate most of the time to within plus or minus 10 per cent. Marketing research in this situation will in no way provide "perfect information" for decision-making. Totals may not agree as they are estimated independently of market and company estimates.

TABLE 9
MRI REPORTS

MRI # Identification	Ref. No.	Cost
Promotion		
1. Total allocated promotion expenditures and no. of promotions for each company	None	$800
2. Itemization of promotion types for requested competitors	Competitors #1-#4	$500 Per competitor
3. Total allocated promotion expenditures for each market	None	$2,000
4. Itemization by company of promotion expenditures in requested markets	Markets #1-#5	$900 per market
5. Itemization by market of promotion expenditures for requested competitors	Competitors #1-#4	
Advertising		
6. Total advertising of each company	None	$1,800
7. Total advertising in each market	None	$3,500
8. Itemization by company of advertising of requested markets	Markets #1-#5	$900 per market
9. Itemization by market of advertising of requested companies	Competitors #1-#4	$900 per competitor
Demand		
10. Itemization by company of demand in requested markets	Markets #1-#5	$800 per market
11. Itemization by market of demand of requested companies	Competitors #1-#5	$900 per competitor
12. Total demand in all companies	None	$1,200
13. Total demand in all markets	None	$1,500

Three types of marketing research are available: promotion marketing research, advertising marketing research, and demand marketing research. These market research information (MRI) reports are listed in Table 9. To obtain them, determine the MRI numbers and competitive and marketing numbers, if required, and insert them on the marketing research input sheet.

MANAGEMENT REPORTS

Two reports other than market research reports are presented to the firm after each round. The first report is the financial statement. It summarizes all cost data for the current rounds and the year to date. The second report is the operations reports. It enumerates current and in-transit raw material and Spartan inventories. It also shows the current and contracted warehouse space in each market.

The operations report should be used for comparative purposes. A comparison of current inventory with currently available warehouse capacity tells a firm whether detention and demurrage charges will be incurred. Comparison of current and projected production schedules indicates whether sufficient raw materials will be available to meet production requirements. If any of the comparisons indicate trouble, the manager of the firm will have to decide on what corrective action to take in its next decision.

RECORDING DECISIONS

For each week, each firm is required to complete a decision sheet set on the spreadsheet provided. The spreadsheet must be handed in promptly at the end of each decision round. They are entered as submitted without alteration. Firms are encouraged to maintain a duplicate copy of each spreadsheet.

McGRAW-HILL/Irwin

Instructor's Manual to accompany Supply Chain Logistics Management by Bowersox, Closs, and Cooper

Please use this postage-paid form to report any errors that you find in this material. Be as complete as possible noting specifically which changes should be made. We will address them in subsequent printings and future editions. Thank you.

Attention: Scott Isenberg

Name _____   School _____

Office Phone _____

Please fold and seal so that our address is visible.